Trail Blazers

Made in
MISSOURI

Trail Blazers

The Free-Spirited and Extraordinary Lives
of Ted and Pat Jones

by Jeannette Cooperman

Contents

Preface

Because both Pat and Ted are gone, this effort to tell their story is, necessarily, an act of reconstruction and imagination. It is based on the Joneses' photographs, letters, tapes, and transcripts; whitepapers, symposia, and SEC filings; several excellent company histories; newspaper and journal articles; and the memories of more than 75 people. I have adhered carefully to all I could discover, but when can all the facts ever be known, let alone the inner thoughts and feelings of two rather private individuals? The only comfort is that they were both the sort to forgive any well-intended error.

Thank you to all the relatives, colleagues, friends, neighbors, environmentalists, farmers, firefighters, financial analysts, educators, curators, and civic leaders who shared their experiences with Ted and Pat. Many of those memories, I stole faithfully but shamelessly in order to weave them into the narrative. Please forgive the lack of attribution and know that you have shaped the telling.

~Jeannette Cooperman

Debt of Gratitude

In 1980, John Beuerlein and Dan Burkhardt were both named partners in Edward Jones. Their first partners meeting would be held at the snazzy new Crown Center in Kansas City, and though a blizzard was coming, the mood on the bus was festive. John Bachmann was there, as were Pete Key, Jack Phelan, Darryl Pope, and Doug Hill, all with their spouses. Headed west, the bus driver glided onto the exit in Williamsburg, Missouri, and the brakes squealed. A man and woman—both short, sturdy, simply dressed—were waiting on the side of the I-70 outer road.

Ted and Pat Jones.

As the managing partner and his wife climbed aboard, Beuerlein and Burkhardt hid smiles. The firm's founder, Edward D. Jones Sr., always dressed to the nines. His son was a farmer through and through, indifferent to luxury, and he had chosen a wife with the same plainspoken ease. Ted and Pat were funny and smart, concerned with big ideas, indifferent to appearances. It was rare, and the two new partners knew it, to find finance and idealism braided so tightly, neither canceling the other.

Beuerlein and Burkhardt worked together for the next quarter-century. They said goodbye to first Ted and then Pat, feeling a profound sense of loss. Forty-one years after that bus ride, Beuerlein called his old friend, both of them now retired, and said urgently, "There needs to be a book about Ted and Pat. Not just a company history—a book that tells their life stories, Pat's as much as Ted's. And we need to get it written fast, before people forget."

Finding support for the project was easy: So many Jones partners still felt a debt of gratitude to the Joneses, and they were immediately on board. Their loyalty made this book possible.

All proceeds will go to Magnificent Missouri, a not-for-profit organization inspired by Ted and Pat. Warmest thanks to the contributors who deferred the costs:

List of Donors

Steve and Nancy Becherer

Roger and Janet Belshe

Tom and Lois Bertsch

John and Crystal Beuerlein

Don and Linda Bolin

John and Kay Borota

Bill and Penny Broderick

Mort and Barbara Brown

Dan and Connie Burkhardt

Kay Bachmann

Jack and Anne Cahill

Brett and Lisa Campbell

Tom and Shay Carmody

Don Carter

Pam and Jared Cavness

Bill and Laura Christensen

Robert and Mary Ciapciak

Steve and Jackie Clement

Tom and Merilee Curran

Carolyn Decker

Kent and Carol Donley

Norm and Laura Eaker

Mike and Bettina Esser

Alan and Ann Fender

Walt and Karen Fucito

Barb Gilman

Jim and Susan Goodknight

Gordon and Jane Griffin

Mike and Marta Grinney

Patty and Carey Hannum

Jim and Sharon Harrod

Randy and Tamara Haynes

John and Riley Hess

Doug and Vicki Hill

Glenn and Pat Hunn

Eric and Mary Inglett

Larry and Judy Jackson

John and Laurie Manwaring-Jatcko

John Key

Bret and Angie Kimes

Loren and Peggy Kolpin

Jim and Pam Krekeler

Ron and Carol Larimore

Michele and Tim Liebman

Rhonda and Matthew Liesenfeld

David and Diane Mayo

Jim and Kathy McKenzie

Jim and Merry Mosbacher

Rodger Naugle

Tom and Patti Pape

James and Carol Pax

Bob and Rita Peichel

Wayne and Carolyn Polston

Darryl and Cindy Pope

Dan and Shirley Power

Leonard and Ruth Price

Gary and Joanne Reamey

James Reeves

Jim and Jan Regnier

Ray and Cherry Robbins

Wann and Mary Robinson

Tim and Susie Rupp

Rick and Rosemary Schachner

Dan and Nancy Schmelter

Steven and Patricia Schreiber

Ken and Patricia Schutte

Phil and Carol Schwab

Jeffrey and Sabrina Sellmeyer

Steve and Diana Seifert

Fes and Mary Claire Shaughnessy

Bob and Patricia Sheets

John and Joyce Sloop

Jane and Chris Smoot

M.L. and Karen Steinmetz

Lee and Sue Theis

Larry Thomas

Craig and Sue Tidball

Steven Van Voorhis

Bob and Gerry Virgil

Steve and Linda VanVoorhis

Lee and Linda Warner

Harold and Elizabeth Weaver

Kim and John Webb

Carol Wechsler and Daniel Middleton

Jim and Stacey Weddle

Steve and Denise Weidert

Steve and Twila Westphal

Price and Tammy Woodward

David and Debra Wortman

John and Susan Yancey

David and Robin Young

Introduction

How to introduce two people as unusual as Ted and Pat Jones? Both born to money, they refused to live accordingly. Sociable and warm, they had no appetite for the trappings of society. They preferred working hard enough to break a sweat, then shooting the breeze with anybody who came out to the farm, whether it was a local blacksmith, the governor of Missouri, the Jones receptionist, or Bud Walton, one of the founders of Walmart.

"Down to earth" is more than a cliché: Ted built what's now one of the world's most widely held and successful financial partnerships, yet all he ever wanted was to be a farmer. Pat whispered horses, planted vast fields of sunflowers, crusaded for environmental issues, and restored acres of land to an 1840s prairie landscape. They lived wholly and freely as themselves.

What gave them the courage? We begin to see the answer in the lives of their spirited and fiercely intelligent ancestors—a nineteenth-century explorer, a Scottish ship's captain, an abolitionist, a world-class architect, an environmental activist. Then we watch Pat and Ted meet young, each sensing that no one else would ever suit them better. We follow along while Ted sails through World War II on a tugboat, brave and impulsive, and Pat blazes her own trail as the first female graduate of the University of Missouri College of Agriculture. We meet the cast of characters who partnered with Ted to create one of America's most powerfully successful businesses; we watch biologists help Pat restore a prairie and invite kids there to learn, get dirty, and have fun.

The Jones farm is another character in the story, evolving from a cattle operation Ted couldn't quite make work into an ecologically conscious refuge for birds and deer, and eventually a restored prairie.

The battle to build the Katy Trail adds a little drama and a happy ending, with cyclists and hikers from all over the world coming to see how beautiful Missouri's landscape is.

The Katy ends near the confluence of the Missouri and Mississippi rivers. Ted and Pat's marriage was a different sort of confluence: a meeting of two strong and independent lives. Theirs was not a soppy romance—they were far too practical—but an enduring love. Instead of attending galas, they invited people out to ride horseback, sit around a bonfire, get sloppy-kissed by the Jones dogs. Instead of living tight, self-absorbed lives, they drew thousands of people into their circle.

Stubborn, eccentric, and a ton of fun to be around, they shared a love of nature that kept them grounded and a curiosity that kept them awake. Ted loved the circus and piano singalongs and real-life spy stories and all kinds of history. "You may never be here again," he would remind any companion who failed to stop at a historic marker. Pat read Shakespeare, listened to physics and astronomy lectures, grew tons of veggies and gave them away. She gave away Ted's money, too, and he gave away the company he fought so hard to build.

Between them, they helped people achieve countless dreams. And the earth itself was better for their presence.

1

A Bicycle Trip

The bike trip will wind 300 miles through the Ozarks. The kids—students from three expensive private high schools in St. Louis—have been promised basic accommodations along the way. Though accustomed to comfort, they are young enough to enjoy giving it up. Each carries a pillow and a sheet on their bike.

One of the girls, Pat Young, attends Mary Institute, which in adulthood she will describe as "a proper school, but not very good," tactfully adding, "It's a good school now." Utterly unselfconscious, she loves sports and horses and cannot be bothered with makeup or gossip or frills. Ted Jones is one of her brother's mates at the Taylor School. A

Ted, second from left, at the Taylor School in 1939.

small private academy, it prepares students for college, often in spite of themselves. Its headmaster is quite a character, and because well-to-do St. Louis is such a small, criss-crossed world, he met and married Pat's aunt, so she knows him well. The boys at Taylor amuse her; she is more at ease with them than with her chattering classmates.

But neither Pat nor Ted wants to think about school right now. They are outside at last, cut loose from classwork, surrounded by nature. And they are both the type to notice what their wheels spin past: limestone bluffs, clear streams, blue-green springs, and tumbling waterfalls.

Ted is broad-shouldered and short, five-five, with a grin that says you can expect anything. Pat's gaze is steady, and she has thick, wavy brown hair and a movie-star smile—perfectly shaped lips, deep dimples, and an easy, throaty laugh. Even when she's not biking, she wears flats for comfort's sake. Ted's swagger is in no danger of being overshadowed.

We can imagine the other kids on that trip: the girls plagued with the usual worries—do they look fat in those shorts, is their new hairstyle cute or a disaster?—and the boys trying to be cool. Neither Pat nor Ted bothers. Both the second of four kids, they live in lovely Clayton homes that are, it turns out, just a few blocks apart. Pat's family home is a gracious four-bedroom on a six-acre lot; Ted's is a five-bedroom, redbrick Georgian Revival. There are servants, parties, trips abroad. But Pat and Ted, both fifteen years old and born only a month apart, keep away from all the fuss.

Pat has not made a checklist for her ideal future, picked out colors for her bridesmaid gowns, or decided what size family she wants. Nor does she have any grand plans for a career. When her yearbook editor asked people to name their Ambition, other girls said things like "to wear a fresh gardenia every day" or "to have a cute laugh," and a few dared serious career goals. Pat's dry answer was that her Ambition was "to be ambitious."

What she really wants is to work on a farm.

Her happiest moments have been on land her father owns near Eureka, Missouri. Pat and her brother and two sisters spend long, golden days out there, canoeing and swimming in the Meramec River, exploring the sandstone canyons. A week feels lost if she can't spend at least a few days at The Shack, the little house her dad built atop a hill overlooking the Meramec River. She likes the vast expanses of land, green and lush, buzzing with critters. The dogs panting as they tear up and down the hill. The horses, grazing in a paddock until she can whisper them into a ride. When she sees the veggies her mom has planted growing fat and shiny in this rich crumbly soil, she wants to grow things, too.

Ted's happiest moments have been on his family's farm, riding the horses and playing with the dogs. As a kid, he took it upon himself to plant a double row of trees—a formal allée, though he did not know the word—down the main driveway. Watching those saplings grow changed something deep inside him. Farming, gardening, horticulture—another word he is not yet tossing about—all of this is as hard as his toughest

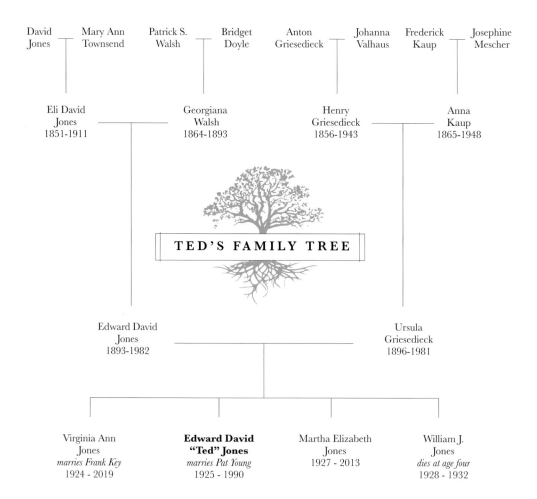

| David Jones | Mary Ann Townsend | Patrick S. Walsh | Bridget Doyle | Anton Griesedieck | Johanna Valhaus | Frederick Kaup | Josephine Mescher |

Eli David Jones 1851-1911 — Georgiana Walsh 1864-1893   Henry Griesedieck 1856-1943 — Anna Kaup 1865-1948

TED'S FAMILY TREE

Edward David Jones 1893-1982 ———— Ursula Griesedieck 1896-1981

| Virginia Ann Jones *marries Frank Key* 1924 - 2019 | **Edward David "Ted" Jones** *marries Pat Young* 1925 - 1990 | Martha Elizabeth Jones 1927 - 2013 | William J. Jones *dies at age four* 1928 - 1932 |

class, but so different from hunching over books of abstract squiggles in an airless room. Instead of tiring his bright blue eyes and pinging facts around in his brain until they slid into the right spot, this pulls everything together—the land and sky, his muscles, his quieted mind, his heart. Farming fills him with a quiet joy.

Do they talk about this yet? They might; they are both forthright, unusually clear about what matters to them. This bike trip suits them: no elaborate social rules or silly expectations, just the freedom and ease of moving across the land.

And a growing sense, for each of them, that they have found someone in whose company they can relax.

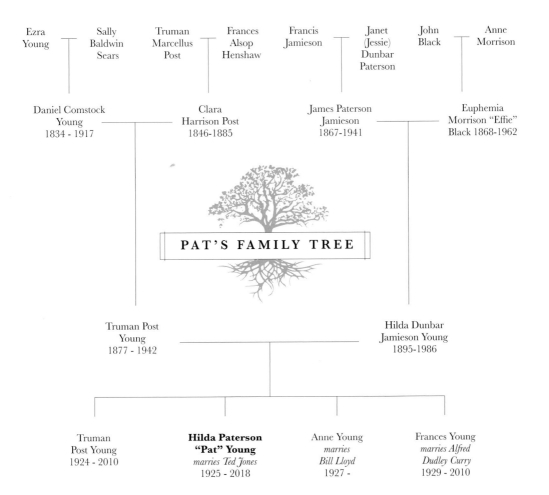

| Ezra Young | Sally Baldwin Sears | Truman Marcellus Post | Frances Alsop Henshaw | Francis Jamieson | Janet (Jessie) Dunbar Paterson | John Black | Anne Morrison |

Daniel Comstock Young 1834 - 1917 — Clara Harrison Post 1846-1885

James Paterson Jamieson 1867-1941 — Euphemia Morrison "Effie" Black 1868-1962

PAT'S FAMILY TREE

Truman Post Young 1877 - 1942 — Hilda Dunbar Jamieson Young 1895-1986

Truman Post Young 1924 - 2010

Hilda Paterson "Pat" Young *marries Ted Jones* 1925 - 2018

Anne Young *marries Bill Lloyd* 1927 -

Frances Young *marries Alfred Dudley Curry* 1929 - 2010

2
—

Scots and Sailors and Abolitionist Preachers

What was extraordinary about Ted Jones and Pat Young began long before they were born. To understand Ted's business acumen, horse sense, and showmanship, we have to go back at least as far as his grandfather. We can trace Pat's love of the land and impatience with dogma all the way back to her great-grandfather.

The Rev. Truman Marcellus Young was called by a congregation in Missouri in the 1850s. Members were divided on the subject of slavery, as was the entire state. Young did not want to live in a slave state; nor did he want to be part of splitting a church. But when the church broke anyway, the delegates asked, "*Now* will you come?" He set one condition: "I have to speak my mind from the pulpit."

And so he became the founder of the First Congregational Church in St. Louis, seven years before formal start of the Civil War.

In 1877, Young was invited to tell his life's story to the general association of Congregationalists at their fall meeting. He began by studying law, he said, and when his thoughts turned toward Christianity instead, he felt "fenced out" by "creeds, requiring as conditions of membership categorical statements of belief on doctrines which seemed to me speculative." He was determined to be honest—with himself and with others. The tension of standing apart from the crowd shaped his life's course, he said, and "certainly prepared me to understand

and sympathize with persons perplexed and distressed with doctrinal difficulties."

Restless, Young went off on his own to Andover in the fall of 1832 and studied sacred literature. He would cherish those solitary, absorbed months for the rest of his life. Lyman Beecher, the father of Harriet Beecher Stowe, began talking with him, helping him resolve his theological difficulties. He spent the winter listening to Supreme Court arguments and debates of Congress, feeling that he was watching an old regime die.

Young left Vermont to take a teaching job in Illinois, which required sailing down the Ohio "along shores frowning with primeval forests or escarped with cliffs pierced with caves." When he reached St. Louis, he saw "a French village of some 6,000 or 7,000 inhabitants, hanging on the edge of a green bluff. It seemed to me the end of the world—the 'jumping off place.'"

In 1833, St. Louis's Third Street was "a bold push westward. Fourth street was quite out of town," wild enough for Young to go out at dawn and scare up the prairie fowl. Remember this later, when Pat gets interested in prairie chickens. Remember, too, how her great-grandfather was drawn toward "a vast primitive wilderness, where no smoke or steam curled in the silent skies and no clang of machinery or tramp of coming millions broke the wide stillness of nature."

From St. Louis, Young made his way to Jacksonville, Illinois, driving through a prairie that seemed a "vast, silent green waste, houseless, manless, the red man gone, the white man not yet entered." Gazing long, he thought of an ocean: one minute flat and smooth, the next "rippling into verdant wavelets, now with a vast sea-roll of gradual rise and fall, occasionally billowing into bluffs that bordered the rivers." The forest at the prairie's edge was "flecked and embroidered with the redbud and the haw," the oak, maple, walnut, and pecan trees "fringed with the sassafrass, the persimmon and the sumach." This place was *so* different from tamed New England that it seemed "a fairy landscape."

In Jacksonville, he married, raised a family, taught college, and watched the seedling maples he had planted grow into great trees, the sentinel elms reach the sky. Fourteen years later, he was called to the St. Louis church. "I was unwilling to lay my bones in a slave state, or commit my family to its destinies," he would later recall. But when he said as much, the church's delegate replied, "Come down and help us remove it."

§

On the maternal side, Pat's grandfather, whose middle name she shared, was James Paterson Jamieson. He was born in 1867 in Falkirk, the cradle of Scotland's Industrial Revolution. Even as a boy, he had an eye for line and form, and a pencil moved surely in his hand. He studied at the School of the South Kensington Museum, then emigrated to Philadelphia in 1884. There, he apprenticed for several architects and did further study at the Pennsylvania Museum and School of Industrial Art.

In 1891, James married Euphemia ("Effie") Morrison Black, also from Scotland. Both had lived for a time in Glasgow, although Effie's family moved to a stone cottage in the countryside, thinking it a healthier place for kids. They grew up simply—it was exciting when Queen Victoria's train chugged past on the way to Balmoral, but those glimpses made it obvious that the world of celebrity was fleeting. The Blacks had more fun picnicking, crossing a wide stream on stepping stones, or tramping in the winter woods, gathering pine, fir, and mistletoe to decorate the house for Christmas. Their annual train ride to Glasgow was to see the shops and pick out one toy apiece as a Christmas present. Their stockings were stuffed with sweets, a fat bright orange on top, and for Christmas dinner, they had meat pie with flaky crust and plum pudding for dessert. New Year's Day brought the "first footing," when friends dropped by for shortbread, seed cakes, and brandy diluted with soda water.

Effie's father, John Black, was a ship's captain in the late 1800s, and he brought home trunks stuffed with presents from India and other distant lands. He also brought cases of pungent ginger root in thick syrup, jars of chutney, boxes of pomelos, and rolls of Tussar silk to make summer dresses for his wife, Annie, and their daughters.

John was a Highlander, born on the Isle of Arran. The Duke and Duchess of Hamilton had an estate below the island's sandstone cliffs, and one day John and Annie encountered the royals out for a stroll. Annie, a staunch Lowlander, refused to curtsy. Her starched-proper mother-in-law never quite forgave her.

Nonetheless, the Blacks spent every summer on Arran, and it was a life Pat would have loved. The older kids climbed Goat Fell, and from the top they could see the Isle of Skye and the Irish coast. By the water's edge, they built sandcastles. In shaded glens, they gathered primroses and maidenhair ferns for visitors to take home. They picked watercress along little streams and ran through fields divided by stone dykes or hawthorne hedges. Out of breath and thirsty, they would stop by their uncle's store, which, Effie's little sister announced, "seemed to hold everything in the world in its small space." In other words, it was a lot like Crane's, the country store Pat would someday visit daily.

John captained the City of Glasgow, a clipper ship in the Merchant Marine, and he set a speed record from Australia to San Francisco. When his company built their first steamship, he was given command of it. Annie swung a beribboned bottle of Champagne, red, white, and blue satin ribbons streaming from its neck, and cracked it open against the bow.

He had inherited his love of the sea from his father, also a ship's captain, who died a hero's death trying to rescue passengers from a shipwreck on the rocky coast of Lyme-Regis. John also inherited a zodiac ring of such solid gold, you could bend it. No alloys had been snuck into that molten metal. According to family legend, the ring was given to him when he delivered two white asses to the sultan of Zanzibar.

Pat's nephew, Truman Post Young, a research ecologist in California, always thought the tale too fanciful to be true. But when he was working and living in East Africa, his interest was rekindled. In Alan Morehead's *Blue Nile*, he found a mention of King Theodore of Ethiopia riding to his doom on a white ass. So, white donkeys *were* considered special. He consulted a friend, an East African historian, and that led him to *Arabian Princess Between Two Worlds*, a book by Emily Ruete. Born Princess Sayyida Salme, she was the daughter of Sa'id ibn Sultan, the sultan of Zanzibar in the first half of the nineteenth century. In her memoir, she mentions a present from her father: a pair of white asses, their tails dyed red with henna. She and her sisters rode them on an excursion to *shamba*, which means "farm," so perhaps a weekend in the country.

Truman grinned. So the sultan *did* keep a pair of white asses in his

stable, and surely they would have needed replacing by the time his
son succeeded him? The family legend just might be true.

John Black kept the zodiac ring but left the sea. It had taken both
his father and his grandfather, and when he fell ill with severe sunstroke
in Calcutta, the doctor warned him that he must stop sailing. Too fond
of his wife and children to risk dying on them, he moved as far from the
sea as he could manage: Minnesota, where one of Annie's cousins had
bought a farm. Luck struck: The land next to their farm was for sale, so
in 1888—the year of a terrible spring blizzard—John and his son Jack
sailed to America and took blind possession of a farm buried
in snowdrifts.

§

When her family arrived in the States, Effie, the eldest daughter, was
already a young lady. She and James took a summer wedding trip to Great
Britain, where he tested his bride's patience by spending hours making
rubbings, drawings, and sketches. The following year, he won a scholarship
that let him return to Britain and go on to France, Italy, and Greece.

By 1900, he had proved his talent in the Cope & Stewardson
architectural firm. When the partners won the competition to design
Brookings Hall on the new Washington University campus, he was sent
to St. Louis to oversee the project. For a while, he traveled back and forth
between Philadelphia, where his first two children were born, and St.
Louis, a grand city at the time, shimmering with excitement as it prepared
for the 1904 World's Fair.

Inspired by the fifteenth- and sixteenth-century buildings at Oxford
and Cambridge, James used the Academic Gothic style in his designs for
Washington University. What changed were the materials: the faded rose
of Missouri red granite softening the buildings and white limestone crisply
outlining the gables and towers.

James had just designed Blair Hall, a dormitory at Princeton
University, in the same style, and he would again turn to Academic
Gothic for buildings at the University of Missouri-Columbia. Versatile, he
also won acclaim for his design of the Edward Mallinckrodt mansion in
Westmoreland Place, which was lauded as "continuing the finest tradition

of the noble French manors of the Renaissance, and at the same time truly representative of life in the present age."

Effie, meanwhile, was setting a spirited example of independence, even hosting a St. Louis Suffrage League luncheon. When World War I broke out, the Jamiesons' youngest daughter, Hilda Dunbar Jamieson (Pat's future mother) went off to work on a chicken farm on Long Island, where she learned to tinker with machinery. She then persuaded an automobile company to let her work in their repair shop, promising that she could work as hard as any man. Clad in overalls, she pulled her weight and left with a certificate of efficiency. At twenty-three, she was chosen to drive an ambulance for the war effort.

Four years later, back home in St. Louis, Hilda fell in love with Truman Post Young, a forty-six-year-old attorney. His family had come early to New England, and it was said that Steven Post had been friends with Uncas, the last of the Mohicans.

As boys, Truman and his identical twin brother Henry had been irrepressible. Their mother had died young, and their aunt, Kate, had come to care for them. Her routine instruction to the maid was, "Go see what the twins are doing, and tell them to stop."

One day, Aunt Kate heard one of the boys bragging, after hearing about his grandmother's Henshaw family tree, that he was a descendant of William the Conqueror. 'Don't you ever tell that to anybody!" she snapped. "Don't you know that man was a bastard?"

The twins surprised her by making it through Yale University, graduating with honors in 1899. Henry became a physician, and Truman went on to Saint Louis University School of Law. By 1906 he was an assistant district attorney; three years later, a newspaper editorial was urging President Taft to pick him as district attorney.

In 1919, Truman lost his first wife, a Mary Institute graduate whose brother had been in his class at Yale. Just twenty-four years old, Kitty had fallen ill with what was probably one of the last cases of the Spanish flu. A fatal pneumonia set in, inflaming and clogging her lungs.

Three years later, Truman proposed to Hilda Jamieson. Unfazed by their nineteen-year age difference, she accepted. The wedding took place at her family home on Pershing Avenue. She wore "cream kitten's ear crepe with touches of old rose point lace," and her tulle veil was caught by a narrow band of orange blossoms. Her sisters, Norah and Louise, were her attendants, elegant in chiffon gowns with silver underskirts. Truman's twin brother was his best man.

After their honeymoon, the Youngs lived for a while in the Warwick Apartments, near Hilda's parents, then moved to a home in Clayton. What they both loved most, though, was the countryside. In his single years, Truman used to put a canoe on a train and, as soon as the train crossed a river, take the canoe off and float for a while. One day he was camping on a gravel bar, and one of the local guys came out to chat. "I wonder who owns this land behind me," Truman said idly, leaning back against a boulder.

"Well, I do," the man drawled.

Truman looked up sharply. "Would you sell it?"

"I might."

They reached an agreement in 1910, Truman buying a ten-acre stretch from the river to the top of the hill. When he met Hilda, he took her out there—maybe as a test, to make sure she would love it, too. "Don't bring in any foreigners," he warned her when they married—meaning that she should not plant any exotic, possibly invasive species. "We have plenty of nice plants here, if you just encourage them. Don't bring in any fancy European trees, or even ones from Illinois." He believed—as would their daughter Pat—in treasuring a native landscape.

Truman also put a log cabin on top of the hill, and soon his friends named it The Work House on Chigger Hill, because he kept inviting them out to help him build a proper house in its stead. He liked the challenge of building things, so he read a bunch of how-to books and built a barn, daring to construct it without internal supports so the interior would be wide open. A good friend who was an engineer promised him it would never work, *never*. He built it anyway, even added a hip roof. The barn stood straight and proud for decades.

3
—

Horse Trading, Vaudeville, and Aristocracy

Though most of Pat's family came from Scotland, the other half of the Joneses' story is spread across Great Britain and Germany. Ted's great-great-grandfather was born in Caernarfon, Wales, a royal town once part of the Kingdom of Gwynedd and famous for its castle. That bastard Ted's wife descended from, William the Conqueror, had ordered it built.

English blood entered the family in the next generation. And Ted's father, Edward David Jones, marries into St. Louis's new-money German aristocracy.

Edward is an elegant man with a horse trader's instincts. Born in St. Louis in 1893, he never knows his Irish mother, who dies in childbirth. This is a second wrenching loss for his father, Eli Jones, whose first wife died soon after giving birth to a baby girl. Giving up on domesticity, Eli sets off traveling, leaving his daughter with her mother's family and baby Edward with a succession of relatives in New York, New Jersey, and Tennessee.

Edward is seven years old when the world crosses into the twentieth century, and he is already prepared to make his own way. His father has sailed to South America, wanderlust unchecked. Eli then works his way north to Panama, lit by the excitement of the new canal being built, and takes a job as a railroad engineer.

When the cousins Edward is living with in Chattanooga decide they, too, will move to Panama, he announces that he is staying put.

He will live at Mrs. Comb's Railroad Boarding House and finish eighth grade.

And so he does. Eventually, he receives word that his father has returned and remarried and is waiting for him in Bellefontaine, Ohio. His half-sister, Florence, writes to him at Mrs. Comb's and says she had no intention of living with their father and will Edward please now burn this letter. He hurriedly complies—and in the process, sets fire to the lace curtains in his room. Smelling smoke, Mrs. Comb's daughter races upstairs, helps smother the flames, then covers for Edward by saying he has taken up smoking.

He packs his few belongings and takes the train to Ohio.

Late to fatherhood, Eli begins to teach Edward about the buying and selling of stocks. Edward will later find—and will carry in his wallet until the day he dies—a card certifying that his father was a member of the St. Louis Mercantile Exchange, a grain exchange that required trading expertise. A common bond, and a prophetic one.

Back in grade school, Edward kept a ledger where he neatly inked the record of every transaction, buying and selling penknives and other small treasures, always at a profit. Stocks, though—this is serious. A world of possibility has opened.

Edward's high school job is tame—he works as a delivery boy for Boggs Grocery. But life gets more interesting when he goes to work for his stepmother's relative, Ole Taylor, known as "the silver-tongued auctioneer of Logan County." Edward studies Ole Taylor's techniques and learns to be both a horse trader and livestock auctioneer.

With all his jobs combined, he makes enough money to pay tuition at New York University, where he intends to study finance. He has some fun along the way, though: He quarterbacks for the high school football team, hangs out with other kids at The Oak on Main Street, and catches vaudeville acts and The Roth Brothers Acrobats at Tom Moore's, where he reportedly dines one evening with William Jennings Bryan. (Or maybe Bryan is at the next table, but never spoil a good story.)

In 1913, Edward goes off to NYU. Half a century later, he will remember all his professors by name.

In 1916, he takes a job selling securities for N.W. Halsey & Co. on Wall

Street. His first territory is the Woolworth Building; he is to call on every single tenant. Then he is transferred to Cleveland, Ohio, to sell bonds.

When the United States joins World War I in 1917, Edward enlists with the Navy. He spends two and a half years as an ensign, assigned to one of the boats that protect cargo ships. German U-boats lurk beneath the ocean's surface, eager to torpedo any American ships that might be hauling contraband.

Home in one piece, Edward returns to work in Cleveland, then switches to Blair & Company, a New York bond house. As their field representative, he moves to St. Louis, the city where he was born.

§

"My name is Ed Jones," the young man is saying into a pay phone, raising his voice over the hubbub of Union Station. "I think my mother was related to you."

"You wait right there," Mrs. Phelan says warmly. "I'm sending my son down to pick you up."

The mother Edward never knew, Georgina Walsh, was Frank Phelan's cousin, born in the same county in Ireland.

Edward and Will Phelan become fast friends. They will be best man at each other's weddings, and when Will is the first to marry, Ed will weep, wrecked to be "losing" his buddy.

There is work to distract him, though. From St. Louis, his territory stretches all the way to New Orleans. One day, he calls on the famous Godchaux sugar refinery, founded a century earlier by a French-born planter dubbed the Sugar King of the South.

"We want to *sell* bonds, not buy them," the Godchaux heirs tell Edward. He nods and, undaunted, offers his firm's services to underwrite and manage the bond issue. The Godchaux men agree—a coup for Edward—but when he asks what his finder's fee will be, his boss snorts: "You're paid too much already."

"If that's the way it is," Edward says, drawing himself up, "then I quit."

He will start his *own* brokerage business.

The announcement hits the newspapers in January 1922: Edward

D. Jones & Co. is open for trading. Its headquarters is a single room on the eighth floor of the Boatmen's Bank Building, a stately edifice built only eight years earlier, with gray granite for gravitas and ornate classical ornament in white terra cotta to lighten the mood.

Inside, in his tiny office, Edward has squeezed a desk, three chairs, and a hat rack. Soon he will expand—into a second room with a bank of telephones. The brokerage business still draws mainly wealthy men—money understands money—and they barely work, because their connections are enough. Every morning, they arrange a few trades, and by midafternoon, they are heading for their clubs. But Edward *wants* to work. He has no desire to be what today we would call a boutique firm, specializing in certain kinds of investments. Taking a well-stocked bar as his analogy, he announces that he intends to sell *everything*, full service, with never a need to tell a client no.

He has chosen a city abuzz with financial activity; the year he opens his company, St. Louis has more firms registered on the New York Stock Exchange than any city outside New York. Bubbling with postwar energy and free of debt, the nation takes a keen interest in the daily dramas and possibilities of the stock market.

§

The woman Edward falls in love with, Ursula Griesedieck, is from a wealthy German-American brewery family. She graduated from the Sacred Heart Convent school and was presented to society with suitable decorum: a late afternoon reception at the Woman's Club on Lindell and, at nine that evening, a dance for three hundred guests. Afterward, Ursula was a sought-after guest at bridge luncheons and dinners; one newspaper account described her wearing pale pink taffeta for a friend's wedding party.

Her older sisters showed up more colorfully. One was already married, she and her husband "prominent in the Union Club set," according to the *St. Louis Post-Dispatch* society page. In 1912, she was accused of leaving her husband because she packed up her three children and moved back to her family home to visit with her parents while he was away on a business trip.

The other sister, Carrie, was described as "one of the prettiest and most popular girls on the South Side." When she became engaged, the society reporter promised readers that her wedding would be "a large and fashionable one."

Ursula's wedding is not. She and Edward are "unattended," notes a disappointed reporter, and they are married "very quietly" at her parents' home in Soulard. A Roman Catholic priest officiates. The guest list is limited to family members. Of Edward, who is three years older than his bride, the *Post-Dispatch* notes only that he is "a nephew of Mrs. F.W. Phelan of 6599 Bartmer Ave. and lived with his aunt."

When the newlyweds leave for the Allegheny Mountains, Ursula wears a three-piece, dark blue traveling suit. Who knows, she might have worn it for the ceremony, too. They honeymoon in Hot Springs, Virginia, probably at one of the historic luxury hotels.

A year later, the Joneses present the world with a baby girl. A year after that, Ted emerges.

4
—

The First Confluence

Born in November 1925, Hilda Paterson Young will be Patty, then Pat, Patsy to her future husband, but never Hilda, a name she loathes and will later giggle about because only the IRS knows her so formally. Pat has an older brother, Truman Young Jr., and soon, two younger sisters. They live off Wydown Avenue at One Harcourt Drive, a big house of light brick with arched windows and an arched doorway. Except for the surprise of dormer windows popping into the roof, the house is graceful and sedate, but the children's happy shouts bring it to life.

Pat, center, at Mary Institute as captain of the baseball team.

Life there is comfortable: The Youngs have an upstairs maid, a downstairs maid, a laundress. Pat and her sisters are taught to carry themselves like princesses and never allow their backs to rest against the back of a chair. As soon as she is old enough, Pat is sent to the prestigious Mary Institute. She

Hilda Paterson Young

10 Years at Mary Institute
Green Team
Soccer, '40, '41
  Captain, '40
Volley-ball, '40, '42
Baseball, '41, '42

"*I can't, I'm going to the shack*"

*P*AT is one of those rare individuals who possess a keen disposition and friendliness to everyone. Her happy-go-lucky nature is combined with a seriousness which makes her succeed in everything she tries and yet keeps her from worrying too much when disappointments or problems arise. She is always calm, slow to anger, quick to forgive, and fair at all times. She is liked by everyone. Pat devotes much of her time to manual arts and her attention to the Shack, that Ozark farm, well known to us all for the rollicking barn dances held there. In athletics her favorite is horseback riding, and no wonder, owning and training a colt of her own. She is also proficient in baseball, soccer and hockey, having a reputation of really being able to sock those balls! Pat has added much to our class and will continue to contribute wherever or whatever she is.

— 61 —

Pat was a senior at Mary Institute in 1943.

makes tons of friends there, cutting through any drama or prissiness in her easygoing way. Her friends come out to The Shack for rollicking barn dances or hike with her through cedar forest, across LaBarque Creek, around small ponds filled with sunfish and white and black bass.

She and her brother and sisters all go out to The Shack whenever they can. Away from their separate friends and interests, they draw close, easy in one another's company.

Summers, the family drives up to Douglas, Michigan, near Saugatuck, to stay in a lake cottage. This is St. Louis's summer colony, and there are other families they know, other kids to meet for swimming and bonfires on the beach. Hilda and the kids stay most of the summer, escaping the city heat and congestion. Truman, like the other fathers, comes up on weekends.

He also takes the family out West several times, once to a dude ranch in Montana. Pat loves horseback riding and is training her own colt. Lean and athletic, she winds up captain of the baseball team, and fans murmur about "the power in the arms of Patty Young."

In the Mary Institute yearbook, her senior photo is pretty but uncompromising; she wears a crew-neck sweater and no jewelry. She wins easily for Best Disposition: "Her happy-go-lucky nature is combined with a seriousness which makes her succeed in everything she tries, and yet keeps her from worrying too much when disappointments or problems arise. She is always calm, slow to anger, quick to forgive, and fair at all times."

"Where will we be next year?" the yearbook editors ask, predicting that Pat will be an "Ambler." They cannot know the hours she will spend hiking, camping, cycling, roaming through farmland and prairie, helping her husband make the Katy Trail possible. But they do know that being outdoors, moving through nature at a pace slow enough to observe its subtle changes, is what feeds her soul.

Ten years hence, the editors continue, Pat will have "proved herself to be invaluable to her country as she is the head of the Animal Husbandry department in Washington."

But first, as she is keenly aware, college of some sort is expected.

§

"The only thing you can give your children is an opportunity to get an education," Truman has said more than once; he is not a fan of the sort of legacy that can turn a child's character rancid. For his kids, education would be their estate. They must learn to do something and then do it.

Pat receives no specific advice; it is entirely up to her to decide. She just has to want to do *something.* And she knows quite well what she does *not* want to do: spend hours in the kitchen, cooking.

She enrolls in the Pennsylvania School of Horticulture for Women.

Did the choice involve a nudge from her mother, who grew up in Pennsylvania and loves gardening? In their twenties, Hilda and her sister Norah started a little landscaping business, finding clients through their father's architectural projects. Later, Hilda worked for the Missouri Botanical Garden. She is bound to envy her daughter the formal classes in botany, floriculture, garden design, landscape architecture, orchard care, and soil chemistry.

But this refined, ladylike curriculum is not nearly enough to sate Pat's hunger to know the earth.

As she dutifully finishes her coursework, she happens to read an article in the *St. Louis Post-Dispatch*, written by Dr. W. A. Albrecht. He is on the faculty of the University of Missouri-Columbia, teaching in the agricultural college. (Ted Jones is away at war, but he studied at Mizzou's ag college the summer before he enlisted; maybe he knew this guy?)

Dr. Albrecht is a soil scientist, and he is convinced that the nation's future rests on the productivity of its soil. He explains in vivid detail exactly how plants pull nutrients from the ground. The university has the oldest continuous experimental field west of the Mississippi River. And the College of Agriculture sits, Albrecht explains, at the confluence of "the glacial soils of the north, the limestone prairies of the Great Plains to the west, the Ozark uplift of granite and cherty dolomites of the Ozarks to the south, and through these ran the Missouri River bordered as it was by the loess of the hills."

This confluence is precisely where Pat wants to be.

§

She enrolls, eager to study the earth beneath her feet. Whenever she asks a question, Professor C. M. "Woody" Woodruff says, "Well, go find out." She takes geology and quite a bit of chemistry; she learns how to test soil and find out what it is made of. Because spectroscopy is brand new, scientists are still learning what the spectroscopic patterns are for the different elements, which she finds thrilling. What pattern does calcium give? What about phosphorus, or lead? They will know soon….

Pat learns about crop rotation; about broom sedge and sweet clover, erosion and subsoil and acidity, root rot, clay, and limestone. With the war over, synthetic nitrogen is now available from the ammunition plants, and there is fresh interest, across the nation, in enriching the soil.

Several of Pat's classes are held in quonset huts, hastily built to accommodate the GIs back from World War II. Mizzou, famous for fun, is suddenly full of mature, serious students. The professors are loving it, Pat can tell. She adores her teachers, a motley mix of eccentric and brilliant people who love the earth as much as she does.

Between semesters, she heads out west to work on an archaeological dig. Pat carefully forks up hard ground, brushes artifacts clean, and boxes them under the tutelage of Dr. H. Marie Worthington, who will later become the first woman president of the Society for American Archaeology. Pat comes home with piles of photographs that become a family joke because there are never any people in them, just hard-baked earth, a rubble of excavated clods. She was in her element that summer.

In May of 1950, Pat dons cap and gown to become the first female graduate of the University of Missouri's College of Agriculture. In September, she will marry the guy who shares her love of farms, animals, and nature. But first, instead of swooning and spending the summer planning her trousseau, she heads west with three of her Mary I friends. They drive out Route 66, a tent and bedrolls stuffed in a ludicrously small car. Each of them has $300, and they want to see Yellowstone National Park, and the redwoods in California, and the Pueblo Indian ruins.

"They tolerate us," Pat realizes bleakly, watching Pueblo dances and learning about various ceremonies. "I think we're kind of intrusive." At Mesa Verde, she hears about their sacred rituals and their people's history, and the full truth hits home: "It's *their* history. Their *place*. And we took it."

Returning from the dry, vast expanses of beige sand, bleached bones, and spiky, relentless cacti, Pat breathes in the wet, earthy fragrance of Missouri's woods. It is August and no doubt muggy, but she sees, with fresh gratitude, the expanses of thick, springy green grass, the sunflowers and black-eyed susans, bright helenium and trailing coreopsis. "You find out that there are green places in the world," she says, "and Missouri is one of them. It's a pretty nice place to come home to."

5

———

Teddy's *Wild!*

Where in heaven's name is Teddy? Daylight is fading, and the five-year-old has vanished. His two-wheeler is missing, too. Ursula and Edward are so worried, they call the police.

An officer finds the little boy sitting cross-legged on the bank of a lake in Forest Park. Silhouetted in the darkening twilight, he looks as serene as the Buddha.

"Your parents are very worried, young man," the officer says sternly. "What on earth are you doing here?"

"I tell you what," the boy says, "I'm watching the water lilies go to sleep."

Ted is what the Brits call a "tearaway." Never a bad kid, but always with a mind of his own. He loves riding in the horse-drawn milk wagon; craves motion, activity, adventure. Frustrated by his propensity to play all day long, never even coming inside for a drink of water or to use the loo, his mother warns him that if he does not check in regularly, he will be sent out to play in his sister's dress.

He shrugs. The next morning, Ann sees him flying down the street in one of her dresses.

Her little brother is *wild*, she sighs.

The live-in nanny cannot keep up.

§

In the photo, Edward and Ursula stand solemn in front of Ursula's parents' home, on Russell Avenue in Soulard. The Joneses' starter home is right around the corner, on Allen Avenue. Already a little portly, Edward looks genial and has dressed with care and style, a carnation in his buttonhole and a linen handkerchief in his pocket. A mink stole warms Ursula's neck, yet her expression is severe, challenging the camera. Ann, their eldest child, is dressed in a gray sweater and navy skirt; Ted, their second-born, wears a matching gray sweater and navy pants. Little Martha and William wear matching dark sweaters with lace-collared shirts underneath.

Martha is so tiny, her nickname is Mousey. The pediatrician wants her to have a cookie every afternoon, but the nuns at Villa Duchesne do not approve of such indulgence. Edward drives out to the school and tells the Reverend Mother, "Give her a cookie. Mary Institute is right around the corner."

Villa was his wife's choice; Ursula is a devout Roman Catholic. And Edward is a devout husband. He takes her to Mass every Sunday at the twin-towered St. John the Apostle and Evangelist, a Romanesque masterpiece built in 1847 in what was then a peach orchard and is now a busy part of downtown St. Louis. After the service, they have brunch at the Missouri Athletic Club, whose name is a little misleading. Steam rooms and squash courts and a gym cater to the athleticism, but the marble vestibule, wood-paneled walls, mezzanine, and ballroom are more reminiscent of a fine London hotel between the wars.

Somehow Teddy will grow up indifferent to both rituals, utterly uninterested in organized religion and clubby society.

§

A rambunctious childhood is complicated by a tragedy Ted will rarely mention. When he is seven, his little brother, William, four years younger, goes out for Halloween and comes home with a double mastoid ear infection. Mousey falls ill with the same infection. Like Shakespeare's children in the Plague, the frail daughter is the one everyone worries about—and the little boy is the one who dies.

His parents' hearts are broken. Ursula becomes tense and

Ted (far left) with Ann, Martha, William, and parents.

hypervigilant. Every Halloween, the grandkids must be bundled into overcoats and hats that utterly ruin the effect of their costumes, at least until they can wriggle out of them without her noticing.

There are material distractions from the pain and worry—the Joneses have a fancy new radio in 1930, and Edward trades a defaulted Rockford Piano Company bond, bought for $25, for a $1,200 baby grand piano. (Ted's sisters learn to play;

he never bothers.) In another of his magic deals, Edward trades a $1,000 Scruggs, Vandervoort & Barney bond for a $750 refrigerator. It is the largest ever made for home use, a General Electric he saw displayed with a pineapple arrangement on the top. Somehow, that pineapple arrangement stuck in his memory. Now neighbors make excuses to come over and gape.

He loves to horse-trade. What Ted loves are real horses. Every Sunday afternoon, Edward takes the kids to the Highlands to ride the ponies. Sidney Rink, a famous animal trainer, is always there, coaxing his troop of jumping mules to do more tricks. He and Edward become friends, and Ted, nine years old to Mr. Rink's seventy-eight, listens open-mouthed to his stories. One of the first Black animal trainers and a member of the International Circus Hall of Fame, Rink has well-worn patience and a million tales about the elephants, mules, goats, and other critters he has taught to steal the show. He lets Teddy drive the goat cart and even takes him to see his cowboy idol, Tom Mix.

Meanwhile, the owner of the ponies is struggling to keep them fed through the Depression. Ted's father offers to buy all fifty Shetland ponies, knowing he will have a place for them to live. In 1932, standing on the courthouse steps, he buys a 740-acre farm in Callaway County for $6 an acre.

Edward brings eight-year-old Teddy with him the first time he goes to check out the land. The road is dirt from "the slab," which is what people in Callaway County call Highway 40, the first ribbon of concrete to run through their land. Edward's car gets stuck in the mud, and the tenant farmer, Fletcher Simms, comes out with a wagon and a team of mules to drag them out of the muck. Fourteen black and tan coon hounds—Teddy needs four fingers twice to count them—lope into the farmyard to offer a greeting. He's never seen so many dogs in one place in his life.

Four horses are grazing, tethered to big old honey locust trees in the yard. Edward mounts one of the horses and pulls Teddy up behind him. Sitting on a gunny sack, arms wrapped around his father's waist, he is ecstatic. They ride all over the farm, taking note of the land's gentle curves, the groves of trees, the hilltop views.

There is no running water, no indoor toilet. Ursula will not stand for that; the place is quickly made civilized, but as a rustic retreat. She enjoys the idea of weekends in the country, but she has no intention of ever *living* out there.

The ponies, on the other hand, quite like it. Before they can settle in, though, Edward seizes another opportunity. The 1933 Chicago World's Fair is about to open, and pony rides will make a fine concession. He sends his new entourage north, and over the next two years, the Jones Pony

Ted on one of the members of the Jones Pony Ranch.

Ranch proves a popular attraction at the Fair. When one of the mares is about to foal, Edward persuades the *Chicago Tribune* to hold a naming contest for the new arrival. The readers choose "Princess Progress."

By the time they return to Missouri, the star ponies—Tiny, Peaches, Frankie, Tommie, Peanuts, Beverly Shadow and Beverly Sundown—have earned their hay and sugar cubes many times over. To round out their diet, Edward finds another deal: oats that a bank repossessed, four cents a bushel.

Weekends now mean long drives to the farm, where there will be a wood fire in the stove when they arrive and, come morning, a country breakfast with sausage and eggs. Ursula won't let the kids drink cow's milk, because it's unpasteurized, so Teddy drinks coffee. He needs the energy when he rides the ponies, especially his favorite, Brownie. One tug backward on the reins, and Brownie stands on his hind legs, and Teddy feels like a cowboy spinning a lasso in one hand.

A little girl from a nearby farm, Jean Smith, comes over one day with her big sister and their parents. They are going to buy a pony from Ted's dad. Seeing a boy riding one of the ponies, Jean strikes up a conversation. Teddy informs her that the pony they are buying, Frankie, got loose during the Chicago World's Fair and galloped up Michigan Avenue with a dozen police officers chasing after him. True or not, he makes a good story of it.

§

In 1937, Ursula's parents book passage for the whole family to sail to Germany. They have relatives in the old country that they have not seen in years, some they have never met. Anna Kauf Griesedieck, Ursula's mother, is with them, but she was too embarrassed to bring her ear trumpet, and now Ursula is exasperated.

"I'm not going one mile farther until she has her horn," Ursula announces, already tired of repeating herself. So Edward, nicknamed Steady Eddie for good reason, gets off the train and goes back to St. Louis. He retrieves the horn and arrives in New York just in time to collect his family and usher everyone to the harbor.

They sail on the *Bremen*, boarding late in the evening. This is an occasion, and Ann, now fourteen years old, is told she must wear a long dress. Well-wishers shower her grandpa, beer magnate Henry Griesedieck, with candies and flowers. Ceremoniously, the

Ted and Ann in the game room sailing to Germany—under Edward's supervision.

family walks across the gangplank—and that is the last they see of young Ted for hours. Wound up like a tin car, he zooms up and down the decks, meeting people, seeing how stuff works.

George Burns and Gracie Allen are on the ship, and they are warmly friendly. The fighter Max Schmeling, heavyweight champion of the world five years earlier, is also a passenger. Just defeated by Joe Louis, he is returning to Germany. Teddy, age twelve, befriends him and cheers him up.

The family is to stay six weeks in Europe. In Amsterdam, they stay at the Hotel Amstelzicht, a 1659 mansion overlooking the Amstel Canal. Teddy gets to know the boatman who glides passengers through the canals. (During the war, the two will remain in touch, and Ursula will send the boatman care packages.)

They move on to Münster, where Teddy's great-aunt lives. The air is thick with tension; on every street, they hear "Heil Hitler." A German officer stops Teddy, who looks German and speaks a bit of the language, and demands to know why he is not in the Hitler Youth.

Even with doom impending, a circus has opened in Münster—one of the small circuses that pop up all over Western Europe. Edward leads the kids behind the scenes to see where the troupe sleeps and rehearses. This is a ritual of his; when a Ringling circus comes to St. Louis, he wakes the children at 4 am and takes them to the train station to watch the circus unload. Later, when the tents are set up, he takes the kids behind the scenes for a tour. He wants to do that now.

A German circus worker stops them.

"Who's in charge here?" Edward asks.

"Who *are* you?" the worker counters.

Straight face, casual delivery: "I'm John Ringling North."

They let him in.

§

In sixth grade, Ted leaves Barat Hall, a Catholic elementary school near the New Cathedral, to attend the Taylor School. Prestigious and experimental, it was designed for boys too restless, high-spirited, or rambunctious for more conventional college prep. William S. Burroughs attended a few years earlier. Ted is a different sort of prototype; instead of being arty, brilliant, and neurotic, he is headstrong, unfiltered, and exploding with ideas.

"I'm Ted Jones, welcome to Taylor School," he will say, shaking hands with a new boy. "What're you in for?"

The school occupies a large, severely classical building at the corner of North Central and Kingsbury. Its founder is Edgar Curtis "Joe" Taylor, a New Englander who was a Rhodes Scholar at Trinity College, Oxford. An excited story in the *St. Louis Globe-Democrat* describes him chumming with the son of the prime minister, taking tea with Lady Astor, and chatting about sports with the Prince of Wales.

Taylor came to St. Louis to teach at Washington University. Here, he met and married Norah Young (Pat's aunt), who is dark, pretty, and amused by the world. Her father's firm has designed them a house near the school at No. 7 Briarcliff.

The faculty will not insist on cramming to bring reluctant students up to speed, Taylor promises. "Many students are boys who have found their regular class work at other schools too much for them and require special attention," the *Globe* notes. But this, Taylor tells the reporter, is "because they have lost interest in study. At least that is usually the case. Or, because they are frankly lazy…. Most ordinary schools are too slow and as a consequence atrophy the interest of the eager student."

In the 1939 yearbook, a boy identified as Jones (only surnames are used) shows up in the Riding Club photo, the shortest in the lineup, slightly chunky and the only one still in short pants. An elegant white shirt collar flops over his dark sweater. We see that he entered the Fall Riding Show but did not place; he was also in the art club and the science club, which took field trips to local companies, walked through a shiny new streamline moderne train at Union Station, and boarded one of the "huge" 34-passenger planes at Lambert Airport.

Two years later, Jones looks quite different, thinner in the face and a bit grumpy. He is in the Public Discussion Club and the Railroad Club, which he and his future wife's brother, Truman Young, cofounded. Next, the two boys will start the Bicycle Club that will eventually introduce Ted to Pat.

Meanwhile, he has launched his first business, buying ninety dozen eggs from Sam Crane's general store in Williamsburg. He brings them back to St. Louis and sells them door to door in University City apartment houses. The fresh eggs are big, shaded a creamy tan or rich pale brown and often dusty with chicken droppings. If one of his customers complains at the dirt, Ted quickly counters with a reminder of how *fresh* they are, straight from the coop…. With his ten-cent markup, he makes $9 a week from his egg route, which strikes him as a handsome sum indeed.

One Arbor Day, the Missouri Department of Conservation presents all the boys at Taylor School with pin oak saplings to plant. Most of these kids live in the city and have no idea where they could plant a tree, so Ted scoops up all the unwanted saplings and plants an allée at his beloved farm.

When he turns fifteen, he begs his parents to let him live at the farm all summer and work with the hired hand. They refuse to let him live there alone, blinking back vivid images of all that he might get up to. Instead, a friend of his father's agrees to give Ted a job with the beef department at Krey Packing Company. He works in the East St. Louis stockyards, helping the head cattle buyer, Speedy Smith.

Soon, Ted can squint at a cow and guess its weight with near accuracy. In the afternoons, he rides back with Speedy to the Krey Packing Company to see the cattle they bought the day before. Often a cattle trader comes along, and they all step into the cooler to see how the cattle dressed out. Every time, the trader says the same thing: "Speed, them cattle was worth the money." The men celebrate with a whiskey.

"Those were kind of rough, tough, crude men working around livestock and wading around in manure all day," Ted will remark later, adding that "they had a heart of gold"—and taught him to cuss with color and precision. "I learned a lot of things from those fellows that I shouldn't have learned at the age of fifteen!"

Taylor School is a man's world, too, but a very different sort. The male teachers, hired because "they can best arouse an intellectual urge in boys," are not rough and frank but bright and socially savvy. One of Ted's favorites, Rupert Allan Jr., will go on to work as Marilyn Monroe's publicity agent, with a client list that also includes Marlene Dietrich, Bette Davis, Rock Hudson, Gina Lollobrigida, Steve McQueen, Jeanne Moreau, and Catherine Deneuve. At Grace Kelly's wedding to Prince Rainier of Monaco, he will corral the 1,600 reporters who mob the wedding, only forty of them invited. Allan stays in touch with the boys, even calling Ted's best friend at Taylor, Harry Willcoxson, years later, before a surgery he intuitively knows he will not survive. "I just want you to know how much you guys meant to me," he explains. "I just wanted to say goodbye."

Harry is a beanpole of a kid, just as sweet and just as irreverent as Ted. Because they were born seven days apart in the same hospital, they refer to each other as maternity brothers. Whenever Ted gets on Harry's nerves, waving his hand imperiously in an attempt to make something happen, Harry says, "Dutchman, I don't want to hear about it!" Used to each other's ways, they will remain friends their whole lives.

"They were not bad boys," Harry's daughter Susan will say, looking back. "Old man Jones would never have put up with bad behavior. They just didn't fit the mold, and their families didn't know what to do with them."

If they could watch these years, the brokers who will be amazed by the latitude Mr. Jones gives his son might understand how even a boulder can be worn down, if the water rushes fast enough.

6

———

Growing Up at Sea

Ted's 1943 yearbook describes him as "an advocate of farming for an occupation, especially as it is done in the 'kingdom of Callaway.'" He is "a true son of the soil," the editors note, and intends to become "a gentleman farmer."

He does graduate from the Taylor School, although a later rumor will insist that he dropped out to fight in World War II. The rumor is understandable; he is impetuous, eager to serve his country. But he is not yet eighteen. Realizing that the war will complicate his yearned-for degree in agriculture, he enrolls in a summer course at the University of Missouri-Columbia. He continues his coursework until the end of October, when his transcript notes that he is "excused from the university." He will not turn eighteen until December 18, but he cannot wait a day longer.

First, he tries to sign up for the Marines, but his eyesight does not pass muster. So he walks across the hall and signs up for the maritime service, the Merchant Marine. First stop: naval training at Sheepshead Bay in Brooklyn, one train stop beyond Coney Island. He and the other trainees wear sailor uniforms, dark blue with red piping, and white sailor hats. They march, row, do calisthenics, swim, do gun drills, learn knots and canvas, practice lifeboat drills. Life gets interesting when they are told to simulate abandoning ship by pulling themselves hand-over-hand along ropes that have been stretched across the swimming pool—which is on fire.

The trainers poured oil onto its surface and struck a match. Now orange blazes above the aqua, and they are supposed to drop into the burning oil, push it away, and swim to the side.

Ted makes it. He survives the spit-and-polish inspections in the barracks every Saturday morning. He secretly loves the formal review that follows, marching on the parade grounds with the band playing. After that, the week's tension snaps, and the guys head for the Pepsi-Cola Canteen, where they can drink free pop and gather up tickets to Broadway shows, Ice Capades, Radio City Music Hall, and the Paramount Theater. Families call the canteen and invite four servicemen to Sunday dinner; churches invite them to dances.

On his first trip to the canteen, Ted scores passes to the Society Canteen at the Fifth Avenue mansion of financier Thomas Fortune Ryan. Only twenty men are invited at a time, and they are served dainty sandwiches while a three-piece combo plays show tunes. There are, "best of all, girls, girls, girls," Ted exults, adding with a sigh, "Very heavily chaperoned—you couldn't pry a girl out the front door with a crowbar."

Saturday nights, he sleeps in the gymnasium annex of a Jewish synagogue. The members have set up cots for a hundred servicemen, and they serve the guys coffee and sweet rolls in the morning.

After the six-month training, Ted is surprised to be asked to stay on a little longer. They want him to teach a class in cable and wire splicing. Tickled, he agrees that he has gotten quite adept at splicing steel cable.

After teaching the class, Ted boards a troop train bound for San Francisco. When they chug into the station at North Platte, Nebraska, the soldiers find a well-stocked canteen waiting for them. Ranchers and their wives have volunteered to staff the canteen, and *everything is free*. Years later, Ted will attend an opening of a Jones office in North Platte, and when he speaks at the town's Rotary Club, he will thank them for their hospitality as if it were yesterday.

His first assignment is guard duty at a former auto dealership turned barracks in downtown San Francisco. With a shore patrol arm band, canvas puttees, a Sam Brown belt, and a wooden billy club, he definitely looks the part, but one of his fellow soldiers is too drunk one night to accept a pleasant request for his pass and ID. The next morning, Ted is reading in the library, and the guy comes in. "You gave me a lot of crap last night," Ted informs him—and the anger he suppressed the night before wells up, and he pops the guy in the nose. Blood shoots everywhere. Ted knows how to wrestle up close to avoid any blows; grappling, they knock over library tables and chairs, and soon footsteps clatter and someone is pulling them apart.

Standing before a lieutenant commander, both men hasten to say that they were not fighting, just horsing around. Nonetheless, Ted is sent across the bay to mop floors for a week, his only consolation the likelihood that his opponent wound up in the infirmary.

The mopping ends with Ted's first real assignment: He will serve in the Pacific on the U.S. Army T.P. 109, a brand-new tugboat. New sheets, new towels—and a new, inexperienced crew. The tug is docked in Oakland, tied up in front of a Russian fish cannery ship that tore a hole in her hull up in the Bering Sea and needs repairs. The 109's crew is under strict orders not to fraternize with the female officers on the cannery ship, lest the Russian men take offense—and take revenge. But one night, crossing the Russian ship's deck to reach the dock, Ted hears an accordion and sees people dancing, and he can't resist. He stands there a minute, keeping time with his foot, and just as he hoped, one of the women beckons to him to come dance. How can he refuse such an offer without starting an international incident? To preserve impartiality, he dances with everyone on the ship.

Once the tug's engine is shipshape, they sail across the bay and tie up near Fisherman's Wharf. Ted falls in love with San Francisco—the cable car rides, the nightly shrimp feasts, the hilltop views, Chinatown…. But they have to leave. They sail out on a Sunday morning, June 3, 1944. Ted has the 8 am till noon watch. He steers the tug away from the dock and right under the Golden Gate Bridge. Then they hit the open sea and he learns that the vessel, as he writes home, "rolls and pitches like a bucking horse." *We'll sink*, he is sure of it, watching the sea rush in through the scuppers and wash across the main deck. He goes back to his bunk and worries about drowning at sea. An hour later, he climbs up to the second deck, sits down on a potato locker, and gives himself a stern lecture: *You chose to be a sailor. You always wanted to be a sailor. You can do anything anybody else can do. Have faith in your ship—you can't get off anyway! Enjoy the experience.*

A new attitude slips into place. In the next fourteen months, he will not allow himself to doubt either the tug's seaworthiness or his own.

§

From that 96-foot tug, Ted sees a big chunk of the world. First stop: Honolulu. They sail alongside a wooden Army tug and two giant steel tugs that are towing a hundred-ton floating crane. The next morning, they hook alongside the steel tugs, and now three of them are towing the crane.

Often Ted has both the first and last four-hour watch. At midnight, he has learned to look for flying fish, their wings as gossamer thin as a dragonfly's, stranded on deck. One minute they are gliding on top of a wave; the next minute, they are dying in a strangely hard, dry place. Ted scoops up the casualties and stows them in the galley refrigerator; the next morning, the cook will fry them up for breakfast.

It was second mate Jake Jacobson, an older Danish sailor, who tipped Ted off about the flying fish. He has all sorts of information, and Ted soaks it up. In return, whenever Jake returns from shore leave off-kilter drunk, Ted runs down and guides the older man around the ancient dock's holes and rotten planks.

Ted loves the sea—its moonlit

Ted at 19 in the Merchant Marine

mystery and morning calm, its plenty, the surprises that charge you with adrenaline, the constant motion. He could make a life of this, he decides. Someone snaps a photo of him, shirtless and tanned, a lean 120 pounds, so boyishly handsome and full of vitality, he would be snatched up by central casting. Years later, Pat will come across the photo and grin: "To the day he died, that's what Ted thought he looked like."

They sail to Funafuti, a coral atoll. Ted grips the wheel hard, guiding it through a narrow channel blasted from the barrier reef. They are caught in the wake of a small Navy crash boat, and the thrashing surf fills his ears as the tide rushes through the channel behind them. Ted steers hard, pulling one way then the other, desperate to keep the tug in the channel. His captain paces the pilot house, snapping commands, waiting as long as his nerves can stand it before ordering the second mate to take the wheel from Ted.

Ten minutes later, they sail into a placid lagoon. Ted breathes a sigh of relief, not at all sore that he was replaced at the wheel. That narrow channel, with a riptide, was terrifying.

"Jonesy, have some more spuds," the captain says at dinner, a manly signal that Ted is all right; he has not disgraced himself.

They leave Funafuti to tow an oil barge to New Guinea. This time, they sail right into a storm so violent, the chain bridle on the barge snaps and it drifts away. The waves are smoking; that is the best way Ted can describe it. Their white crests are blown off again and again by gusts of wind, and rain is hitting the pitch-black water so hard, all he can see is spray.

The next day, they find the barge. Ted kneels on deck, directly below the cable, to coil some heavy lines. He hears a noise and glances up just in time to see the first mate yell and fall backwards, knocking someone down behind him. The cable has jumped out of its guides and is swinging wildly. Ted sees one of his shipmates, Sparks (Kenneth Phillips), in midair, nearly upright, only his head bent over as he plummets toward the sea. Did he jump overboard to avoid the cable or did it knock him off? Ted looks back and sees his friend, second mate Jake Jacobson, pinned beneath the cable and half overboard himself.

Ducking under the cable, Ted starts to pull it to starboard, then reconsiders and pushes it to starboard from the other side. This frees Jacobson, and Ted rushes to help lift him off the upraised fantail before the cable can swing back. Dodging its arc, they carry him to a cabin while the others frantically search for Sparks. Sharks swim in these waters. The last glimpse of him, he is bleeding heavily, and he sinks rapidly out of sight.

His body is never recovered. Jacobson dies that evening; the cable smashed into his head before he went down, and the damage is too serious to survive.

Ted and his shipmates give depositions to Army authorities at Espiritu Santo naval base in the New Hebrides Islands. Then they sail on, sobered by the loss.

§

The tug loads up on fresh mutton from Australia. Most of the crew members groan, but Ted actually likes the stuff, especially when Phil, the cook, spices it up in a curry over rice. Ted is also fine with the frequent breakfast of baked beans and hotcakes (though less fine with powdered eggs). When the sea is so rough that plates slide off the table, Phil tethers a giant pot of baked beans to the stove, wires its lid to the pot, and serves nothing else until the storm subsides.

In the southern waters, the nights are spectacular. Now below the equator, Ted can no longer see the North Star; instead, he gazes up at the Southern Cross. Taught by Jacobson to watch closely at night, Ted watches porpoises dive through the bow wave and playfully circle the boat, their sleek bodies glowing with phosphorescent light.

The next yell of "Landfall" comes late at night, when they reach Milne Bay. Seasoned, the captain mutters that "safety lies in deep water" and circles all night, towing three barges, so he can use daylight to navigate the minefield and the tricky channel. In the morning, they are led in by a pilot boat. Many of its Australian crew members, relaxed in their regulation short pants, are shirtless and barefoot. They "boil a billy," which Ted now knows means a cup of tea, and splash whiskey into it, and somebody pulls out an accordion and somebody else a harmonica, and they all sing.

Ted will be suggesting singalongs for the rest of his life, eager to be transported by music and camaraderie.

§

His naval training comes in handy: One day Ted splices an eye in a two-inch steel cable. The captain looks dubious, not convinced the eye will hold, but shrugs and walks away; there's no time to secure it further. They leave port, heading for Manila. In the middle of the night, the barge they are towing sinks.

Ted's splice holds so strong, the barge nearly brings the tug down with it. Finally, one of Ted's shipmates grabs an ax and swings it hard to sever the cable. The barge glugs down alone.

In fall 1944, the tug sails for the Philippines to join the Battle of Leyte, an amphibious invasion led by General Douglas MacArthur. The Philippine Islands are strategically key; they were taken over by the Japanese in 1942. Now a convoy of old, slow ships—Ted suspects some saw World War I—is making its way to the islands to lend support after the surprise invasion. The tug is traveling loose, not towing anything; it comes alongside the barges to check the lashing lines on their cargo.

On the landing beaches in San Pedro Bay, a large, natural harbor, the bows of the heaviest ships sink into the sand, and suction holds them there. The tug spends days pulling landing craft off the beach. One day, two bulldozers push a ship's bow while they pull from astern. Finally the ship breaks free—and comes toward the little tug at full speed! This is just the kind of excitement Ted relishes—as long as he lives to tell about it.

The war is heating up, and when they head back out to the ocean, Ted watches dogfights overhead between U.S. planes and Japanese Zero planes. One Japanese plane angles in low and drops a bomb on a liberty ship anchored near the tug. Ted's crew fires at the plane, as do other ships nearby. Hit, it veers and tries to fly into another liberty ship, destroying it in a final act of glory—but misses and crashes into the sea.

Soon the U.S. troops control the air. Ted is fighting his own war, though, with a new captain. "You've been getting too damned smart, and I'm the man who will take it out of you," the captain informs him.

"I don't know about that," Ted says slowly, "but I do know that the first mate's responsibilities are to see to it that every lifeboat has ten gallons of canned water, five pounds of ship's biscuits, et cetera, *per man*. I also know that these rations are not on the T.P. 109. I'm sure the port director ashore will be interested."

The captain glowers. "I don't run ashore every time something comes up on board ship."

"I don't either," Ted agrees, "but I am too far from home to take any crap from anybody."

The captain's revenge is to make Ted polish every inch of brass in the pilot house. Ted tosses all the brass polish overboard. The captain buys more at the next port and tells him he must also paint the pilot house. So he paints the brass radiator first.

The captain sputters with rage. "You told me to paint the pilot house," Ted says innocently, "and I thought I should paint anything that might glisten in the sunlight and give our position away to an enemy plane."

This has become a game. The underlying problem is a serious one, though, and other crew members are also suffering under this captain's whims. When they dock in the Philippines six weeks later, the second engineer gets roaring drunk, goes to the captain's cabin, and beats the hell out of him. The next morning, the entire crew submits their resignations to the port authorities. The captain and the second engineer both disappear; no one knows where.

This is Ted's chance, though. While the tug is docked in Manila, in June 1945, he enlists, finally old enough, in the Army. Two months later, the United States drops the atomic bomb and ends the war with Japan.

Ted with an Army buddy in Japan, 1946

Assigned to the 24th division of the Army of Occupation, Ted is one of the first soldiers to land on a home island, Shikoku. His job is to go from village to village collecting weapons. Often people turn them over voluntarily, with courtesy. Ted is thorough, though; if ground looks freshly dug, he excavates to make sure nothing has been buried. At a school, he finds weapons hidden under straw in a cloakroom; he and his mates also find a cache of weapons hidden under bags of rice in a warehouse.

They need not carry guns, though. Because Emperor Hirohito has told his people the war is over, everyone honors that decree. Ted will later marvel to Patsy about this, just as he marvels to his parents about the fine woodworking at the Japanese naval barracks; the well cultivated, terraced farms; the luscious tangerines they somehow manage to grow even in a

climate that gets so cold, he sleeps in his long johns, wrapped in a wool
sleeping bag inside a waterproof one.

One day he visits a Japanese family, sits on the floor, sips tea, and
listens to piano music with them. Another day he bathes in the warm
springs at the community bathhouse, then eats cold fish and turnips with
chopsticks and drinks hot sake.

"A lot of the fellows are buying kimonos," he writes to his mother.
"Would you like one? Do you think Grandma would like one?"

Pride warms the letters: He has done mapmaking for the intelligence
officer, spliced high tension lines, prepared for possible insurgency. But a
little weariness is creeping in, and sometimes he is wistful: "We have been
eating Spam for a month. I recall the time Uncle Will took me to lunch at
the Pierre in New York." He is reading his parents' letters avidly: "I know
exactly where you are going to put the pond, and I think you picked a
good spot." Once, he mentions receiving a letter from Anne Young, but
there is no mention of her sister Pat. "Have Martha give my regards to
Patty Lawton," he writes. "I would like to go to a dance with her right now.
I think I am going to have to put that kind of thing on my post-war list."

Within six months, he has been promoted to first sergeant. Army life,
like life at sea, suits him. He has met men of different colors, creeds, and
backgrounds, listened to their stories, made room for their world views,
worked tightly and smoothly with them when a mistake could have
been fatal.

"I think I grew up going to sea," Ted will say later. "Some of the best
education I ever got was as a sailor and as a sergeant in the Army."

§

Ted has been sending his paychecks home to his father, who promised to
invest them in government bonds but has found a better deal buying bonds
in the Hydraulic Press Brick Company. A brick empire founded in St.
Louis, by 1890 Hydraulic was the world's largest manufacturer of pressed
brick. Now it is in default—but owns valuable real estate all over the
country. One of those lots will become the site of the Pentagon.

A nest egg, a good and secure job, prospects…plenty waits for Ted
back home. But one night, alone for long bleak hours on the night watch,

he thinks about a future off this boat, a home of his own, a woman to sleep with every night. He makes a decision: He is not going to live in some genteel suburb like his parents. He will live on the farm, where life is honest and simple and gentle.

And while he cannot yet be sure of this, he has already met the woman who will share that life.

7

—

Enough of New York

Ted returns home and resumes his studies at Mizzou, where Pat is finishing her degree in soil science. But he manages only a few months of study before a bout of appendicitis, and his father takes advantage of the interruption to urge a different path.

For once, Ted complies. He withdraws from the university, and in April 1947, he takes the train to New York. Probably the Pennsylvania, his favorite. If you stay up late and watch, you can see both ends of the train at once when it chugs around Horseshoe Curve.

In Manhattan, he rents a $2 room at the YMCA, then applies for a job at the New York Stock Exchange. He is hired as a page, the lowest possible entry-level job. Carrying messages back and forth, he listens to the conversations of brokers and reporters, and what he hears shocks him. These guys don't know any more about which stocks are going to go up than the man in the moon. The whole thing's a crapshoot, their advice no more than a guess.

He is not cut out to be a speculator, he realizes. The uncertainty unnerves him. He likes the idea of *investing*, but in solid, known, established companies.

After a few months as a page, Ted apprentices at Josephthal & Co., a correspondent firm of Edward D. Jones. He starts in billing, then moves to the margin department, where he makes friends with Gene Martin, another margin clerk. Missing the sea, Ted often suggests a walk to the docks of the East and Hudson rivers on their lunch hour. Ignoring the No Trespassing signs, he and Gene walk right up the gangplanks. When a guard approaches, Ted does not wait to be questioned. "What kind of cargo is she handling?" he asks. "What about the insurance papers?" He keeps talking until the guard, assuming the young men are there to insure or inspect the cargo, steps aside.

Not once is he stopped.

With his usual hearty interest in good but affordable food, Ted scopes out the options and finds the era's version of fast food, "a hurry up, stand up kind of restaurant" called Seaberg's. Its motto, customers joke, is "Eat it and beat it." Sliding onto a stool, Ted studies the menu hanging on a signboard, then gives his order to one of the craggy-faced older men waiting tables. They all look like they've hit rock bottom at least once, but the white aprons spruce them up a bit. He learns to order efficiently—"I'll have the No. 2, codfish cakes with peas and a cup of black coffee." The waiters write nothing down. When they return with his tray, they put a marble in a box labeled No. 2, because the inventory control system is counting the marbles. Ted knows this because, always curious about process, he has asked. It fascinates him that there is no check: You just sing out the total you owe, and the cashier takes your money. Every once in a while, he forgets to add in a piece of pie, so he tacks it onto the next day's bill.

"How can you run this place and know whether people are quoting the right figure on what they ate?" he asks the manager.

"Well, most people are honest," the man says, "and they sing it out. In time, we notice somebody who's cheating regularly. After all, every day we balance the books, and we've got inventory control on what we serve. The truth is, it doesn't pay us to write down the check, and the waiters we've got wouldn't get it straight anyway." Ted, who has been learning cashiering, likes the common sense of this.

Next, he moves to the research department, learning how to analyze securities. A man who works in Josephthal's wire room drills him every afternoon to prep him for the New York Stock Exchange exam. He passes.

The man who runs the direct wire to St. Louis, Mr. Hagen, shakes hands with Ted and intones, "We welcome you into our midst with all its rights and privileges."

§

The YMCA helps Ted find a room for rent, living with a family on Central Park West. The family has a small son, and there is a lovely young woman, a relative, who comes every day to babysit. When Ted comes home from work, the two of them often take the baby to Central Park together. Ted smiles to himself when he sees people glance at him with a young Japanese woman and a Japanese baby, trying to figure out what at the time would be an unusual scenario.

A few months later, he moves to a rooming house for men at what he calls "a very fine address" on 71st Street a few doors from Park Avenue. (Interesting that he even takes note, this man who will live on a farm and beg his staff to reserve him an inexpensive hotel room whenever he travels.) His $240 monthly rent includes breakfast and dinner and feels like "pretty high living," he tells friends, even though his room is so small, he has to close the door to the hall and put his suitcase on the bed every day. The twenty-two men who live there have the service of a butler and his wife, and Ted savors the luxury of putting his laundry out once a week and seeing it come back clean and folded.

Residents can invite a date for dinner; she will then, of course, serve the after-dinner coffee. One of these young women turns out to be the daughter of a man who, as chairman of the board, guided the largest ad agency in the country at the time, J. Walter Thompson. She is dating Gabe Hauge, assistant state treasurer for New York, and Gabe is writing speeches for Governor Thomas Dewey's presidential campaign. In the evening, Ted often keeps Gabe company as he listens to his candidate on the radio. With a copy of the speech in front of him, Gabe underlines in red pencil any phrases Dewey does not hit with sufficient oomph.

It is the summer of '48, and Dewey is running against Harry S. Truman, the incumbent but also the official underdog. One night, the guys at the rooming house all write their predicted winner on a slip of paper, then toss it into a hat. The votes are counted. Twenty-one of the twenty-two name Dewey as the next president. The lone man who picks Truman is in the advertising business, and he has run some kind of straw vote campaign showing that Truman will win. They all laugh at him—until November.

By the morning of Truman's surprise victory, Ted is back in St. Louis. He has done his apprenticeship. He has realized just how vehemently he dislikes big cities, and this has renewed his determination to live on the family farm. Young enough to be idealistic, he is still appalled by just how little the brokers know about what they are doing. Their casualness with other people's money startles him.

If he can't be a full-time farmer, he intends to be a very different kind of broker than these New York fellows.

8

——

His Own Company

Ted's father began his career selling bonds, and when the stock market crashed in 1929, he returned his focus to bonds. He scooped up one company after another as they declared bankruptcy. He bought federal farm credit bonds for ten cents on the dollar; that was how he acquired the family farm, paying just $6,000 for a 750-acre farm originally appraised at $60,000.

In 1932, Edward voted for a Democrat for the first (and no doubt the last) time. Franklin Delano Roosevelt had pledged to end Prohibition, and Edward's father-in-law presided over the Griesedieck Western Brewery. Edward had watched the company make do by selling soda water, root beer, and ice through the long, dry desert of Prohibition. He had urged his father-in-law to take his company public before the amendment was repealed, and Henry had agreed.

FDR won the election, and when he signed off in 1933 and corks popped all over the nation, Griesedieck Western had immediate capital. Revving up its production lines, it could barely keep up with the demand for Stag beer.

In 1941, Edward bought himself a seat on the New York Stock Exchange. (Until 2006, the NYSE was a private company, and trading on the floor was a privilege that required you to pay.) The price of a seat was meant to fluctuate with the strength of the U.S. economy, and Edward being Edward, he had been watching closely. In the 1920s, the price of a seat had reached $625,000; when the market crashed, it fell to $68,000. Edward managed one of his deals, paying just $21,000 for another man's vacated seat.

The following year, he moved Edward D. Jones & Co. a few blocks west, to an office at Eighth and Olive that was strategically located above a nut and candy company. The aroma soon had everybody punch-drunk, but they wouldn't have long to enjoy it. In 1943, the president of Boatmen's Bank, Tom K. Smith, called Edward. Whitaker & Co., a venerable St. Louis brokerage house, owed the bank roughly $50,000, secured by drainage bonds, institutional bonds, and a Jewish synagogue issue. Nearly all those bonds were in default, and the bank examiner was pestering Smith to clear the loan. "Eddie," he said, "if you'll take this off my hands, I'll finance you."

So Edward paid off Whitaker's loan and bought the company, thus making Jones, by association, the oldest brokerage firm west of the Mississippi. His timing was excellent: World War II was gathering a deadly momentum, and the Office of Price Administration intended to take over the Edward D. Jones office space and its heavenly fog of almond and chocolate. Edward moved four blocks east to the Whitaker offices, which were tucked inside the old Everett House Hotel at Fourth and Olive.

Four stories high, the building was slabbed with cool marble from an abandoned Mormon temple in Nauvoo, Illinois. A printing company occupied the top floor, and when its huge press cranked up, the brokers watched the light fixtures swing above their heads.

As soon as the acquisition was final, Edward summoned all of Whitaker's staff—the sales force, secretaries, everybody down to the messenger boy. If they stayed with him for six months, he promised, he would guarantee their salaries and sales commissions. Then, he said, "we will sit down and exchange ideas, and if you want to leave me or if you can do better, that will be either of our options."

They all stayed.

§

The year after he bought Whitaker, Edward was forced to take over the brewery as well as his own expanded brokerage house. At only forty-seven years of age, Henry Griesedieck had startled everyone by dying.

Now Edward had to spend every morning in Belleville, Illinois, at the brewery. At lunch time, his chauffeur drove him across the river to the Jones office, where brokers teased that he was doing this in the wrong order. Wouldn't it better to wind up at a brewery in late afternoon?

Ah, but he was not there to relax. Within three years, Griesedieck Western was the thirteenth largest brewery in the nation, quenching American thirst with pale gold cans of clean, malty, ultra-cheap Stag.

The company had some fun with its Stag blimp, but there was a bit of a kerfluffle: The startling appearance of this giant and very odd bird and the vibrato of its whirring engine so alarmed a dairy farmer's herd that he filed suit, swearing that the trauma had stopped his cows from producing milk.

Nonetheless, Stag, which cost only a dime, was St. Louis's top-selling beer. In 1949, when Arthur Godfrey complained on air that a strike in New York was depriving him of beer, Edward offered to send him all the Stag he can drink.

In 1950, Edward bought the upscale Hyde Park Brewery, too. Griesedieck Western was now the nation's eighth largest brewer.

Edward admiring the number #1 selling St. Louis beer of the late 1940s

§

Many a night, Edward and Ursula went out for a swanky candlelit dinner with the Phelans, only to have Edward excuse himself before dessert. He had to make it to the Chase Hotel by 9:45 so he could introduce a pair of pugilists or present the Winner's Cup to Gorgeous George. A sought-after impresario at wrestling and boxing matches, Edward reveled in the color and schtick of these gladiatorial contests. He even bought an interest in Chillin' Charlie Riley, aka the Finney Avenue Fashion Plate. A featherweight prizefighter, Riley was as fond of fine threads as Edward, but was also a contender. One urban legend even has his ignominious, unexpected defeat at the gloved hands of Willie Pep serving as cover for the Great Brink's Robbery. Supposedly the guards were boxing fans, glued to the radio broadcast of the fight and oblivious to any unusual noises. The robbers got away with $2.7 million, rather more than Edward's take on the fight, which was less than ten grand.

It makes a fabulous story—except that the fight was January 16, 1950, and the robbery took place at 7 pm the next day.

§

St. Louis's two top beers grew in parallel, Budweiser selling for fifteen cents and Stag for a dime. But in 1954, Bud lost its first-place national rank, and Anheuser-Busch threatened to cut the beer's price to a dime to regain at least local supremacy. This did not bode well. Edward swiftly arranged to sell the brewery—something Ursula had been urging him to do—to the Canadian maker of Carling beer. With the help of Gus Griesedieck, a cousin who was an astute lawyer, Edward finessed one of his ingenious deals, selling the vats, hoppers, and kegs for almost $10 million but retaining the corporate identity. Stockholders could either liquidate their holdings and pay hefty taxes or retain their shares in Griesedieck, which would now be a closed-end mutual fund instead of a brewery. (The fund would stay healthy until it closed in 1976.)

The night Edward finalized the sale, he came home and exclaimed, perhaps to shore up his resolve, "I cannot run two businesses!" His daughter Ann nodded; she had sensed the drama in the air. "Don't tell anyone until it hits the press," he added.

Frank Finnegan, who had joined Edward D. Jones the year before, noticed a change in his boss after the sale. "He was the happiest guy in the world," Finnegan would recall later, "because now he could be with us all the time."

He was also shrewd; the bottom would drop out of the beer industry soon after the sale. No matter; he was free. On a trip to New York, a waiter asked for his drink order. "Hell," he said, "give me a Budweiser. Everybody else in the world is drinking it."

§

By midcentury, Edward owned quite a few companies, among them a wholesaler called General Grocer. On Saturdays, he took his grandson, John Key, to visit all of General Grocer's customers, little mom and pop grocery stores dotted around St. Louis. John dashed up and down the aisles while his grandfather checked in with the owners.

Late on a Saturday, Edward would finally relax, sitting on his screened-in porch listening to a ball game on the radio. In 1953, he sent an exuberant telegram to Gussie Busch to congratulate him for buying the Cardinals. In 1962, Edward wrote to the legendary announcer Harry Caray and received a quick response: "It is a pleasure to write to the man I always refer to as the smartest man I have ever known in the brewery business. Kidding aside, it was nice of you to take the time to write your letter of October 3. While we didn't have a good season, the final three games did provide an exciting finish." After signing the letter "Harry," he added a postscript: "How come you didn't buy a ball club with the $18,000,000 and when are you going to clue me in on some of those red hot things your firm handles?"

9

—

A Confluence of Lives

In October 1948, Ted comes home to St. Louis and becomes the eighteenth broker in his father's firm. Patsy is still at Mizzou—where he wanted to be. He will marry her, he knows that now, but they are biding their time until she graduates.

Ted lives at home with his parents, or at least, that's where he stows his stuff. After a week's training in marking up over-the-counter stocks, he goes on the road. That Sunday night, he drives to Hillsboro, Illinois, and by Monday morning, he is standing outside the Montgomery County Bank, psyching himself up to make his first call.

He spends most of every week on the road, selling securities in small towns across central Illinois. In addition to Hillsboro, his territory includes Litchfield, Jerseyville, Carrollton, Whitehall, Roodhouse, Winchester, and Pittfield, and he drives 150 miles a day, knocking on doors, working out of the trunk of his car. He drives through blizzards, fords creeks, gets his engine soaked and frozen and has to have his car rolled down the street to a mechanic. Nights, he stays in shabby old hotels, asking for a (cheaper) second-floor room. For $2.50, he can usually get an iron bed, clean sheets, and a communal bathroom. It's not so different from the Army.

Gradually, he gets the hang of this selling thing. With his apple cheeks, slanted brows, clear blue eyes and mischievous grin, he has plenty of boyish charm, and he is learning to use his gift for storytelling and his showman's love of props to make investment strategies clear. Still, it's slow going—yet his checks, he notices, are fatter than they should be. He confronts his father. Edward is making sure his son receives commissions—even when they are premature.

"I will not take charity," Ted snaps. "And if I have to work for this company, I'm not going to stay in St. Louis. I'm moving out to the country."

He rents an office over a hardware store in Montgomery City, Missouri.

By now, he knows that the only way to do business in the rural Midwest is through referrals from satisfied customers or pillars of the community. Like a modern-day Lewis or Clark, he explores the territories of Hillsboro, Warrenton, Moberly, Hannibal, Mexico, Bowling Green, Fayette, Macon, Louisville, Kirksville....

One day, he is picked up by the Warrenton police because he does not have a peddler's license. He calls his father long-distance from the station, not sure what to do.

"Get a peddler's license," Edward says, "and keep calling on people."

§

In 1949, soil experts from the U.S. Soil Conservation Service Agency come out to the Jones family farm in Williamsburg. They run soil tests, examine the cropping system, note where erosion is occurring. Ted wants an organized farm plan. With the experts' advice, he starts a program, picking up rocks, filling in ditches, sowing grass to forestall erosion, spreading lime and fertilizer. He's getting the place ready.

Next, he proposes to Patsy (only he calls her that) in a cemetery. She will later forbid him to reveal the setting at parties.

Pat and Ted cut the cake, September 29, 1950.

They set a September date. Then, with his bachelor days scheduled to end with summer and his fiancée motoring on Route 66 with her high school friends, Ted decides to spend the summer of 1950 in Europe with a pal, Ralph Cohen. While they are in Austria, the Korean War begins. Ted's stomach clenches. Now a second lieutenant in the Army Reserve, he is sure he will be called up. Right away, he reports to the appropriate overseas office, but he is told not to worry yet, just check in when he goes home. To his sweet relief, he is never called.

Pat's father died years earlier, so Hilda gives an evening party to announce her daughter's engagement. The wedding takes place on September 29, 1950, at Pat's family home, 415 North Hanley. Effie, her grandmother, is there, and so is Ted's grandmother on the Griesedieck side. Pat's sister Anne has flown in for the occasion, and Pat's sister-in-law is there…. Except for a few close friends like Harry Willcoxson and his young wife, it is very much a family affair. Ted has a razor-sharp short haircut and a solemn look; Pat wears a taffeta dress with a fitted bodice and a Queen Anne collar. Beneath the band of taffeta holding her fingertip veil in place, her hair looks, well, a lot like it looks every other day.

The brief ceremony takes place in late afternoon. Dispensing with attendants, Ted and Pat stand in front of a fireplace mantel laden with white autumn flowers, fern, huckleberry, and burning tapers. The Rev. Dr. Thaddeus Clark, pastor of First Unitarian Church, officiates, and Pat is "given away," though she hardly would have thought of it that way, by her uncle, Dr. Edward Curtis Taylor, Ted's former headmaster.

Both Pat and Ted are twenty-four. On the wedding certificate, his handwriting is bigger, a little flourishy but not grandiose. Pat's writing is small, tight, less loopy, more reserved—but the ink is darker and heavier. A graphoanalyst would have fun with the implications.

There is no grand European honeymoon, no flashy resort or tropical paradise. The newspaper announces that "Mr. and Mrs. Jones will motor through the Ozarks on their wedding trip." It is, after all, where they met.

§

Home from their Missouri honeymoon, the newlyweds move into a little cabin on Hilda's land in Eureka. They stay through the winter of 1950, but the following spring, they rent an apartment in Montgomery City near Ted's little office and, more important, the Jones family farm.

Their rent is $32 a month, and the apartment is on the top story (really, Pat tells friends, the attic) of a large frame house. They have a separate entrance, which sounds dignified but requires climbing a wooden stairway on the exterior of the house and clambering through what used to be a dormer window.

For four years, they live in this apartment, coping with frozen pipes every time the weather turns cold. Every weekend, they are in Williamsburg, cleaning up trash on the farm, tearing down old buildings, preparing to live there year-round.

Ursula is not best pleased by this decision. Indeed, she and Edward refuse to sell Ted the farm. Furious, he takes Pat on a trip to the West Coast and, while there, applies for a job selling securities with another firm.

Alarmed, his parents soften their attitude. Despite plenty of evidence to the contrary, Ursula insists on blaming Pat for the harebrained scheme. Farms are quaint for summertime or autumn weekends, but they are not meant to be a permanent abode, and as a woman, she should know that.

Ted has most definitely not married, as many do, a woman just like his mother. Both are smart and independent, but Ursula is stern and uncompromising. Her husband calls her Queenie, and indeed, "she looked like Queen Victoria," one of her granddaughters will later observe. "Very German—sensible shoes, dessert at every meal." She reads avidly (that trait she does share with Pat) and insists that one's hands must be clean before reverently picking up a book. But she is also surprisingly girly and can even be frivolous; she loves to shop, and the clerks at Tiffany's knew her by name. Every winter, she takes the train south to Pompano Beach, Florida, to spend the coldest months at the Sea Ranch resort, and she sends boxes of clothes back to her grandkids. For the girls, she always sends three sizes of the same dress, and when she is in St. Louis, she has linen dresses custom-made for them at the Woman's Exchange.

For herself, Ursula chooses conservatively, navy or light gray. She searches high and low for comfortable shoes, because arthritis has left her feet gnarled, tender, and burning. The day she finds an especially forgiving shoe—a Delman, one of the oldest salon brands in the country—she asks the clerk to send her five pair.

"Mrs. Jones, how would you like to pay for these?" he inquires politely. Her response is to hand him her card—not a credit card, as they do not yet exist, but her engraved personal calling card. It suffices.

§

When Ted makes his obligatory weekly appearance at the Jones office in downtown St. Louis, he learns technique from Al McKenzie, a genius of a salesman who became a broker in January 1929 and somehow stayed optimistic. As the catastrophes of the Great Depression mounted, a banker in Illinois told Al, "Don't give in to what's going on. Cows are still having calves." He set his jaw and managed to make a good living for his wife and six children, and now he says only, "The first few years were difficult."

Monday mornings, Al takes Ted and a few other young salespeople to the Missouri Athletic Club for breakfast. As he teaches them the principles of sales and the value of mutual funds, the young brokers stick a few of the MAC's famous caramel rolls in their pockets for lunch, because nobody is making a whole lot of money yet.

At the time, mutual funds are considered a last resort; "real men" pick their own stocks, or let their advisor pick. But Al thinks they're a solid and responsible choice, and he keeps telling Edward, "We need to start a mutual funds marketing and training department."

Finally, in exasperation more than agreement, Edward says, "Oh, okay, fine, just do it!" In time, mutual funds will be the largest sector in the company's retail business. Six mutual funds will constitute the bulk of Ted's investment portfolio. He will carry a card in his pocket that bears the list of six, and he'll pull it out to show other brokers.

"This business will pay you a premium for honesty and for poise," Al tells the young men. He teases them—but only about their strengths, so everybody can enjoy the banter.

Al is firm about right and wrong—he has been dubbed "the conscience of the firm"—but he has a soft heart, and you can bring him to tears with "Edelweiss." He has six kids of his own, and when the neighbor kids converge to play softball on summer evenings, he coaches, making sure every kid gets a hit. The garage is center field, he tells them. If you hit a line drive and it breaks a garage window, it's an automatic double.

§

The rest of Ted's education consists of trying stuff, researching ideas, reading avidly, observing. Conventional wisdom does not impress him. As a result, he sees things differently than other people—and notices opportunities they might miss.

After a day in the downtown office, he swings by his parents' home—out of filial duty but also for the food. Pat is a healthy and indifferent cook. Ursula keeps Pfeiffer's pastry shop in business, and she always fills a cookie jar with iced oatmeal and windmill cookies. "Teddy always sticks his hand in there first thing," she informs her daughter Ann, smiling fondly. "Pat doesn't buy this kind of thing."

Edward and Jack Phelan, mid-1950s—the Jones salesforce begins to expand.

A few cookies, and Ted is back on the road. So is Jack Phelan, who joined the company in 1950, right after college. "Go ask Uncle Eddie for a job," his mother said, so Jack called to make an appointment, and Edward said, "Come on over now." When Jack came in, Edward fired three questions at him: "Did you graduate? Have you had your shots? Did you go to the dentist? Okay, start Monday."

Jack knows Ted from spending days at the Jones farm when they were both kids. They shared a few memorable summers at sleep-away camp, too. Then they lost touch.

Now, they will become each other's staunchest allies. Jack starts out with a simple job, watching the tickertape and marking changes on the chalkboard, nearly forty feet long, that displays all the quotes for the salespeople in the Board Room. Rows run across that board: Stock, Close,

Open, High, Low, Last, High/Low. The big blue-chips of the Fifties—
Rexall, U.S. Steel, Walgreen, Warner Bros., Brown Shoe—are all up on
the board. Jack climbs the short ladder at the end of the board and moves
across the walkway, a white jacket over his shirt and tie to catch the
chalk dust.

At their desks, brokers reach for the heavy handsets of their black
rotary phones, spin the dial. Clients sit in chairs, chatting with them
as they work, watching the board. The constraints of privacy have not
yet arrived.

Soon, Jack's days at the board are over. He has earned the job of
salesman—and he was born for it. While Ted travels to small towns in
Missouri, Jack's in his VW wagon traveling to small towns in southern
Illinois. Saturday mornings, they're both back in the downtown office, and
they trade stories. Jack tells how a client in Olney suggested they have
dinner together. They had a beer first, and then the man called the Hotel
Litz down the street, and the next thing Jack knew, a kid was riding up the
street on a bicycle with a tray balanced on his head and two dinners on
the tray.

Ted talks about seeing an underwriting for A.B. Chance common
stock and deciding to go to a little town called Centralia and see if he can
scare up some business. He has learned that whenever you reach a new
town, you stop at the gas station and ask who the five richest folks in town
are. This time, he stops first at the Standard gas station—he needs gas
anyway—and asks the mechanic to check under the hood, oh, and check
the battery, too. When the guy returns to show him the dipstick, Ted says,
"Hey, I'm up here selling stocks and bonds, and I've got some A.B. Chance
stock. Who should I call on? Who's got some money?"

"Mr. Chance," comes the answer, and Ted sighs. "He's the one *selling*
the stock." He's not giving up, though. He asks the mechanic to wash his
car and rotate his tires and see if he needs new ones (the prospect of a
lucrative sale). When he returns to pick up the car, he sees a telephone
book hanging from a greasy string and snaps it free. "Okay, come over
here," he calls to the mechanic. "Bill Alexander. Has he got any money?
What about Henry Anderson?" They work their way through the phone
book. (It's a small town, and people know who's loaded.) Then Ted goes to

the phone company, buys the station a new phone book, buys himself one for a quarter, and transfers all his checkmarks.

He works on the A.B. Chance offering for three weeks, parking his car at the station and walking through town. One evening, when he walks back to pick up his car, the mechanic calls, "Hey, did you call on a Mary McKenzie?" He points at a woman climbing the steps to a nearby house. "There she is, just home from work."

Ted approaches her and explains his mission. "Edward Jones isn't handling it," she says crisply. "Stifel is the principal underwriter."

"You're right," he says, realizing she must work there. "But I'm talking to a lot of people here in Centralia. I wanted to see if you wanted to buy some stock. We're about to run out."

Alarmed, she tells him she has a list of people who wrote the company expressing interest weeks earlier. He takes the list from her and assures her he will take care of these people. And so he does.

"I felt like a thief in the night," he tells Phelan, unable to believe his luck.

In temperament, these two make a perfect team: Ted the shit-disturber, Jack the smoother-over, preppy and confident and sweet. He might show up in green corduroys with a pink sweater over his shoulder; Ted will be wearing a plaid shirt and the eternal khakis. They critique each other, share tips and failures, commiserate.

When they begin to play larger roles in the company, they start getting together, along with their wives, at the Phelans's house every Monday evening. Pat drives in from the country, her dog in the back of the station wagon, and the two couples have dinner, the men scheming about the future of the firm. "Jack, someday this firm will have cream stations all over the Midwest," Ted says, referring to the milk stops where every little railroad picks up cans of rich cream. They are on the same page, but the older partners are a few chapters back, not at all sure Ted's ideas make sense.

"He will be a good boss," Jack assures the older men at the firm. When Ted and his dad clash, Jack arbitrates. As far as Jack can see, Edward is a very fine salesman and almost an aristocrat in manner, but Ted has more street sense; he's a true entrepreneur. And his vision of expanding the company to offices in small towns across the country, reaching people who don't have access to a fancy brokerage firm, makes total sense.

§

Every weekend, Ted and Pat work on the farm, chopping persimmon sprouts out of ditches, clearing and planting. Pat makes a uniform of flannel shirts and jeans; Ted favors worn khakis that have shrunk to well above his ankles and a tired (but starched and pressed) Brooks Brothers shirt.

Once they move to the farm year-round, they start work in earnest. First they tear down the crumbling two-story farmhouse Ted refers to as Pneumonia Alley. It was built before the Civil War, and its soft brick was probably made on site by enslaved Blacks. The knowledge sits heavy.

Before Ted and Pat build themselves a new house, though, they put in a pond, choosing as their site an eroded ditch so big you could, in Pat's words, "lose a horse." Spotting a big crow's nest makes the name easy: Crow Pond. Later, they will put in Teal Lake, Duckweed Pond, Wood Pond, Lotus Pond—seventeen lakes and ponds total. Eventually, as their understanding of prairie landscape changes, they will convert all but four to wetland. But Crow Pond will stay, and it will always be Pat's favorite place to swim.

In 1953, the pond priority addressed, Ted and Pat build themselves a smallish, practical house. They will have a metal roof, they decide, so they can hear the rain, and so they will never have to reshingle it. They argue over ceilings—Ted wants them high, but Pat knows their furnace will be working overtime come winter.

Thus begin decades of experimentation. They terrace, grading a hillside into a series of shelves to slow the runoff. They plant more and more trees. Ted learns what he needs to know about farming by reading everything he can find and talking to farmers all over Williamsburg. He lays out and plants contour crop strips.

Pat mows the six trails regularly, using these solitary hours to inspect the foliage and watch for birds and wildlife. Eventually, she will have a top of the line John Deere, nicer than you'd see on a golf course, but for now, she mows all the trails with a small tractor mower and a bush hog. She does all the maintenance herself, changing the oil, greasing the gears, and scolding Ted when he does not keep up with *his* tractor's maintenance. Meticulous, he finds the chore too messy.

All this hard work would make most couples cranky, but these two enjoy it. The mutual tolerance of a good marriage is taking root. Friends, neighbors, colleagues—nobody hears a harsh word exchanged between the two. They are cheerful in their exasperation—Pat is a Democrat, for God's sake, and Ted is…Ted. They stay gentle with each other, respectful.

People close to them worry that Pat will feel deserted, stuck out there on that farm all by herself while Ted travels around selling investments all week. Instead, she is serenely content. The horses and dogs are company during the week, as is the land itself, and come Friday, Ted livens things up for the weekend. They go camping, visit friends, go out to dinner, plan big shared projects for the farm, catch up on each other's week. She has an ability, unusual for a young wife in the Fifties, to be interested and engaged by others, yet self-sufficient, comfortable with her own company.

Pat's preferred kitchen, with Ted and neighbor Peggy Van Dyke.

§

As they work, Ted and Pat learn the farm's history.

The surrounding region, Callaway County, was created in 1820 and named for Captain James Callaway, an early settler who was killed by the Osage.

A man named James Callaway Anderson, born in 1792 near Leesville, Virginia, settled the land in 1832. Was he any relation to the first James Callaway? Ted intends to find out.

Eventually, he will dive deeper into the genealogy, unrolling twelve feet of brown butcher paper and printing in neat script, using markers of different colors, all the family trees of previous farm residents. He is intrigued by Achilles Moorman, 1713-1783, who might have been a Quaker.

When the Civil War came, Ted learns, one boy was living on the farm, Thomas C. Anderson, and he enlisted with the Confederacy. Captured, he was told he could be paroled if he promised not to take up arms against the country again. He returned to the farm—and immediately joined the guerilla military forces. He spent the rest of his life with a price on his head, even though he married into a prominent family from Columbia, Missouri.

In the antebellum years, the Rood family farmed the land, and they did a good job of it. But when land in the Missouri Bootheel opened up, they left.

After World War I, the United States heartland, "breadbasket of the world," prepared to feed all of hungry Europe. The farm's next owners planted wheat on every acre. But by the Twenties, the monocropping had drained all the richness from the land, and wheat's price had bottomed out.

The land, overfarmed and rutted with ditches, was abandoned.

By the time Edward bought the farm, it was overgrazed and eroded. Green with "cheat grass," Pat guesses, knowing how easy it is to make ground look lush with a thin layer of grass that looks luxuriant until you mow it and find all the bald patches.

Still, the place was a bargain. And she likes how much it mattered to her father-in-law that this wasn't somebody's family farm, and he wouldn't be displacing anyone by taking on the property.

They explore the farm's cemetery, noting that only one grave has a headstone. A young woman named Judith Clark Moorman, twenty-seven years of age, was buried here in the 1830s. And the graves nobody dignified with a headstone? Pat and Ted don't want to think about it. By 1860, enslaved people made up at least 25 percent of the county's population, far more than in most other parts of Missouri. Back then, this area was Little Dixie.

§

In the early years of marriage, holidays mean driving into the city, and before the superhighways, that means a two-and-a-half-hour trip each way. Pat and Ted drive to the farmhouse atop the hill in Eureka to celebrate with Mima, the family nickname for Pat's mother.

Hilda fell in love with the wilderness her husband bought, and since his death in 1942, she has continued buying land; by the time she dies, the original nine acres will have grown to one thousand. She ignores the furrowed brows of her lawyer and tax accountant, especially when she buys a lush chunk of land in the LaBarque Creek watershed and they cluck, "That's just too expensive." Its value will grow exponentially, but Hilda does not know that and even if she did, would not bother making the argument. She loves the land for itself; loves it as much as Truman did. Now that he is gone, she will continue what he began.

Truman's identical twin comes regularly to check on his brother's widow, but she finally asks him to stop. Working outside, she will look up and see a man arrive, and grief and love will cancel reason, and for a sweet, then bitter instant, she will be sure Truman is alive again. Seeing his ghost at regular intervals is just too hard.

In 1952, she moves out to Eureka permanently, building herself a house atop the hill, overlooking the Meramec River. Far nicer than The Shack, it has a big fireplace and a huge kitchen with a nook big enough to hold a picnic table. On regular weekends, her fast-increasing flock of grandkids eat at the picnic table and hold enthusiastic food fights. Then they all run down to the LaBarque Creek.

At Christmastime, the kids drag a sled into the woods to cut down the tree. Hilda is in the kitchen, opening the doors of her twenty or so cabinets to find the candles, the special Christmas platters, the silver serving pieces, the olive tray. At Thanksgiving, someone is always standing by the stove stirring the giblet gravy while she tends to the candied sweet potatoes (free of heretical marshmallows) and homemade cranberry sauce (none of this stuff in a can!). At Christmas, they always have a pudding, boiled with candied fruit and served with a hard sauce just as it was on the Isle of Arran. Hilda pours brandy on top and sets it aflame.

Her long mahogany table needs all three leaves for these holidays, and soon there are enough kids to require card tables on the sides as well. Sprigs of holly decorate the platters, and at each place setting is a pastel cup, like a mini-cupcake liner, filled with nuts. There is a little wine, too, for the older kids. Hilda always asks one of the men to carve—the turkey at Thanksgiving, the ham at Christmas—and she is never happy with how he manages. But she raises her glass nonetheless, making a Scottish toast, and the meal begins. Hopeful brown eyes watch every bite; as many dogs as people attend these dinners. Later, the sons-in-law go outside to smoke and commiserate about the strong, spirited Jamieson women they married.

Though never lavish with hugs and kisses, Hilda makes anyone feel welcome. When people drop in, they find her in jeans and a blue oxford shirt. Always, she has homemade cookies and ice cream waiting—peppermint, chocolate, and what she calls butternickel. She rarely eats any of it herself, but she makes enough to keep a ready supply on hand.

She keeps things simple. All her shoes, dresses, and hats are shades of her favorite color, blue, so everything mixes and matches. Energy should be saved for what matters: animals, the outdoors, the environment.

One day, she takes her granddaughter Melissa out to a half-finished cement structure on the Meramec. The Army Corps of Engineers, her archenemy, wanted to dam the Meramec River, and Hilda fought to stop them. How can you dam a river that's surrounded by caves and sinkholes, anyway? The lake won't hold water!

Walking on the low cement wall and seeing how far the government got before Mima helped shut them down, Melissa feels a ripple of pride. It is good to be part of this tradition.

§

Ted and Pat also share holiday meals with Mommy Jones, the surprisingly familiar nickname the grandkids picked for Ursula, and Bobo, their name for Edward. Martha is there, and Ann and Pete Key walk over with the kids. They live two doors down from Edward and Ursula, with a household of Phelans in between.

"You didn't want to sit next to Mommy Jones," one of Ann's daughters will recall in adulthood. "It would be a long, formal dinner, and you had to be proper. You also had to dress up and wear everything she'd ever given you."

At Christmas, though, the kids wear a costume. Every year, Ursula picks a different theme—cowboys and cowgirls once, which tickles Uncle Teddy—and they dress up for a family picture. During dinner, the French doors are kept firmly closed. After dessert, they are swung open, and it's "like FAO Schwarz opened a store in the living room," in the words of one of the grandkids. (All the presents have in fact *come* from FAO Schwarz.)

Ted's big sister, Ann, takes Pat under her wing. Martha is the classic Auntie Mame, hardly the nurturing type. Busy with her own life and no longer "Mousey," she always has a date, a party to attend, a trip to take. Her tomboyish new sister-in-law mystifies her, so she focuses on Ann's kids instead. The jazzy single aunt with a sportscar, she treats her nieces to exciting shopping trips to New York or brings them on the train with her to Chicago to see a new show. Martha will live in the family home until old age, and her mother's frowning opinions of Pat's and Ted's lifestyle will rub off.

§

For New Year's Eve, there are no family obligations. An early photo shows Pat and Ted with two other young couples, everybody laughing. Ted has a funny smirk on his face and has donned a top hat, though no one is dressed up. One young woman wears a twinset and pearls; Pat's skirt is schoolgirl plaid.

This is most definitely the Fifties. In the role of young wife, Pat is low-key, even docile. She has learned to race in from her gardening, rinse the mulch from her hands, and quickly slice up some onions to sauté. That way, Ted will say, "Mmmm, smells good," instead of "What have you been doing all day?" Not that he ever would. But she was shaped by her time, and she wants him to at least *think* a home-cooked dinner is well under way. She's good at casseroles,

Ted (in top hat) and Pat on New Year's Eve, 1950s

at least. Especially hamburger casseroles. Ted loves hamburger. And if she keeps it simple, she has time to do what she loves.

10

The Jones Men

Here is Edward D. Jones, clad in a light straw hat and light summer suit, his bow tie dark to match his hatband, his shoes dark and shiny, a fine linen handkerchief or silk scarf in his pocket. "When I dress my best, I feel my best," he likes to say—and he always dresses his best. His shirts are whiter than snow, his shoes shinier than ice, and he has his nails buffed at his club. The minute you see him, you know he has a position of some stature.

Edward and Ted with Bull and Bear

Here is Ted Jones on the same summer day. He is wearing his perennial khaki trousers, a short-sleeved gingham shirt, and soft suede Hush Puppies. If he needs a nicer (but still short-sleeved) shirt and a tie, they are not likely to match. He has been indifferent to wardrobe since infancy (witness his mother's ineffectual threat to make him wear his sister's dress). Ted is as smart as his father but does not look the part, and that is mainly on purpose.

The two men look alike, short and stocky with ruddy complexions. Edward's face is squarer, and though he has the same affable charm, his eyes are sharper. Ted grew up with steady parental presence, comfort, indulgence, and security, and though his mind is restless in its curiosity, constantly springing ideas, he lacks his father's hypervigilance, and his eyes are merry.

Edward is never anything but "Mr. Jones." Ted is always "Ted."

Both men walk fast, their gait purposeful. Both have quick tempers, triggered not by minor irritations but by signs of dishonesty or disloyalty. For all his elegant demeanor, Edward once punched and flattened a salesman who cursed him. When he tips into one of his rare rages, he can be heard three blocks away. "Now we're going to have some fireworks," the brokers think when his rebellious son joins the firm. But nobody hears a word.

Over the years, that discreet silence will break only a few times, once when they are arguing about whether to bring in younger partners. Darryl Pope, one of the first of those partners, says it is "like two giant dinosaurs in a room making all this noise, and then the door would open and Mr. Jones would come out sort of red-faced, and then Ted would come out red-faced but he would kind of smile."

Luckily, father and son share a similar sense of humor—and neither holds a grudge.

Edward learned early to be cheerful. By all reports, he was a sunny child who never complained—a lucky disposition when you must live with distant relatives. "Learn to laugh," he instructs new hires. "Learn to keep trouble to yourself; nobody wants to take it from you." "Enthusiasm sells things. Keep a smile on your face and be enthusiastic." "A laugh is better than medicine."

Ted has the same cheerful nature, though his seems more a birthright than a learned strategy. He is willing to work hard; those months sweating on a tugboat in the Pacific showed him that he thrived on it. But he is convinced that hard work should be fun. "We're going to work hard and make this company succeed," he tells Pope. A beat later, he grins. "But if it doesn't, it's been a lot of fun, hasn't it?"

§

In a way that today's high-powered executives have forgotten, both Jones men know how to play. Edward counts among his friends the wildlife adventurer Dana Brown, who wrestled alligators instead of business rivals, and several St. Louis business owners. He plays horseshoes with four buddies every Saturday. When they go on fishing trips, they stick packets of whiskey sour mix in with the plastic worms, feathered lures, and sinkers in their tackle boxes.

Ted and his dad also share the winning trait of being genuinely interested in other people. Ted is the one famous for his stories, but Edward has plenty of his own—like the time, during his Navy years, when he went ashore for R&R and somehow found himself at an Irish wake. "So here we are, toasting his memory, and the guy pops out of the casket alive…."

His determination to succeed, combined with the Griesedieck family connection, adds gravitas. At one point, Edward sits on twenty-two boards. Ted avoids such honors; even at his own company, he squirms every time a meeting outlasts his attention span.

Edward wants his people to have the very best and never skimps on a motel room or travel expenses. Ted wants them to be as frugal as he is.

Despite his aristocratic bearing and French cuffs, Edward is no snob. He does not claim a private office; his desk is on the floor of the Board Room with everybody else's. Ted is the one who seeks a little privacy, putting a wooden desk in the corner of an unused conference room for himself, maybe just to concentrate his restless attention. And Ted is the one dazzled by graduate degrees, maybe because he treasures knowledge but never finished college. His father emphasizes associating with successful people, but he does not insist on refinement and advanced education. His clients include a beekeeper, several prizefighters and at least one saloon proprietor, and his hires often have colorful backgrounds: One played pro baseball; another played the trombone for a living.

Both the Jones men respect simplicity; each watches the dizzying advances of his time with a wary mix of awe and nostalgia. "Modern living has brought tremendous advances via television, Band-Aids, ready-mix cakes, steel-belted tires, Geritol, credit cards, Bufferin, Anacin, and Hungry Jack biscuits," Edward remarks in 1976. "The past is gone, but it was comfortable, pleasant, and uncomplicated. Medicine chests used to contain a bottle of iodine, a spool of adhesive tape, a roll of bandage, a bottle of aspirin, a jar of Vicks, and often a box of baking soda for brushing teeth."

Both men believe in treating their sales force with fairness and with— well, Edward might say "deep courtesy and respect"; Ted might say, "I've got your back as long as you work hard and stay honest and loyal." The biggest difference between them is the conservative formality of the father, who moved into a world where he had to behave in certain ways, and the casual forthrightness of the son, who grew up with the keys to that world and chose not to enter. He would have been bored silly there. He was fine with oldschool ways, Brooks Brothers clothes, and conservative politics, but he needed color, action, and a looser, more playful sort of camaraderie.

"Ted did not like high society," financial advisor Brad Seibel observes. "He was smart enough to be there"—when he had to be—but it was not his scene. That said, "he was comfortable anywhere. He would do just as well on the floor of the exchange, at the capital in D.C., or chewing a piece of hay, leaning against a stall in a barn somewhere. He was at home anywhere in America."

§

While they keep the peace in public, father and son have plenty of clashes in private, and the differences at the core of their personalities always simmer. One day Edward is chatting with the receptionist, Jean Burnett, and he tells her he doesn't know how healthy it is for Ted to be living out there in the country. She hides an involuntary smile; it seems far healthier than urban life.

Early on, Ted confides to Jack Phelan that if his father had forced him to work in the St. Louis office, he would have quit. Not once does he complain about his commute, which drops to ninety minutes each way as the highways improve.

By and large, he and his dad go their own ways. Every once in a while, they are seen leaving together, both dressed up, probably for some social occasion or family celebration. But even their desks are situated in different parts of the office. Roughly once a year, they argue forcefully enough that Ted has to troop out to Bellerive Country Club and let his dad, a member, buy him lunch and be persuaded to give up some share or aspect of the firm. If they disagree, Ted resigns: "All right, by God, I'm out! You just run it yourself." Then his dad concedes, and Ted returns to the office and groans that he's had to go through the ritual all over again, even though his father "has more money than he knows what to do with."

When father and son disagree about company policy, Ted reminds himself that his father began as a wholesale broker dealing with other brokers, not the general public. That makes a difference. Also, Edward was focused on improving his station in life from a young age, and he lived through the weirdness of the Great Depression, when tragedy created unusual deals and bargains. Ted began life in the elite world his father attained, then drew powerful lessons from the rough old guys at the stockyards and the sailors and soldiers from all walks of life. His era has been more stable, a time of postwar solidity and optimism, not crazy bargains.

Also, he likes to stir the pot.

§

Watching Edward on horseback, Ted swung up to ride behind him as they survey the farm, Pat chuckles. "That's the closest they've ever been!"

Yet the animus never takes over; if it had, Ted would have shunned his father's interests instead of embracing so many of them. They both have a sweet tooth, perhaps thanks to Ursula's insistence on dessert at every meal, and they can sniff out donuts or a birthday cake anywhere in the office. They both love horses—and horse trading, both literal and metaphorical. The year before he dies, Edward gives his son a book called *Mister, You Got Yourself a Horse*—and sticks a note inside about his own early experiences. The most legendary is his brief courtship of a young woman whose father happened to own five fine horses. After Edward professes his sincere intentions toward the daughter, the father agrees to sell him one of those horses. Edward turns around and sells the horse to a buyer in New York. The next time he arrives to pick up his girlfriend, her father meets him at the front door to inform him that he is no longer welcome.

Ted is less of a trader—he keeps his horses and refuses to speculate on stocks. What he has is horse sense, a practical wisdom that lets him size up any person, any situation, any opportunity.

Like his dad, he loves the Wild West and peppy, high-energy

entertainment. Back when he was traveling, Edward caught a vaudeville show in every town. Now he dons a seersucker suit and takes his granddaughters, pretty in pastel sundresses, to the Muny every summer. To entertain the little girls at intermission, he folds the program into origami birds.

Ted loves musicals, too, but even more, he loves ragtime music, Dixieland jazz, and the family legacy: circuses. In his traveling days, Edward's father bought an interest in a circus in Mexico City, and the stories are family legend. One day, for example, Eli Jones found the circus manager distraught because the female equestrian, Josie LaMott, was throwing a tantrum, insisting she would quit if she did not get a raise.

"What would you do if she died?" Eli inquired.

The manager shrugged. "Put somebody in her place."

"Well, then. Just pretend that she is dead."

Years later, that was code between Eli's son and grandson: If Ted worried that a broker might quit without an offer of bonus or partnership, his father drawled, "Well, son, just put him over there with Josie LaMott and pretend that he is dead."

The circus has a powerful hold over the Jones men's imagination. Edward was once thrilled to be asked to help halter a giraffe, and he looked for years for a circus to buy. "Stop the car!" he would call out while driving with a friend. "There's a circus in town!"

His notion was to sell one share of stock in the circus with

Sisters Martha and Ann with a circus friend— and Ted

each ticket, so the circus would belong to those who truly enjoyed it.

His son will wind up doing something quite like that with their company.

11

Taking Wall Street to Main Street

In 1955, Edward makes his son a partner in the firm and re-emphasizes the need to expand in *cities*.

"Why would we want to go to a large city?" asks his new partner. "Everybody else is there. I want to be where Merrill Lynch *ain't*."

Quietly, Ted keeps refining his dream.

Then, in 1957, he gets word that a big block of common stock for Mexico Refractories will be available for sale. Ted has spent a lot of time in Mexico, Missouri, renting one of Ruby Dillar's rooms "for traveling men" and sitting on the porch swing in the evening, chatting with whoever walked past. It strikes him that this offering might be a good chance to promote himself in town, so he buys an ad in the *Mexico Ledger*: "Mexico Refractories. Common Stock. Bought and sold. Write E.D. Jones. Williamsburg, Missouri." Then he borrows the newspaper's Pope City Directory and sends out postcards to every employee of Mexico Refractories with the same message. He wants people to write to him, not call, because then he'll have their names and addresses.

A week or so later, J.B. Arthur, president of Mexico Refractories, concerned that Ted's ad may be viewed by regulators as an attempt by the company to drive the stock higher before the offering, asks to meet with Ted. He wants the ad pulled.

"Mr. Arthur, are you telling me not to run these ads, or are you *asking* me not to run the ads?" Ted inquires.

"I have no power to tell you not to run the ads," Arthur concedes, "but I would appreciate it."

"In that case," says Ted, "I will go right over to the newspaper and cancel the ad, and I won't ask any questions."

What he doesn't know is that the company's stock is in registration with the Securities and Exchange Commission, and the principal underwriter is Reinholdt & Gardner, the Jones company's big rival in St. Louis.

The due diligence meeting is held in St. Louis at the Noonday Club, and Ted's father attends. At the cocktail reception that follows, Arthur asks Edward if that was his son who called on him in Mexico.

Why, yes, Edward says, probably not even sure what transpired.

Arthur turns to a partner at R&G and says, "Russ, Mr. Jones's son is a personal friend, and I want Edward D. Jones to get as much stock on this offering as they want. I don't care who you have to take stock away from, including Reinholdt Gardner. Mr. Jones's son has done me some favors."

Swelling with pride ("puffed up like a pigeon" is how Ted puts it), Edward takes a ton of stock. When Ted hears how much, he starts to sweat. His dad will expect him to sell every bit of it.

He goes to Frank Kister, a client and good friend who is the founder and president of the Savings & Loan Association in Mexico. Ted explains that he has a big block of stock to sell, and he needs somebody local to help him. Kister recommends Warren "Zeke" McIntyre, a guy everybody likes and respects.

Zeke sells the stock so effectively, Ted asks if he'll continue working for Jones. There in Mexico, not in St. Louis. (And definitely not in Boston, which is where Edward wants the firm to go if it must expand.)

Warming to the idea, Zeke sets up an office in a roomy closet above Scott Five & Dime and starts placing orders on an old black telephone, going through the operator to make long-distance calls to St. Louis. "If you want to buy them in the valley and sell them at the peak, pick up the phone and call ol' Zeke" is his sing-song slogan—he has just become the self-proclaimed marketing department of the firm. He holds business meetings at the local diner or the Rotary Club.

It is that easy. The firm of Edward D. Jones has opened its first branch office in Mexico, Missouri, population 12,200.

Ten years later, the company will have 62 offices in small towns throughout the Midwest.

§

Months after Zeke opens his office, Frank Kister asks Ted how much they're making in Mexico. When Ted gives him the figure, he chuckles. "You're in the wrong business. You shouldn't be in the business of talking to me about selling stocks and bonds; you should be in the business of opening offices like Zeke's all over the country."

Ted has an auditor doublecheck the numbers and, yes, Zeke's office is definitely making a profit. So Ted hires a broker to open an office in Jefferson City.

A huge market waits, untapped, because the old-money investment brokers in big cities have never deigned to go out to the country. People in small towns save plenty of money, but they have nobody close at hand to help them invest it for the future. Brokers don't *see* the money, because these folks just tuck the cash away; they don't drape themselves in furs and drive sports cars. Anybody looking only at the surface misses the opportunity Ted has recognized all along.

How many more offices do you plan, someone asks Ted.

"I want 300 offices making $500 a month," he replies instantly, a number that probably sounds sweeping and grand, more of a dream than a possibility.

§

Ted's strategy is fresh, and in a few decades, it will look cunning. The impulse is genuine, though: He just plain likes small towns. The people tend to be thrifty, hardworking, family oriented, and forthright. Everybody knows everybody, so you can go far on reputation—and people without integrity sink fast. This is where he wants to be and how he wants to work.

"If you go where there's no business," his father warns, "you'll get poor." But Ted doesn't think so—and in any case, it's a risk he doesn't mind taking. He envisions strong-willed, entrepreneurial financial advisors scattered across the nation, working independently, with no need to compete, no backbiting or infighting or jockeying for advantage, no Board Room schmoozing to waste their time, no secretary as a buffer, no hierarchy people can use to bump problems up or down. Just the advisor and the client.

Soon he has opened dozens more of these small-town offices. People at other brokerage firms scoff, calling Edward D. Jones & Co. "The Bumblebee That Couldn't Fly." A one-person office? Why bother? City brokers hear that an office has opened on the second floor of an old building in a podunk town and decide that's all poor Edward D. Jones can afford.

"Let 'em think so," Ted says, grinning.

His father winces.

§

John Bachmann's first job at Jones is an internship in 1959. He sweeps floors and makes deliveries. Then he moves up to monitoring stock quotes on a big drafting table.

He pays his tuition for an MBA in finance at Northwestern University by overhearing a customer make a remark about American Motors, then going to the library and reading up on the company. He buys stock, sells it six months later, puts all the money into H.J. Heinz, and watches it quadruple.

By the time Bachmann finishes the MBA, he has plenty of job offers, the most serious one from a bank in Chicago.

"You can work for the bank, and they're going to offer you more money than we are," Ted says. "What are your ambitions?"

"I'd like to be a partner in the firm," Bachmann blurts.

Ted nods. He intends to recruit more young people with advanced degrees, professionalize the firm. "If you're going to come into the business, come now," he warns. "Don't go out somewhere and say, 'I'm going to get a few years of experience and then come in.' You'll never."

Bachmann joins the firm, set on making partner—but with no clue about what will follow.

§

Also in 1959, another young man, this one from a small town in southeast Missouri, applies for a job at Jones. Darryl Pope worked for a year at a Kroger grocery store, then came to St. Louis and tried selling Collier Encyclopedias door to door. When he went home and told his dad he'd made only one sale in five weeks, his dad said, "You get right back up there and get a real job!"

Jones had posted an ad for a margin clerk, which meant penciling what a customer bought on a little lined card. After Darryl takes a typing test and a math test (Ted finds interview chit-chat insufficiently revealing), the decision is made. "Okay, we're gonna give you a try," Ted says. "We pay $200 a month. We are going to hold your first two weeks' pay, because then if you quit, you will have two weeks' pay to live on. You'll have to work some overtime, but we'll give you supper money."

Darryl's first job is erasing cards so they can be reused. He goes home covered in shreds of red eraser. But every day, as he erases, he pesters his boss, asking questions. Sometimes his boss explains. Other times, he sighs, "Just erase the card, would you?"

The firm is in an old building at Fourth and Chestnut, and rats scamper across the basement's dirt floor. Every once in a while, someone must descend to fetch old files; one guy keeps a hammer in his desk for the occasion, and if a rat darts forward, he swings it wildly in warning.

When the fire marshall threatens to shut the place down, Bachmann— the future managing partner of the firm—carries almost ninety years' worth of old documents out of that basement.

§

Another college intern, John Hess, remembers, as a kid, sitting on Mr. Jones's lap when his father, a client, brought him along on visits. Things are less cozy now that Hess is working in operations for the firm; there is much to learn and absorb in the very adult world of finance.

One day, Hess is hard at work when he feels a shadow loom behind him. He turns to see Edward, who is not smiling. Edward demands an explanation of Hess's job. He gulps and explains that he stamps in and logs the securities, then delivers them to waiting taxis so they can be couriered to the airport.

"Then can you explain these two envelopes?" Edward asks, producing them from behind his back. "You sent all the Midwest certificates to the New York Stock Exchange and all the New York ones to the Midwest." A pause, while the words sink like stones. "Do you know how much that cost this firm?"

Hess shakes his head, mute.

"More than we are going to pay you all summer!"

It is a hard, good lesson. Hess does not let himself act that carelessly again. At the end of the summer, Edward calls him to his desk and says, "You've done well. I'm giving you a bonus, and I want to have you go to grad school in New York. I'll take care of it."

§

John Hess's summer job might have been simpler if FedEx had existed. In the Sixties, there is still a cumbersome physicality to doing business. In their small-town offices, brokers start the day staring at a skinny little tickertape streaming from the side of their teletype machine. They slide a little metal clip onto their finger, so they can easily rip off a bit of tape, lick its gummy back, and stick it down. Meanwhile, the teletype cranks out a continuous feed of data and messages. In the winter, static electricity animates the paper as it unfurls, and instead of obediently dropping into a basket on the floor, it festoons the wall.

Once they are up to speed, the brokers make their phone calls, then head out to knock on doors. A friend at a rival firm informs Jones rep Stan Cunningham that all this knocking is beneath the dignity of a broker. He should know better. He is demeaning their profession. Stung, Stan mentions the comment to Ted, who waves it off as nonsense.

A year or so later, an article comes out in *The Wall Street Journal* quoting Ted, who remarks that some brokers feel it is beneath their dignity to knock on doors. "Those brokers do not need to bother to apply at Edward D. Jones & Co."

Tickled, Stan calls his friend and says, "Did you know you were quoted in today's *Wall Street Journal*?"

§

One of Ted's brothers-in-law, Pete Key, comes to work for Jones and becomes one of the firm's anchors: an amazing stock picker and the head of the wire room, where wishes and promises turn real. The teletype machines sit on a raised platform in the center of the room, mixing clackety and chugging noises into such a cacophony, the firm enclosed the room with glass-windowed walls. The "wire girls" (this is the Fifties) sit on either side of the platform, tearing off orders and questions as they stream from the machines. Brokers cajole these women with candy or flowers when they need urgent favors, and the operators knit booties when a broker's wife is expecting.

The teletype machine kick out a continuous tape, less than an inch wide, backed with glue. A wet sponge sits in a dish just below the tape's exit, making it easy to moisten a section of tape and press it onto a "wire pad" half the size of a standard sheet of typing paper. The sheet of paper is then placed on an eight-track conveyor belt that will speed it to its destination in another part of the building.

If the wire pad contains an actual client order, the wire operators place it on one of the belt's westbound tracks, and it will slide through a cut in the wall that separates the wire room from the trading room where the orders are executed. A trader will pull the order off the belt and enter the instructions into a machine that connects the firm to all the major exchanges. Once the trader receives confirmation of the trade's execution price, the filled order will be sent east, back to the wire operator, so she can send a confirmation wire back to the branch with execution details for the client.

All non-trade wire communications travel east from the wire room to the various operational and administrative departments of the firm. This is as high as the tech goes, mid-century. The wire system will remain intact until 1979, when it will be replaced with a flashing, beeping computer system that needs no sponge.

The wire room buzzes with electricity, urgency, and laughter. Everybody adores Pete Key, because he knows how to cut through the stress and and tedium and keep the atmosphere light.

Another brother-in-law, Bill Lloyd, who is married to Pat's sister Ann, also works for Jones. In 1960, it is decided that he will open an office in Pueblo, Colorado. The first Jones office west of Missouri. To accommodate Lloyd and stretch the firm's reach, Ted decides to expand the network, investing in a telegraph wire that will run all the way to Colorado. They can add offices in between.

Edward is livid. "What's my son doing?" he yells at Jack Phelan. A Jones office that far west? How can they afford this? "Get out there and stop him!"

Instead of obeying Edward and going out to Colorado to rein Ted in, Jack just calls: "Ted, your old man is raising hell. You need to come back here."

"Just hold him off," Ted says. "I'll be back soon enough." He sounds unconcerned, even happy. "We're gonna string offices all the way back to St. Louis."

When Edward hears this, he mutters something about going broke first. What he does not yet realize is that the additional offices, strategically placed along that wire, will help absorb the fixed cost of the wire to Colorado. Besides, Edward might want the company closely held, but Ted wants it to spread out. While his father cools down, he hits the road, looking for the right sorts of towns for a branch office and the right people to place there.

Financial advisors regularly joke about Ted's site selection process, saying that he goes to a town's main street and finds a café, and if the food's good, he opens there. This is not entirely wrong, but he does have other criteria, and he will refine them over the next three decades. Nobody should open an office in the town where they grew up, for example. "They'll always remember you as the kid who climbed the water tower and painted your name on it. You've got to go someplace where nobody knew you as a kid, so you can have some credibility." Nobody should be working in the place where they hope to retire, either.

For the offices between St. Louis and Colorado, he picks Dodge City, Hays, Great Bend, Manhattan, and Goodland in Kansas, and Ponca City in Oklahoma. He incubates the new offices, fussing and brooding over them as they come on line.

When Frank Finnegan says the string of offices "sounds like a stupid idea," Ted replies with uncharacteristic patience: "Frank, you're just not seeing the picture I'm painting."

§

"Ted, I want to bring your sisters in as partners," Edward announces in 1962.

Ted gives him a level stare. "That's interesting. What are they going to do?"

"They're not going to do anything."

Tempers flare—Ted's first, then his father's. Soon both men's faces are brick red. Ted says, "Well, if that's what you're going to do, then you're going to do it without me. People who don't work here shouldn't share in the profits."

He has quit the firm.

Granted, he has stalked out of the office before. When two strong-willed men are clashing over the future, sometimes quitting is the only way to speed a resolution. Most of the time, though, Edward just has the switchboard operator ring Ted at the farm, tell him all is forgiven, and ask him to come back again.

This time, he knows that won't be enough. There is no word from Ted for three weeks. Finally, Edward sends Jack Phelan out to the farm. Jack can charm and soothe in a way the Jones men cannot. The message he bears—"Ted, there's a lot of work to be done, please come back"—is the most dignified way Edward can think of to concede defeat. His daughters will not become partners.

It's around this time that Ted confides to Jack Phelan, "Someday I would like the workers of this company to own the business."

§

In 1963, the company moves up the street to the old Cotton Belt building at Fourth and Chestnut, originally the Planters House Hotel. Its famous bar saw the concoction of Planters Punch and, later, the Tom Collins. Wealthy cotton farmers brought their families here so they could eat and socialize and dance in warm candlelight during the bitter cold winters. Notable early residents included Abraham Lincoln (where *didn't* he sleep?), Jefferson Davis, Andrew Jackson, Ulysses S. Grant, and Charles Dickens. The meeting that ultimately kept Missouri in the Union during the Civil

War occurred at the hotel on June 11, 1861.

Edward D. Jones & Co. moves in at a gentler but still historic time. In his first month with the firm, Darrell Seibel gets swept away from his desk: "Come with me," Ted says, walking him over to the Old Courthouse and pointing to the steps. "This is where Dred Scott was standing when they sold him."

Seibel looks at the steps and shudders at their brutal history. For reprieve, he glances toward the river and sees a welcome distraction: a pile of lumber and equipment. "What's all that mess down there?"

Ted explains that St. Louisans have voted to build a new national monument, a sculptural steel arch to symbolize the role of this place as the gateway to the West.

The firm has moved just in time; its location, right next to the Old Cathedral, is the perfect vantage point to watch the Arch rise. Edward keeps a pair of binoculars in his desk drawer. He knows all about building something from the ground up.

And his son knows all about exploring new territory.

Market updates in the Board Room, circa 1962

§

November 22, 1963. Women in the wire room are typing in their usual flurry. A teletype rattles in. Somebody yells, and the room goes quiet. Darrell Seibel read the message aloud. President John F. Kennedy has been shot, Gov. Connelly has been shot, and Jackie, who was sandwiched between them, is unharmed.

The teletype is full of slashes. When you make a typing mistake you have to hit slashes or Xs and say DISREGARD, and there are a *lot* of slashes. Whoever typed it was in a state of shock, Seibel realizes.

People are sobbing. Somebody gets word to Ted. Surgeons have been called to the Dallas hospital. So has a priest.

After Kennedy's funeral, Ted and Pat, still dazed with shock that anyone would dare assassinate a U.S. president, walk out to the little cemetery on their farm. They agree on a site and have a huge boulder brought in, a commemoration. Sure, Ted is a Republican, but he is quite fond of Kennedy, and this was *wrong.*

§

In 1967, the New York Stock Exchange tries to take away the commissions that brokers at small firms receive when they send orders for larger firms to execute. Blazing mad, Ted writes to the committee chair: "Mutual fund buyers are not found on Wall Street or in the NYSE Luncheon Club, nor do you meet them by attending the annual outing of the Bond Club of NY…none of the ponderous machinery of the NYSE means anything until the salesman gets the order."

The SEC board relents—temporarily. But soon the split commissions, called "give-ups"—an important source of revenue for Edward D. Jones & Co.—are gone. Ted goes looking for new revenue, and the company's brokers learn better ways to sell bonds, move into municipal bonds, and sell real estate through limited partnerships. The diversity more than makes up the difference.

Still, the late Sixties are rough years. Trading volume skyrockets: In 1965, five million shares a day change hands on the New York Stock Exchange; by 1968, *twelve* million shares a day change hands. A lively market sounds like good news, but that flood of orders hits a bottleneck. The financial industry is muddling along, most firms not yet computerized, and manual bookkeeping requires multiple copies, a blizzard of paper that cannot be managed at this pace, for this volume. Orders keep piling up, and there are long lag times before they can be executed, and everybody's making mistakes. Operations snarled by the back-office crisis, the New York Stock Exchange limits trading, staying open only four days a week.

Firms are panicking, looking to foreign money or complicated financing schemes. Most brokerage houses save themselves by going public, but Ted vows, "That will never happen as long as I'm alive. The people who run the firm should own it. Not stockholders."

In 1968, he realizes that he has to take over. The company needs more resilience, tighter bookkeeping, better control of its finances, if it is to stay afloat. And so he begins to act as managing partner, with hardly a word exchanged.

Ted brings in experts to analyze the company's books and forestall any future problems. A management consultant recommends losing thirty associates, about a third of the firm. The layoffs are so bitterly painful, Ted resolves never to resort to that again. Years later, a *Forbes* article will highlight the Jones company for not laying off anybody when all its competitors did.

For now, though, the damage has been done. His father summons him to lunch and thunders, "You have destroyed what I built!"

Gulping down an indigestible meal, Ted holds his ground. He did what he felt had to be done. He is working late, sometimes even staying overnight, sleeping on a cot in his office that is reminiscent of his military days.

Though he rarely backs down from his dad, he defers in other ways. As managing partner, he draws no attention to himself, does nothing to distract from his father's social position. For years, the company will grow, and Edward will continue to take credit for Ted's ideas. This will not bother Ted one bit. The people he cares about know what he's done, and as for the "downtown bluebloods," he doesn't run in that circle anyway.

§

The next crisis hits directly, a bomb through the window instead of the air raid sirens and scattered shrapnel the entire industry has come to expect. Because Jones is such a staunch supporter of mutual funds, the funds often return the favor by calling when they want to add a stock to their portfolio. Jones receives a bit of revenue by executing the trade—but is required by the New York Stock Exchange to pledge a percentage of its own capital against the value of the trade. One day, a number of mutual funds issue so many of these orders that Dick Christensen walks up to Ted with "Good news, bad news. We got all this business today, but it absolutely exceeds our ability to pledge capital. If we can't find more capital by the seven-day settlement date, we'll be out of business."

The crisis is ironic, given that business has never been stronger. But the SEC's capital requirements do not bend for coincidence, and for the first time in its history, Edward D. Jones is in danger of violating them.

Ted goes to the trading room. "Call all the mutual fund companies and tell them we're not accepting 'buys,' but we'd like to have 'sells.'" Then he goes to the wire room and asks Pete Key if his friend Dayton Mudd, whose father was high up in the JC Penney company, will meet with them. Like, *today.*

"This will be a short-term investment," Ted explains to Mudd, who is about to become the first non-working partner in the company. A partnership can pledge not only its own capital but also the value of its partners' personal accounts, and Mudd will place $1 million of JC Penney stock in his new partner account.

Crisis averted, Ted works nonstop to replace Mudd's million and remove him from the firm, so they will again have only *working* partners. "We can't go through this every time business volume gets high," he mutters. "We've got to find a way to raise our own capital and let the people who *work* here own a piece of the profits." He begins to look for a solution.

1 2

Partnering Up

The terror of the paper crunch, all those other firms going out of business, has shaken Ted. He needs more than salespeople now: He needs solid infrastructure, sharp systems, and capable partners. He leans hard on his father, pressuring him to relinquish some of his shares in the company so they can bring in more young partners like Pete Key and Jack Phelan.

Edward D. Jones needs fresh blood and new energy, and it needs the reliable, internally-sourced capital that would come if more partners were allowed to invest in the firm. The whole industry is ravenous for capital, because to cope with rising volume, it needs expensive computer systems, and to pay for those systems, brokerage houses need to diversify, offering a new mix of investments and services, all of which require infusions of capital to launch.

After yet another shouting match with his dad, Ted prevails. In 1970, he brings John Bachmann back from Columbia, Missouri, where he has been running his own office, and makes him a partner. Along with Edward and his original handful, the partners now include Ted, Jack Phelan, Pete Key, and Bachmann—and Ted is not yet satisfied. In 1971, he adds Darryl Pope, Bill Christensen, and Tony Puglisi—none of them salesmen. This is groundbreaking, because both Ted and his dad have kept such a tight focus on sales alone. But now they know what happens if the firm tries to go too fast and can't process all the business. They need to guard against errors and lapses in service, because that will alienate their customers. So they need a leadership team that collectively possesses every skill required.

Ted keeps pushing for younger partners. Without them, the firm will be controlled by a handful of older, very wealthy people, and everybody else will sit around waiting for them to die off. Besides, Ted wants the company to grow, not just tread water. He's convinced that when you share ownership with people, they behave differently, taking fuller responsibility for the firm's success.

In 1975, he adds a professional accountant, Bill Hauk, and three other new partners, bringing the total to seventeen. He is selling these partnerships at book value—a bargain-basement price—and when he believes in someone and knows they are strapped for cash, he steps in to make a partnership possible.

"I'm kind of a communist," he jokes. "I want the workers to own the means of production. But I want them to pay for it!"

§

Ted's generosity is strategic: never a handout, always a vote of confidence. Soon the partners begin to grasp the plan's structural brilliance. As a partnership, they can act faster, but they can also be more judicious, thinking long-term. If you're playing with stockholders' money, you're more likely to be a gunslinger, Ted knew. When you're playing with your own money, your attitude toward risk will be more conservative. By the same token, because they are accountable only to themselves, they don't have to make short-term decisions that will show stockholders a quick profit. They can shape their own culture, adhere to their own values.

Best of all, "with all of us together as a partnership, we're in control of our own destiny," remarks Doug Hill, "and no one can swoop in and take us over the way they've taken over most of the publicly owned brokerage firms."

§

The firm still needs a backstop of additional capital, though—and Ted still wants to share ownership with more of the associates—he refuses to call them "employees"—of the firm. When he and Bill Borgstadt, an astute and congenial partner who lives in Warrenton, drive in to the office together, Ted opens up about the dilemma, and Borgstadt urges him to allow far more salespeople to invest in the firm. Ted wants to do just that, but isn't yet sure how. He talks it through with Bachmann, too, and when the younger man sees a huge ad in the newspaper announcing that Lamson Brothers, a firm in Chicago, is doing a limited partnership offering with some of its own employees, he carries the paper straight to Ted. This is something that has never, to their knowledge, been done before. And they already have a relationship with Lamson Brothers, which is their correspondent firm when they need to trade commodities on the Chicago Stock Exchange.

"I think they've figured it out," Bachmann says.

Ted nods. "Get them on the phone."

The Lamson Brothers rep says yeah, they're excited about this new source of capital. But when Bachmann asks if he and Ted can come meet with them, the guy says, "Is your business good?"

"Really good," Bachmann replies.

"So's ours, and I don't know that we even have time to visit right now. Do you have any Wite-Out?"

Bachmann's not sure where he's heading. "Er…sure."

"We'd be happy to send you these documents, and everywhere it says 'Lamson Brothers,' you can just white that out and type in 'Edward D. Jones.'"

§

Once the lawyers have pored over the forms, the Wite-Out is carefully painted on and blown dry. By 1974, Jones is announcing its first limited partnership offering. At a time when other investment firms are merging or collapsing, they have found a strategic way to raise permanent capital and build loyalty at the same time. Ted is sharing ownership in a big way, now—something he has wanted to do for more than a decade—and the company can continue to grow.

In 1976, Ted approaches Larry Sobol, who he hired as corporate counsel fresh out of law school. Sobol has put together a fat compliance manual and reviewed all the contracts, and now Ted wants him to find a way to invite even more associates to become limited partners in the firm. This time, the opportunity would be open not just to financial advisors but to anyone who has worked hard for the company.

Sobol does his research and comes up with a plan, and Borgstadt, who taught college courses in finance and earned a master's in accountancy, does the financial review. Soon capital is flowing into the firm from its own members, and the associates who become limited partners are the ones reaping the rewards. The rest of the industry is having another meltdown, with brokerage firms going public, merging, or borrowing money to keep their firms afloat. But Ted is doubling down: We are going to remain a private partnership, and we are going to let our partners share the profits. (And, as he would cheerfully remind them, share any losses.)

§

The quakes and tremors of the Sixties and Seventies have shifted the very structure of the securities business. Long-established firms like Merrill Lynch are abandoning their traditional partnership structures in favor of public investors. Exotic and esoteric means of finding capital have come into vogue. Smaller firms are merging by the dozens or simply going out of business because they can't raise enough capital. The stock market is moribund, and even the chairman of the SEC calls the individual investor "an endangered species."

It is in this environment that a small firm in St. Louis, one that deals *only* with individual investors, has developed a method for raising capital that is revolutionary—and goes almost unnoticed, outside the small group of partners who work with Ted to make it happen.

Fifty years later, the genius of raising capital with your own associates and letting them be the ones to profit from the returns will seem obvious. By then, Jones will have thousands of limited and general partner investors, and its offices will cover North America, with 19,000 advisors counseling millions of investors. But in the early Seventies, opening ownership of the firm to those who work for you is a bold and unprecedented move, its success far from assured.

§

When a limited partnership offering is made in 1980, Jim Weddle—who will someday lead the firm—is not on the list. His is the first name *below* the line they have to draw. He grits his teeth and decides he will work even harder. Three years later, at the next offering, he is included, and at the end of the same year, he is offered the chance to become a general partner and move to St. Louis, where he will train new financial advisors and work with Jack Phelan, his mentor, to expand relationships with mutual funds.

By now, the Weddles have a two-year-old, and Stacey is eight months pregnant. They have just bought their second home, out in the country with three acres and an orchard, and they are putting the finishing touches on the nursery.

"Honey, is this what you want to do?" Stacey asks.

"Yeah, but I don't know if the time is right," he says carefully.

"Just let me have the baby before we move," she says cheerfully. "We can find another house."

§

Edward Jones's current managing partner, Penny Pennington, remembers hearing "Raise your hand if you're a limited partner" and watching all the hands go up. "Now raise your hand if you *want* to be a limited partner"— and all the rest of the hands went up.

She was home recuperating from breast cancer surgery when Doug Hill called with her first limited partnership offering, and the pride washed away all her recent misery. But what followed was an even greater sense of responsibility: She was now an owner in this company.

§

Historically, all investment firms began as private partnerships. But as Ted, with his love of history, is keenly aware, one of the causes of the Great Depression was ending that requirement. Partnerships became corporations, and as the margin rates plummeted, it became tempting to take huge risks because now you were risking other people's money and not your own.

After the Depression, the Securities and Exchange Commission was created and brokerage houses and their sources of capital became more highly regulated. But by the 1970s, after a few decades with no major financial disasters, the laws relaxed again.

It is possible to go public—and because investments are becoming more complex and requiring more capital, the partnership format is less attractive. By going public, brokerage firms can rake in ten or twenty times the book value of the partnership.

Jones is one of only a handful of investment firms that remain private.

"We are responsible to our clients, but we are accountable to ourselves," Weddle will later explain, "and that is a huge strategic advantage. We are not building shareholder wealth; we're building client wealth. We can think independently, and we can make long-term commitments which often are extremely expensive but position us to continue to grow." His favorite example is the way other firms all added online, do-it-yourself discount services. Bachmann is eventually taken to task in the *Wall Street Journal* because of this incredible financial opportunity this backwoods firm was turning down. No, he tells the reporter firmly, Jones isn't going there.

"We made that decision in part because we could," Weddle says. "We didn't *have* to go for every marginal dollar in profit."

§

Ted feels sure that with this partnership structure, the firm is pioneering an approach other businesses might want to copy. Years later, Spencer Burke, a lawyer and, for a time, a Jones investment banker, will study family-owned and privately owned companies. Reflecting on a handful of success stories, including Jones, he will lay out the conditions necessary to grow a company into a billion-dollar entity: Owners must be willing to make a financial sacrifice, selling their stock to employees at less than fair market value, with no tax benefit. Employees must have leadership skills—and enough money to buy in. There must be an appropriate governance structure, a succession plan, ways to enforce the values and principles at stake, and a refusal to accommodate points of view that could destroy what has been created.

Also, the company must refuse to sell outright. Over the years, Ted listens to one offer after another, letting the potential buyer speak their piece before he firmly declines. He is flattered, but he never takes the offers seriously—not even when they talk about giving him "ten times book value." He wants the company to stay intact, owned by its own associates.

But how to stop them from selling sometime down the road? Other owners have sold to their employees only to have the employees turn around a month or two later and resell the firm for four times what they paid. Edward D. Jones is going to become so big, at some point, that anybody would be tempted to sell their shares.

To remove that temptation, Ted, who has not yet turned fifty-five himself, makes a rule that partners must begin divesting themselves of their shares at fifty-five. They have to sell down 10 percent every year until they are sixty-five, at which time they must step down as general partners. He wants people moving down the bench, making room. He's seen too many firms fail, he says, because "all they had was a bunch of old guys sitting around collecting checks, and that would be so frustrating for the young people that they would leave."

§

Bill Hauk, who does the Joneses' taxes, is not the least bit surprised that his client made a rule requiring himself to divest his holdings in his own company. Ted just isn't greedy. In the Eighties, tax rates will be high, and all sorts of perfectly legal tax shelters will pop up, and Ted will ignore them. He does not *believe* in sheltering much of your income. Tax deductions for charity, absolutely, but nothing elaborate. This reluctance is rooted in Ted's patriotism, Bill decides. Every year, Ted asks what percentage of his income he is paying in taxes, because he wants to make sure he's paying a fair share.

Ted thinks of charity as nearly useless, when it takes the form of a handout that only camouflages the core problem. He will give huge sums in order to make sure kids of all races and backgrounds have education, opportunity, jobs. But he doesn't believe in doing things *for* people. He believes in making it possible for them to do the work themselves.

He measures his business's success by its growth, not by how much money it generates for him. And he does not take off points for failed experiments. At Jones, they test ideas, and if something flops, well, mistakes don't end the world. They fix the goof, dust themselves off, and say, "We're not going to do *that* again."

§

Once Ted has settled the partnership structure, he asks Borgstadt to come up with a way to standardize the branch office accounting so everybody is pulling the same weight. This means taking a few perks away, and Borgstadt sets his jaw and begins making phone call after phone call, calmly explaining the rationale. Aggrieved, some of the brokers complain to Ted, and one is so vehement, Ted tells Borgstadt this guy is exempt from the new rules. Furious, Borgstadt takes his stack of paperwork down to Ted's office, drops it on his desk, and says, "If we're not going to do it right, *you* make the calls."

Fifteen minutes later, Ted comes up to Borgstadt's cubicle, face bright red, and slams the stack of paperwork on *his* desk. "I called and told the guy there would be no special deals. You make the calls."

With the playing field even, Ted sets up a bonus program to reward the hard workers. He likes competition when it's external, not internal; he does not want a firm of winners and losers. So he gives the same payout to every broker and keeps the bonuses consistent. When the firm sends top salespeople on incentive trips, he just sets a sales goal and says that anybody who hits it can go. Because he keeps things simple, without an elaborate hierarchy or favoritism, everyone knows where they stand.

He is clear with the regulatory authorities, too. Appalled by the lack of branch office managers, the SEC commissioner asks how on earth the Jones partners think they can supervise a broker out in the Kansas wheatfields when there's nobody there to watch what he's doing. How do they know he's not cheating the customer?

Ted looks the guy in the eye and says, "Sir, we have the will at our firm to comply."

He hires an auditor who goes out to each branch office once a year and performs an audit stringent enough to satisfy the most exacting SEC review. Profit does not get in the way. More than once, Ted has fired a top producer, each time for some failure of integrity that at another firm might not even be noticed.

§

Governance of the firm stays simple, too. The managing partner runs
the firm. There's a Monday Group of trusted advisors that morphs into
a management committee, but because Bachmann is allergic to titles, it
remains the Monday Group. And that's the structure. Period. No votes
taken, just input and, in most cases, an eventual consensus. Either way,
the managing partner bears the ultimate responsibility. The managing
partner can admit or dismiss a general partner or adjust their interest
in the partnership.

Bonuses are not automatic. When there is sufficient profit, the bonuses
are generous—but wily. Ted based them not just on how much somebody
sold, but on how profitable the branch office was. This gives the broker
an incentive to keep expenses down.

The structure of the firm makes everybody dependent upon
everybody, and the financial incentives are aligned because all
associates are paid out of the same pot. Most investment firms have
separate profit centers, and lucrative areas like investment banking or
wealth advisory services pull in cash while the rest of the firm stays
spare. At Jones, the only way for associates in any part of the company
to earn bonuses is if the whole firm makes money. Investment banking,
for example, is not a separate division, something a 1999 Harvard
case-study on Jones will remark upon. All underwriting fees and other
revenues go back into the general pool. Because brokers are not pitted
against one another, they share marketing ideas and collaborate. The
support staff is well aware that when the brokers succeed, everybody
benefits, so they lend the brokers as much support as possible. At times
of crisis, everyone has something at stake, so everyone pitches in to find
a solution.

There are not conventional budgets, notes Norman Eaker, a CPA
and longtime Jones partner. "Everybody else in the world has a budget,
and people manage to the budget. We have guidelines, so we don't
use resources in a stupid way," but none of the games that come from
overestimating costs on purpose, overspending at the end of the year,
and jockeying for budget allocations.

At one of the big Jones meetings, Ted talks about "dividing the pie," holding up a normal-size pumpkin pie as a prop. Then an assistant he has primed rolls a utility cart out with a giant pie on top. "The pie," Ted announces with a flourish, "is getting bigger."

At one point, his father owned 80 percent of the firm. "Now he owns 3 percent," Ted tells Bob Gregory, "and he made more last year with that 3 percent ownership than he has ever made in his life. He resisted me all along; he thought he wasn't going to make any money."

Coincidentally, Gregory also owns 3 percent of the company, a fact that still blows his mind: "Me, the son of a blue-collar guy who worked in a cleaners, and who never owned a stock or bond in his life."

13
—

Crisis After Crisis

On May 26, 1970, the Dow Jones hits the lowest point of a bear market at 663. With people yelling comparisons to the Great Depression, President Richard Nixon calls financial experts to the White House the very next day. The appearance of action shoots the index up 32.04 points, its biggest jump since 1928, and it continues to rise. The bear market is over, the crisis averted. But Wall Street is still, as John Brooks puts it in *The Go-Go Years*, "hanging by its fingertips."

The decade opens with ruin for many investment firms, among them one of Jones's competitors, Dempsey-Tegeler. Its net worth is now a negative number, and it will have to liquidate faster than a witch melts in water. A special trust fund is set up to compensate its customers for close to $18 million.

Watching the debacle from St. Louis, Edward tells a local paper, "I don't think good management should have to pay for bad management's mistakes. I want to preserve the integrity of the industry, so I'll pay my share. But this thing is getting out of hand with all of these dead fish floating to the surface."

By the end of 1970, one-sixth of the brokerage firms registered with the New York Stock Exchange have been forced to either merge or liquidate. Yes, they were tested by the market's wild dips, but crazily, the real challenge was the pileup of paperwork, which threw record-keeping into chaos.

In 1973 and '74, the stock market drowns again, dropping by 43 percent. Edward D. Jones & Co. has just moved out to Westport, settling into a whole campus of buildings—and now revenue looks precarious.

There is "cold comfort in many economic forecasts," Edward acknowledges, but he reminds the brokers not to fall into nostalgia's trap, mistily remembering the tremendous yields of earlier years. George Washington's "good old days" included a long, divisive war opposed by a third of the nation and rampant inflation followed by a depression. Lincoln's "good old days" contained one of the bloodiest wars of all times.

Ted is hardly feeling misty-eyed. He stops all expansion and experiments with a four-day work week, cutting costs wherever he can. His own work week is 24/7; he's sleeping on a cot in his office.

By now, he has surprised the graybeards and proved to be an excellent manager, fair and surprisingly steady. He can make a decision and stick to it; as long as it is fair, he is comfortable. He does not try to be all things to all people, and neither does the firm. Jones goes out of its way to avoid fads. Face-to-face communication means better relationships with clients and fewer misunderstandings within the company.

At meetings, Ted always sits in the front row and takes notes—even when he's been to the same meeting in a different location—to set an example. Born curious, he asks everybody for input about everything. When the company receptionist, Jean Burnett, gives him a ride to the airport, he asks her opinion about shop-from-home tv shows and whether downtown is ever going to come back. Always, before finalizing one of his zillions of ideas, he sounds people out, talks it through, and if the idea is too zany, lets people talk him down.

The way his brain works? Try something, try it, try it, and then if it doesn't work, get rid of it as fast as you can. Often he gives up too soon; impatience and impulsivity are his worst enemies. But he sees things fresh, unswayed by general opinion, and he picks up on small details others miss.

Ted doesn't think he's smarter than everybody else, Darryl Pope decides. He's just *determined*. If he has a solid idea, he's going to pursue it. But he gives others the same freedom. And while he is quick to challenge people, he reels out a slack rope. "Even if he didn't agree with it," Bob Gregory will recall, "a lot of times he would let you do it so you could make your own mistake, or sometimes he thought he would learn something too."

Ted walks power's tightrope with perfect balance. "Nobody ever worked *for* Ted," Bill Borgstadt will observe. "You worked *with* him—unless you argued with him in public, and then you found out who the boss was." Others say they never forget Ted is the boss, but it never makes them feel uncomfortable or forces them to censor their opinions. He enjoys other people's points of view (though he feels no obligation to accept them as his own).

Often he hands the same project to four or five people, and they run into one another in the hallway, each holding the same document, waiting to report their findings. He grins when he sees their accusing expressions. "I knew if I told five of you to do it, one would."

He has never cared much about getting credit himself, so he doesn't see why anybody else would be affronted. All that matters is that stuff gets done.

§

Some of Ted's urgency is existential. In 1972, he was diagnosed with melanoma—a fast-growing cancer that can be deadly. The doctors did an exploratory operation on his left side, cutting him "from A to Izzard," as he joked afterward. When he woke up, half-conscious, his body zigzagged with stitches and a porcupine of drains and tubes, he was sure he was dying. He couldn't even turn in bed to reach the call button.

Like the fear he felt that stormy night, tossed on black waves in a tugboat, terror took over. Once again, he took back control. Why fear death? It was normal and natural and would happen to every single human being. Alone in that hospital room, he asked himself a series of questions: What *was* the meaning of life, anyway? Why are we here? What really matters?

Love. Beauty. Truth. Those were the answers that came to him. He thought about Patsy and all they had shared. About beauty—not of a woman or a child or a pretty sunset, but of character. He had known only a handful of people with that kind of beauty—a Black preacher and Teamster who worked for his father; two neighborhood farmers and their wives. As for truth, he kept hearing that line from Patsy's favorite playwright: "To thine own self be true." He had always tried.

Now he is well again, and he burns to experiment and expand. He keeps the firm's atmosphere friendly and old-fashioned, though. Out front, Jean Burnett takes people's kids onto her lap and lets them pull the cord and push it into the right opening on the switchboard. If the boss wants to call somebody, the kid slides right off her lap. Ted is not a time waster; the minute he ends one call, he wants the next one, and she has to be ready. If he calls in from out of town, he does not like to be put on hold; when he calls in from Europe and she tries, he hangs up on her. "You pick up on this line while I'm talking to him," she instructs whichever person he's trying to reach, "and you start talking at the same time."

She might have thought Ted all business, impatient and demanding— except for all the contradictions. Like the day he sees her pay for an intern's lunch because she has found out the young man is broke. "I don't want you doing that," Ted tells her firmly. "The firm will be glad to see that he has a good lunch." From that day on, Ted pays for the intern's lunch himself.

People are beginning to trust that not only can Ted lead the company, but he has their back. When a client accuses Wylie Beeler, a financial advisor in the home office, of selling short without his knowledge, Beeler is so indignant, he tells the man to go to hell. When Ted is drawn into the dispute, Beeler worries that his outburst might cost him his job. But instead of casting blame, Ted produces all sorts of records for the client, who is still not satisfied. So *Ted* loses his patience and tells the man he can call the SEC if he likes, they'll check it out, but he is not to disrupt the firm any further. Placing the man's hat firmly on his head, he tells him to leave.

§

By now, Edward is the company's elder statesman, its resident source of wisdom. He offers practical advice to every new hire: "The stock and bond crop never fails. Set aside an hour each day to do your thinking. Associate only with successful people." Just as playing tennis with a good partner improves your game, associating with the best prompts you to do your best.

Doug Hill joins the firm young, and when he finally convinces Ted and Jack Phelan that he is ready to go into the field, Edward puts his two cents in, striking up a conversation in the men's room. "Doug, Teddy tells me you are going to the country. You are awfully young. Are you up for some advice?"

Hill waits eagerly, expecting pearls.

"Number one," Edward says, "when you go out to Dodge City, you have got to call on people with money. You are young, and you will tend to call on young lawyers and doctors, and at best, they will buy a hundred shares, and you are going to go broke. Two, you have got to ask them for their business. You have to ask for the order. Three, you have to ask for that order with enthusiasm. When you are shaving, practice your presentation. It is your responsibility to convince these people, and enthusiasm sells. Four, don't be afraid to ask for help. Ask for referrals. Five, take an hour every day and think about how you are going to invest your clients' capital. If you do a good job investing *their* capital, you will never have to worry about your own." He pauses for breath before his grand conclusion: "Always do what is right for the customer. It's all the business plan you need."

This all seems a bit too simple to young Doug Hill. He moves out to Dodge City, Kansas, and one day he goes into a drugstore, and the druggist is busy filling a prescription, and people are lined up waiting. "This guy is too busy," Hill thinks. "I'll go talk to that nice lady at the cash register." He makes the best call in the world on the white-haired lady, who tells him regretfully, "I don't have any money."

Hill is walking out the door, feeling like at least he tried, when Edward Jones's words ring inside his skull. It's like the older man has materialized and hit him over the head with a beam of wood. He turns around and asks the clerk if the pharmacist will mind if he goes behind the counter and talks to him.

"Now, you're cookin'," she says. She marches him behind the counter with one hand on his shoulder, which makes him feel like a kid caught stealing candy until he hears her say, "Now, Harold, I want you to talk with this young man." Mr. Jones's first point has been made.

Next, Hill drives to Coldwater and calls on the brothers who own most of the area's wheat and run a factory as well. When he walks in, a guy in bib overalls yells, "Hey, Richard, there's a suit over here who wants to talk to you." Richard comes over, and they talk. Ten days later, Hill returns ("The suit's back!") and Richard greets him warmly. "Hey, Doug! I went home and told my wife that finally we were having young people move *into* the area instead of leaving. She asked what you do for a living?"

Once again, he has done it wrong. Nervous at that first meeting, he talked with Richard about everything in the world and never asked for his business at all.

Decades later, Hill will become the managing partner of the firm. He will have little cards printed up with the founder's advice and will invite him to talk to training classes at every possible opportunity.

Edward will continue to come into the office every day until the day he dies. He might leave for a long lunch, but he takes pride in arriving earlier in the morning than anyone else. In bad weather he stands near the door, heartily greeting his snow-caked colleagues as they clomp in. He trades stock tips with his cronies, and he cultivates other sources within the company, asking young brokers questions to figure out just what his son might be up to and not divulging.

He may not even realize just how loyal his son is. Exasperated by all the confusion between Edward D. Jones and A.G. Edwards, regional leaders ask Don Bolin, who is close to Ted, to beg for a name change. Bolin does not relish the mission. He chooses his moment carefully and brings up the familiar concern, explaining how many problems it causes.

Turning to look Bolin in the eye, Ted says, "Edward D. Jones is a very, very fine name, and as long as I'm alive, that will be on the door."

§

When Rodger Riney was a civil engineering student at Mizzou, he hunted for an unpaid internship over winter break because he wanted to learn more about the investment business. One firm after another told him no. "If he'll work for nothing, send him on in!" was Ted's response—and it began a long chapter for both of them.

Riney graduated in 1969 with a civil engineering degree and an MBA. He had an offer from Bethlehem Steel for $1,100 a month and an offer from Ted Jones for $400 a month. "Naturally, I took the $400," he told his startled parents and friends.

He starts off in the Board Room, tearing off the Dow Jones tickertape every five feet and tacking it up on the wall for the salesmen to reference. The best training, though, is watching Ted operate. In a dozen different ways, he refuses, daily, to dilute or compromise his vision. When people say, "Gee, Ted, if you put a second person in an office, think how much more money you'd make—you've already got the teletype and the rent paid"—he shrugs, saying only, "I will not let salesmen get in arguments about whose client walked in the door."

Ted stays focused, and he keeps things simple. If money gets low, he tells everybody to come in on Saturdays and make phone calls. He looks at you with a penetrating stare. And while he's soft in many ways, fatherly and kind to anybody down on their luck, he's no pushover. Business is rough and tumble, and if somebody hires away one of his salespeople, he finds a clever way to retaliate.

He also regularly wages war with regulatory authorities. Edward D. Jones is a different sort of duck than other investment firms and is often put at a disadvantage by the rules set for them. He fires off letters with his usual directness. "Edward D. Jones & Co. does not take a 'holier than thou' attitude toward the securities industry back office problems," he tells then Sen. Stuart Symington. "We have had many errors and many knotty problems in our bookkeeping areas. Slowly but surely we are working out of our bookkeeping maze. At the present time the biggest problem we have, and it is an industry problem, is making delivery to our retail customers who are your constituents." He goes into specifics, then all upper-case: "WE ARE AT OUR WIT'S END."

Ted begs with endearing frankness, but he also knows how to be firm. To the Comptroller of the Currency, he writes, "In this instance, Mr. Saxon, it is my conviction that our position is right and that the position taken by your office is wrong."

He can also be audacious, sending the chairman of the SEC some "light reading" about the securities industry and adding that he will not "make any exposé of any facet of the securities industry; God knows we don't want any more investigations, at least not for a little while."

§

Ted's eyes are a clear sky blue that never lose intensity. They hold the light, and when they focus on you, there is no ambiguity. He locks on you, all the distractions fall away, and he reads your character, tests to see how much substance is there. As the conversation proceeds, he edges closer, making sure you're catching his point. It can make you nervous.

The bluntness, too, takes some getting used to.

"I'm not really a bond guy myself," a broker says chattily. "I'm more of a stock guy."

"You don't like bonds?" Ted says, his head coming up sharply. "I'll give you five minutes to love the bastards."

His tone can be rough, but there is nearly always mischief in the crinkle of his eyes, and the slanted brows, each aimed upward toward the center of his forehead, give him a leprechaun look that matches his sense of humor.

"If I can ever help you with anything," he'll say, "please call me *direct*. I have never believed in the chain of command."

When a young man keeps choking on the licensing exam, Ted takes him up to New York and introduces the examiner to him as some guy from the stock exchange that they're going to have lunch with. Ted settles them both down for a chatty, friendly lunch, and the examiner asks the young man all sorts of questions, and he knows every answer, and at the end of lunch, the examiner says, "Congratulations. You passed."

When a young rep sells two bonds that go bad, a customer, furious, prints up thousands of flyers that say all sorts of derogatory things about him. The local newspaper picks up the story, and then it hits the radio. He is ruined. Ted drives out to his office and spends two days there—right around Christmas—doing a live radio interview, speaking to a newspaper reporter, giving a talk at the Rotary Club, saving the guy's reputation.

When Jim McKenzie's dad dies, Ted calls three months later, right when he knows the grief will rebound. "Jimmy, how are you?" Jim says he's fine. "No, Jimmy, how *are* you?" Ted talks about his own father, how much they shared of life and work. "You and your father had much of the same. It's been a few months since your dad died. How are you doing?"

Sometimes he does a simple kindness, like returning with a box of Kleenex for somebody with a terrible cold. Always, he stays matter of fact.

Crossing the street with Shawn Daily, a veteran financial advisor who is forging right into traffic, Ted pulls him back and teases, "If I get hit and end up in the hospital, you're paying *my* bills. If you're in the hospital, I'm starving to death." Daily laughs, but the acknowledgment makes his day.

Learning it's a young broker's first wedding anniversary, Ted has a cake ordered and decorated. For a secretary's twentieth work anniversary, he asks various partners to wire congratulations company-wide and call her personally, then adds, "Darryl Pope, please put in the mail tonight one of the posters on Hawaii so she will receive it in two days." Ted has told the broker she works for that the company will split the cost of a trip to Hawaii for her.

He uses fun as a thank you. When the firm sees a good profit, he sends everybody—and their spouses—to the Tan-Tar-A resort at the Lake of the Ozarks. To even any financial inequity, he gives each person a $50 check for spending money.

On another occasion, he sends the company's longtime receptionist on a trip to Switzerland. Jean Burnett pronounces the trip the thrill of her life and, remembering his sweet tooth, brings him back as much Swiss chocolate as she can fit into her suitcase.

At a dinner party, Ted grabs a tray of hors d'eouvres from a broker's wife and starts serving them to the guests.

One day, a broker can't get her car started. Somebody offers to help her jump-start the engine. She gets back into the driver's seat and waits—and then she looks in her rear-view mirror, and there's Ted pushing, too.

Granted, he has to *get* pushed many times. He drives an old diesel Mercedes that breaks down so often, his father blurts, "Good God, Ted, would you buy a new car? It's getting embarrassing!"

§

Pat stays as far from the corporate scene as she can, but she does put in an appearance when she knows it will mean a lot to Ted—at the annual partner's meeting, for example. Even then, her appearance is hardly that of a CEO's wife. Barbara Webb, the company's events coordinator, takes one look at Pat—no bright lipstick, no cocktail dress, just flats and a skirt and a turtleneck—and grins. This is somebody real.

Setting up a buffet for the partners, Webb sees Pat's hand reach for the Brie. One of her favorite cheeses, it does not show up in any dairy case near Williamsburg. The two women chat, Pat a little shy but so interesting, brimming with ideas. When Webb asks what Pat studied in college, she says, "Dirt."

At the end of the evening, Webb murmurs to Pat, "There's some Brie left over. Would you like to take it home?"

"Oh, absolutely! We shouldn't waste it."

From that night on, Webb always makes sure to order an extra wheel of Brie for Pat to take home.

Ted puts his travel arrangements in Webb's capable hands, and once she flies with the Joneses to a partners' meeting in Florida. People dress up to fly in these days, and Webb has on her nicest outfit. She even splurged on a new piece of luggage.

Ted lugs theirs out of his trunk: two ancient suitcases and a cardboard box tied shut with twine.

Running the company has made no alteration in the way he carries himself. When Terry Hall goes to an Iowa steakhouse with Ted, he sees chicken-fried steak on the menu and his mouth starts watering, but he figures he should order something a little more sophisticated. He orders a top sirloin. So does Ted's driver. Ted orders chicken-fried steak.

Taking him to lunch in a Tex-Mex restaurant in Orange, Texas, Ron Cowling apologizes ahead of time: "Great food, but the place is a dump." To his relief, Ted loves the restaurant: "You can't get Mexican food like this in St. Louis, Ron!" They order more of everything.

The only gap in lifestyle between Ted and his sales force is that they tend to be fancier. For a partners meeting, the men make sure their suits are pressed and their dress shoes gleaming, and the women carefully pack new cocktail dresses in tissue paper. The night of their big restaurant dinner, it begins to drizzle, then sleet, then snow. Shivering in bare dresses and suits, they wait for the private bus outside their downtown St. Louis hotel. Up come Ted and Pat in heavy boots and old farm coats with hoods and gloves. "I don't know about the rest of you," Ted says with a twinkle, "but we're going to be comfortable."

§

Rodger Riney makes partner at Jones—but not because he is a good salesman. He is, in fact, a terrible salesman, and he admits this cheerfully. But he has lent all sorts of management support through the compliance department, human resources, and branch development.

By the late Seventies, the discount brokerage business is revving up; it is now a distinct segment of the brokerage industry. Edward D. Jones & Co. briefly toys with the idea of providing the service, with extremely low overhead and bare-bones service, to undercut Merrill Lynch and other full-priced competitors. John Bachmann strenuously advises Ted to resist that temptation. The company would be competing against its own sales force.

Riney sees the discount business a little differently, liking the fact that it is based on a do-it-yourself price and carries none of the risk of giving advice and being responsible for what clients decide to do. For him, it's a perfect fit. He decides to leave Jones and start his own discount brokerage. When Ted, loathe to see him leave, suggests that he let Jones be a minor partner in the venture, Riney thanks him but says that if he's going to fail, he doesn't want to do so in front of his old colleagues. Ted nods and wishes him well.

Riney manages his discount brokerage, Scottrade, the way Ted taught him, staying focused, opening office after office, plowing almost every dollar of profit back into the company and, when he makes money, spreading it around so all employees taste the reward.

Years later, he will sell Scottrade for $4 billion.

§

Warren Akerson and Darryl Pope are explaining to young John Beuerlein that Ted wants him to become a partner. "You just give us $25,000 of your savings," Pope says, "and we make it $25,000 of our capital." Beuerlein swallows hard. He's making a little over $18,000 a year, and he's trying to pay off his student loans, and he and his wife have saved $5,000 but it's for a down payment on their first house, and she's pregnant with their first child.

"I'm honored," he says, "but I'm embarrassed to tell you, I don't have $25,000."

Pope smiles. "No problem. All you have to do is come up with $5,000. We've got banks that will loan you the rest."

Should he use the down payment? It's exactly $5,000.... No. He can't. "I'm sorry," he says. "I don't even have $5,000 to put down."

Pope's smile widens. "Well, it's bonus time, you know." He reaches into his breast pocket and pulls out a $5,000 check. "You can hold it for a few minutes, but what Ted would like for you to do is turn it over and sign the back, because we'll use this to buy your partnership."

Is this really happening? Beuerlein starts to let himself feel excited. Then Warren says the bank will need collateral, and his spirits sink again. "I don't have any."

They nod, unsurprised. "Ted knew you wouldn't have any collateral," Pope says. "He told us to tell you not to worry, that he would pledge his personal investment portfolio against your loan."

Beuerlein finds out he's not the only partner Ted has backed. Quietly, the boss also gives people loans at times of personal crisis, helps with scholarships to make sure kids get to college, makes all sorts of investments in his associates. "One minute he's tight as tree bark," Beuerlein says, shaking his head, "and the next he's the most generous person you would ever hope to meet."

§

In 1976, Al McKenzie makes the biggest sale yet in the history of the firm: $1.2 million. But the company is seesawing between this ability to pull in profit and the need to process the paperwork. The problem is industry-wide, but it is acute at Jones, which is growing fast and has small offices scattered around the country and technology that is still pretty basic. Darryl Pope agrees to take over, and he moves his predecessor's desk into the open and starts peppering people with questions: How does this work? How does *this* work? What do we need to do better?

Ted stops hiring salespeople for about half a year, letting the firm catch up. He wants to get it right, not keep growing for growth's sake. In this way, as when he trains a dog or rides a horse, he has patience. He doesn't believe in pushing to meet others' expectations, and he's not about to jump into a fad. The world is fast computerizing, but at Jones, the teletype machine still clatters away….

By 1978, even Ted can see it's time to change. The wire room in the St. Louis headquarters is now a hub with spokes going out in all directions. Over those teletype wires, messages sputter in from 300 offices. The lines act like telephone party lines—recipients are looped, so any information typed in from any office along that spoke is sent to all twelve or fifteen brokers on that line. Because only one person can use the line at a time, they sit there waiting, hoping to get onto the line, then tap out their order with agonizing slowness, the machine only able to take ten characters per second. If an order is truly an emergency, they hit the **BREAK** button, which freezes everybody's carriage, and a bell dings three times on every machine. But everything is starting to feel like an emergency, because it's taking hours to execute each order. The days of the teletype are numbered.

Terrified of gridlock again, Ted charges John Bachmann with finding a new telecommunications system.

Bachmann gathers information, compares, narrows, looks into having a system custom-designed for Jones by Hewlett-Packard. Every time he begins to tell Ted what he's learning, Ted yawns and says, "John, just do it."

Jack Phelan and Pete Key, late 1970s, with teletype operators

What looks like boredom is, Bachmann eventually realizes, laced with fear. The project will cost $3 million, which is three-quarters of the firm's capital. This is a "bet the farm"—or rather, "the firm"—proposition. Ted knows it's necessary, too. He wants to open more offices, and they can't do that if they're communicating with Styrofoam cups and string.

Bachmann forges ahead. Then he has a long talk with the vendor he has chosen, who is finding the project more complicated than anticipated.

"We're going to break these people," a worried Bachmann tells Ted. "There is no joy in having a system knowing that it destroyed the company that built it for you."

Ted nods agreement. "Just remember: A contract is nothing more than a guide between people." They tear it up and draft a new one, building in a profit margin for the vendor. In return, the vendor gives them a more exciting system than Ted even knew was possible.

Luckily, he has always been good at delegating. He'll put together a decision-making group he deems competent, then, if the problem lies outside his expertise, he'll exclude himself from the meetings. If you don't have specific knowledge about a problem, he tells himself, why interject your worries, cautions, fears, and uninformed opinions?

His trust in Bachmann pays off. Jones has just become one of the first firms in the industry to move from its old eight-copy forms, carbon sandwiched between the layers, to paperless transactions. The pricey new telecom system will not need to be replaced until 1990.

§

While Bachmann is overseeing the new system, he looks for a tech expert, the firm's first. He interviews Rich Malone, and Ted meets him and makes only one comment: "I don't need partners to share the profit. I need partners to share the *work*."

There will be plenty: Malone is starting a tech group from scratch, all by himself. By the time he retires, twenty-eight years later, Jones will have a tech force of nearly 1,000 people.

For now, he is told he must learn everything about the way Edward D. Jones does business and how the firm is different from others in the industry. Luckily, Malone's cubicle is next to Bachmann's and just a few cubes over from Ted's. He learns patience from Bachmann, who refuses to use technology to eliminate people. Eliminate positions, fine, but only when you have another role for that person at the firm.

From Ted, Malone learns to keep a tight focus on what your true business is. He's watched other companies lose sight of that and nearly go out of business, and he sees Ted resist pressures daily that could swing the firm off course.

Instead of all the measurements and matrices Malone has used in previous jobs, he now has only one: What does it cost to provide this technology to an advisor in a down market? The firm has to be able to manage through those lows. So they stay conservative, but even so, they are constantly automating, adding more terminals. "Hewlett Packard can't build the machines big enough and fast enough for us," Malone realizes, and they switch to IBM. Soon there are intelligent work stations, and Jones is one of the first firms using laptops to keep its brokers mobile. Luggables, they're called, because they weigh about eight pounds, and it's exhausting dragging one through an airport.

Ted's father is dubious about all the tech expenditures, so one day Ted invites Malone to lunch at Bellerive Country Club. Ted sits back while his dad probes the new chief information officer's background and expertise, confident that now they will chat when they see each other in the office, and his dad will be able to trust the firm's brave new future.

14

Handing Over the Reins

John Bachmann started at Jones as an intern, sweeping floors while his brain filled with ideas. By 1972, he was the person Ted trusted to take notes at an important strategic planning meeting. Bachmann took down all the partners' ideas, the details, the stats, the possibilities. Then he wove them into a concise, bold memo. "Our growth will be limited by our ability to handle it, rather than any lack of opportunity," he wrote. This was a turning point, a chance to seize opportunity before their "patent" on the small office was stolen by competitors.

"At the moment, we don't need more new ideas"—Ted and his notebooks full of jottings?—"as much as we need the planning and administrative machinery necessary to carry out proven ideas on a greater scale," Bachmann continued. The suggested goal? One thousand offices. They might want to study the trajectory of McDonald's or Holiday Inn, not Goldman Sachs. And they would need a master plan, new administrative procedures to manage a firm that big and complex, new hiring and training and compensation plans.

That was the boring stuff, in Ted's opinion. But he did like the sound of one thousand offices. Over the next seven years, he leaned harder on Bachmann. In 1979, as the industry's new complexity and the firm's increasing size change the kind of leadership it needs, Ted realizes that a new managing partner is needed to execute his vision. The many planning meetings and discussions with his partners have made his decision, if not easy, obvious. John Bachmann is the right choice to take the firm to one thousand offices—and more.

But already? Ted is only fifty-four. Is he worried that the cancer will return? Jean Burnett gets his doctor in Kansas City on the line for him at regular intervals so he can have dutiful check-ups to make sure there's been no recurrence. Since his recovery, though, he has thought even more carefully about the future of the firm. He wants to make sure he's around to ease the transition.

He also knows he is out of his element. Ted's genius is to take a major problem and simplify it to half a page. But the new problems can't be simplified. Ted's leg jitters when he has to sit through long meetings or listen to reports that drone on. Human resources, compliance, SEC regulations, audits by the New York Stock Exchange—all that takes time away from interacting with human beings, which is where he shines.

He also wants to see the 304 branch offices triple in number, and he figures Bachmann, with his careful market research, can make that happen.

Bachmann teases that Ted makes too much of his scholarly bent; later, he will even theorize about it, calling Ted "a remarkable man who had an exaggerated respect for formal education, perhaps because he never graduated himself." This is both true and absurd, depending on what day you ask. Ted values intelligence of all sorts. He began asking Bachmann to write research reports because he recognized the academic aptitude, and now, as he steps down, he confides to Jack, "I don't think I can be as effective as someone more scholarly." On the other hand, Ted had a deep respect for anybody who is smart *without* a fancy degree, himself included. There isn't a shred of elitism in him, and he's always skeptical of overrated, overblown credentials.

Bachmann just happens to deserve his.

§

In September 1979, Ted calls Bachmann into his office and tells him that as of January 1, 1980, he will be responsible for running Edward D. Jones & Co. He has already taken over technology and operations; now he will be in charge of the entire firm.

Ted will remain, working as hard as ever, and everybody, including Bachmann, will continue to defer to him as their leader. But he will doggedly pursue the details that make the firm work, and Bachmann will do all that big-picture strategic planning Ted knows is needed. "Whatever you do," he tells Jack Phelan, "if you ever catch me trying to tell John what to do, you've got to get me out of his office."

At a partners meeting at the Kansas City Athletic Club, Ted announces his successor. Jim McKenzie hears the news and smiles. The previous July, Bachmann and his wife joined the McKenzies for a charity tennis tournament. Jim took him aside and listed all the strengths and weaknesses he had observed. "John, for what it's worth, I think you ought to become the next managing partner," Jim concluded, never dreaming the change was imminent.

Before Ted reaches his bombshell, though, he tells the partners that he's just gotten back from a Security Industries Association meeting in New York, and Edward D. Jones came in "among the top two or three best managed firms in the industry." Bache had lost money every year for the past seven years. Dean Witter Reynolds and Paine Webber had each lost money in five of the past seven years. Only Jones and Merrill Lynch had been consistently profitable.

Ted lists the innovations the firm has made in its offerings, its recruiting and training, its limited partnerships. "Change in our industry has worked to our advantage," he says. "Do not be afraid of change."

He has handed himself the perfect segue.

"John Bachmann has the youth, energy, experience, and the long-range outlook on the securities business to make an ideal managing partner. He will have 100 percent of my cooperation. I will now work for him in any job he gives me, and I know you will give him 100 percent of your cooperation and loyalty."

Edward D. Jones, Country Broker

The former and current managing partner, John Bachmann, *New York Times*, 1982

1 5

All Creatures Great and Small

On the way to the Jones family farm, the fields are pale with wheat stubble in winter, a mossy bright green in spring. The road is rippled like old glass. You pass a ramshackle barn, then turn onto the long drive that leads to the farmhouse.

Ted spends long hours working in the city, but this is what he has wanted since boyhood: to be a farmer. He was nudged into a very different life, making money grow instead. But when he registers at conferences or hotels or fills out his income tax form, he lists his occupation as "farmer."

Pat wants to farm, too—at least plant crops in a few fields. But the government regulations madden her, with all their price supports and allotments and set asides. So many *rules.* She likes the idea of growing something somebody wants, but it is no fun being told what to plant. Eventually she settles on buckwheat, sunflowers, sweet corn, sweet potatoes.

She and Ted love the farm every bit as much as they thought they would. For Ted, it's the independence—you make your own decisions, free of interference, and you work your behind off, and it's all up to you. Sometimes Mother Nature foils you; sometimes you get lucky; always, you do your part. You sweat, you experiment, and you shrug off the parts you can't control.

For Pat, it's the freedom, and the magic in the earth itself. You work

it, wet it, sprinkle seed, and up comes a field of sunflowers. She takes
her huge vegetable garden seriously, putting in lettuces, asparagus, green
beans, and always tomatoes and peppers so she can make her own hot
salsa. Anything she and Ted do not eat, she cans or gives away. For the
deer, she puts in food plots and places they can forage; for the birds, she
makes sure there is plenty of shelter, water, and seed. In time, she begins
to plant wildflowers, too, bringing them in tubs from Missouri Wildflower
Nursery and dotting them in little native gardens all over the farm.

She and Ted each create their own wetland area. Ted brings in a
bulldozer, making a perfect slope of twelve inches from top to bottom.
Pat's is a natural wetland. Between the two, eleven species of amphibians
find a home—although some of the salamanders will only live in Pat's
wetland.

Every spring, Ted will dry out his marsh and plant Japanese millet to
attract migrating ducks in autumn. When their snack is ready, he mows a
strip down the center—"the runway"—before flooding the pond eighteen
inches deep. He wants to give the ducks a soft landing. Soon mallards,
pintails, gadwalls, baldpates, and blue- and green-winged teal discover the
rest stop.

§

The first step for the Joneses, though, is to sop up some of the red ink.
The farm does not have to rake in huge revenue, but they don't want it
to swallow money and spit nothing back. Ted decides to try a livestock
operation, and he brings in a young neighbor, John Martin.

"He calls me his partner," Martin marvels to his wife. "Introduces me
that way, like I'm a broker at his firm or something." Their deal is that Ted
puts up the cash, Martin does the labor, and when they sell the cattle, they
split the profits. Just twenty-four years old, Martin already has cattle of his
own, so with Ted's added on, he is running more cattle than practically
anybody in Callaway County.

The first year, there are no profits. "John, I'm ready to settle up," Ted
says, "and you lost $38,000." He's matter of fact about it, assured and
businesslike. Martin's stomach drops. Yeah, we *bought high and sold low. But
they tripled in size! Surely…*.

124
Trail Blazers
"I doubt if you have that," Ted continues. "I'll tell you what. I'll write that off, and we'll just go round again."

Martin comes over to the Jones place on weekends now and again, helping out, knowing in the back of his head that he owes Ted $38,000. Also, Ted is fun to talk to, brimming with circus stories and bits of history. The next year, they make a little money, and Martin's share is about $30,000. These are lousy years for the cattle business. Ted casts about for other ideas, ways to improve or supplement what they are doing.

One of his experiments is buying a farm up north in Kirksville, Missouri. His nephew, John Key, does some work for him up there. After an especially long, sweaty day, Ted takes him out for dinner. "What do you folks do?" a chatty waiter asks.

"We tear down barns and sell the wood back East," Ted answers instantly, elaborating on the details of this amazing business he has just invented until the waiter is ready to quit his job and start tearing down barns himself.

For all his pranks, though, Ted is consummately fair. When he buys the land in Kirksville, he researches a fair price and offers it, warning the agent that he will take no counter offers. Then, instead of making the standard deal landowners make with fulltime farmers, he says, "For every year you farm, you will get 5 percent of the profit when we sell the land." The standard deal—in which the farmer provides the machinery, Ted provides the fertilizer and seeds, and they split the harvest—does not strike him as fair, because machinery depreciates and land appreciates.

Pat's nephew Truman Young also gets hired to help pound the Kirksville farm into shape. Truman and another kid are supposed to yank out an old fence and put in a new one. Itching to get back to Colorado, where he can work construction and make a lot more money, Truman works for a while as a favor, then makes his exit. Ted is furious—but mollified as soon as he hears Truman has a better paying job lined up.

After all, it was Ted who instilled Truman's work ethic—or at least polished it up. When Truman was still in high school, Ted hired him to clean out the barn. After pulling out all the junk, Truman swept between the barrels and other bits that were destined to stay. "What are you doing?" Ted demanded. "No, *no*. You take everything out, clean it, and then put it all back." Truman tried cleaning Ted's way and realized, "Sometimes the longer road gets you there better than the faster one."

§

Pat watches Ted's cattle operation with some amusement. If he's out of town and somebody needs to get the cattle off the road, she'll pitch in; there aren't as many farm boys on the Highway Patrol anymore, and there are ways to ease cattle off the road and ways *not* to. But unless there's an emergency, she'd really rather let Ted handle this enterprise, just as she lets him handle company business.

Branding the cattle is an experience. Ted has chutes and alleys set up, but when 400-pound animals are trying with all their strength to get away, no setup is perfect. The EDJ brand proves a nightmare: The inner circle keeps blurring. And the work is exhausting. One day, six guys are working, Ted alongside them. Because he's so short, he builds himself a pyramid of driveway rock about ten inches high so he can reach the levers and close the gate. Everybody else keeps

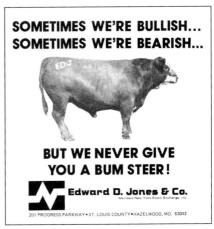

It's easy to see where the inspiration for some of the early Jones ads came from.

stumbling over the rock pile, which becomes a running joke. But they get it done, 250 cows branded in a single day.

The next ordeal is vaccinating the cattle. Another farmer helps him out, a taciturn fellow who's always puffing on a pipe. Ted thinks pipes are a fiddly waste of time, but whatever. They are determined to get the whole herd vaccinated, and at two in the morning, they are still at it, lifting up each animal's tail to take her temperature before inoculating her. They develop a rhythm, lapsing into silence as they focus on moving the cows along. Suddenly Ted bursts, "My God, what's in your mouth?"

The thermometer is between the tired farmer's lips, and his pipe is sticking out of the cow's rear end.

§

Harry Willcoxson brings his wife and kids out to visit so often, and they have so much fun, that when Ted gets wind of a farm for sale five or six miles away, he calls his old friend right away. Harry is interested—as are lots of other people. So Ted has a chat with the old farmer, Howard Tate.

"I have a friend who would love this place," Ted says, "and as a matter of fact, he's a direct descendant of Daniel Boone." This is true, and it intrigues Mr. Tate. When the Willcoxsons come out to see the farm and the four kids bounce in delight, he softens. And then Ted distracts some other potential buyers by talking about investments while Harry talks business with the owner. Deal done.

The Willcoxsons pile their four kids and sheepdog into a ten-by-ten-foot cabin. No electricity, no running water—but a deck where they stay up past bedtime, watching fireflies and telling stories.

Like schoolboys again, Ted and Harry plant white pines together, so many that they get out of hand. "Harry, you really should cull some of these," Ted says.

"Ted, God looks after this land," Harry replies.

"Yeah, Willcoxson, but even God needs help sometimes."

Which is as tight a summary of Ted's theology as anyone could ask for.

§

By the Seventies, the farm is terraced, and strip-cropping systems are in place. In April 1978, *Progressive Farmer* runs a feature about Ted experimenting with sod-planted corn. Eager to cultivate land that for three decades was only grazed by cattle, he and John Martin tried this method. "It converts pasture land into corn land," Ted tells the reporter with some excitement. "It converts land that cost $6 an acre in the 1930s into land that will grow as much corn as expensive Illinois corn land."

He's hoping this will provide income the cattle did not. The first harvest is ninety bushels, easily as much as conventional farming would yield. "I think a combination of sod planting and irrigation may prove to be a winning combination for Missouri's rolling hills," Ted concludes.

§

All Pat's jackets have pockets, and nearly all those pockets contain a few milk bones—or the leftover crumbs. Dogs add their energy to the farm, barking, playing, slaloming around the horses. Max the Weimaraner, the first dog they allow in the house, learns tricks from Ted and trots after Pat everywhere she goes. When her nieces and nephews are over and Pat sits on the floor to play board games with them, Max drapes himself across the game board, wanting her attention.

Ted and Pat with the resident dogs of the mid 1980s.

Over the years, Bonnet, part cattle dog but not a famous intellect, comes to live with the Joneses, as does Effie, named for Pat's Scottish grandmother. Angus, a black and white Australian shepherd, rides shotgun in the John Deere Gator (half golf cart, half all-terrain vehicle) that travels over logs, through ditches, and across creeks running fast enough to foam. Like Jocko, a previous Aussie, Angus will not countenance anyone else's presence in the front passenger seat.

Later, Pat gets Clara Belle, an affectionate cocker spaniel. And she will end her life with Gunner, rescuing the tiny, lionhearted Jack Russell terrier from a shelter just two days before he is due to die.

Pat always gives the pups plenty of freedom to roam the farm—then worries if they don't come back in an hour and goes out to look for them. She has never been much for giggly girlfriend stuff or lunching with the ladies; her best friends are her husband and her dogs.

§

For Ted, too, animals are a source of joy. Also of sport—for his quail hunting, he has a couple faithful Llewellyn setters, black with white spots; a Brittany spaniel; and a beagle. He reads and rereads James Herriott's gentle novels about a country vet. "They have the cutest little Basset hound brand-new pup I have ever seen," he will write, a non sequitur in a memo reporting on a new broker's performance. When he composes his famous letter explaining why he feels like the richest man in America, he says of his four dogs, "Two love only me. One loves everybody. One loves no one but is still very loyal." He is secure enough to respect that.

D-Boy Garner, a teenager who lives on a nearby ranch, grows up hero-worshipping Ted, at least as much as he's willing to hero-worship anybody. Ted's the kind of guy who can see a rock laying in the drive and, if there's a little bit of silence, pick up that rock and create a conversation. He can come up with anything and get you involved in it. It's a shame, D-Boy thinks, that he doesn't have kids.

D-Boy trains the little Brittany spaniel as a bird dog for Ted, who brings her with him in the Jeep whenever he shows people around the farm. Every time they reach a spot with quail in the brush, she points, and Ted beams with pride.

As for Pat, she has a way with her. D-Boy watches her spend time with the horses and sees how they respond, whether it's a farm horse or the high-stepping saddle-bred horse Frances VanDyke gave her. "Classy horse, real smooth gait—you could drink a cup of coffee while you rode that horse," he recalls later. "Pat raised a colt out of that saddle mare, looked a lot like the mother."

He keeps a pack mule at the Jones place, and Pat gets a kick out of the loud hee-haw. She's never in a hurry, D-Boy notices. Slow and casual, just moves at her own speed. It relaxes the critters. When Ted walks out to the paddock, his energy stirs up the horses, and they go a little happy-crazy. Pat walks into the meleé, and they calm immediately.

One of her special horses is Pie, blazed with a wedge-shaped white patch, but her all-time favorite is Currant, a white Arabian, pale as fog. They buy him in the late Sixties, and they hire D-Boy to break him.

D-Boy works Currant all summer on his family's ranch. "He's just a two-year-old; he doesn't know anything!" he realizes. Anytime he and his dad go anywhere on horseback, D-Boy rides Currant. This is a new experience; the Garners are quarter-horse folks, and D-Boy's dad snickers at this small, thin Arabian horse. But Currant comes along nicely, working the cattle slow and quiet and easy. One day, D-Boy's dad announces, "I want to ride that little Arab." After that, it's hard to get him *off* of Currant.

Smart and steady, Currant can pick out the best way through terrain or brush on his own. He never gets tired. And as independent as he is, he will do almost anything Pat asks.

Not so much Ted. *His* favorite is a big gray, mottled with white and called, for some unfathomable reason, Cheddar. The Joneses' foodie names puzzle John Martin—especially when he meets Chutney, because he's never heard of the stuff.

The horse that's always around, like a backyard dog, is Molly, a fine mare, gentle through and through. Kids can climb all over her, and she makes no objection. But she is never actually ridden. One day, Pat's gone, and John thinks, "I've never really saddled a horse. I think I'll try it."

The attempt is short-lived. When Pat comes home, he says, "I tried to ride Molly," and the fireworks bang and sputter: "Oh my God! She's never had a saddle on in her life! You'll break her back!" Pat is fiercely protective of her animals. Just ask D-Boy, who grows up to be a farrier and has to work with her watching over his shoulder and yelping in protest at the slightest discomfort when he shoes one of her horses.

The next time she and John tangle, it is because he has moved the horses to a field of clover so the cattle can graze for a while. Now, it's true, horses can sometimes gobble up all the clover at once, and it'll hurt them. But this is just for a little while….

"Where are the horses?" Pat asks the minute she returns.

"I kicked them out," he says cheerfully. "They're in the clover field."

Pat bends her knee and swings hard, kicking gravel against the side of the Jeep while she yells at him to never, *ever* do that again. It takes weeks for them to be amiable again.

§

Second only to the animals, the Joneses love their trees. Ted's first act on this land was to plant the allée of pin oaks as a schoolboy. When he brought his bride to the farm, he picked up where he'd left off.

First, they brought out a friend of Ted's who was a forester. He walked through the woods. "Well," he said heavily, "I just hate to tell you this,

but you haven't got a tree worth
anything." Previous owners and
tenants had cut down every tree
with lumber worth selling. Then
they'd let the rest of the trees grow
willy-nilly, with no attempt to thin
them and plant the right sorts in
the right places.

Step one would be putting
enough trees around their new
house to have some shade.
Then, they could have some fun
reforesting.

Together, over several years,
Ted and Pat plant short-leaf and
white pine trees. Ted likes the

The oak allée that Ted planted as a child
still lines the drive at Prairie Fork.

sharp, tingling fragrance, the deep-breath calm of a pine forest. Pat loves
all trees, even the thorny honey locusts they inherited. "Have you ever
been stuck by one of those thorns?" she asks a city dweller cheerfully.
"They can go right through the sole of a shoe!"

Schooled by the best deal-maker in town, Ted strikes a deal with the
Missouri Conservation Department: "I'll buy you one of those new tree
planters, provided we can use it on our place first." The mechanical tree
planter is a new idea, and it beats making thousands of holes by hand.
They pull it with the tractor, driven by Pat. Ted sits in back, on the planter,
and as the plough opens a furrow, he drops the seedling in. Then the
slanted wheels close the furrow. He still has to straighten some of the trees
by hand, tamping them in place, but they can plant dozens of trees at a
time. One year, they reach a thousand.

Later, Pat will laugh about her own turns in the planter: "I was never
very good at it. I'd get mine too close together. They're supposed to be
about six or eight feet apart—and if you're really good, you'd get them ten
feet apart, and they'd live."

Ted also asks Martin to help him plant, maybe hoping he will be less
impulsive than Patsy. But Martin can barely stand it: "Why ruin this great

cattle farm with all these trees? It's so much easier just to mow it!" In moral indignation, he tosses every third hedge tree over his shoulder.

Once they have put in as many saplings as Ted sees fit (without knowing how many Martin tossed aside), he donates the machine to the Missouri Department of Conservation as a "private land" planter. It proves so useful, the agency acquires twenty-four more, two for each forest district in the state. They are loaned to landowners to encourage reforestation projects.

As soon as the pine trees are tall enough, Ted and Pat begin inviting all the Jones associates out to the farm every December. The 1960 invitation takes the form of a prospectus for "1000 Christmas Trees, Jones Pine Forest, Inc. (a subsidiary of E.D. Jones Farms)."

"These trees have not been approved or disapproved by the Securities and Exchange

PROSPECTUS

1,000 CHRISTMAS TREES

Jones Pine Forest, Inc.

(A subsidiary of E. D. Jones Farms)

THESE TREES HAVE NOT BEEN APPROVED OR DISAPPROVED BY THE SECURITIES AND EXCHANGE COMMISSION. COMMISSION PERSONNEL HAVE NOT CLIMBED THESE TREES.

	Price to Public	Underwriting Discounts and Commissions	Proceeds to the Company (1)
Per Tree	Plenty	Hardly worth mentioning	What's left after paying salesmen
Total	100%	99%	1%

(1) Before deduction of expenses

Offered in Anticipation of Christmas

These trees are offered one to a customer, subject to prior sale and change in price. It is expected that delivery of trees will be made on Sunday, December 18th, 1960, in the Pine Woods of the Corporation located at Williamsburg, Callaway County, Missouri.

PAT AND TED JONES
(A Partnership)
Members - New York Stock Exchange

The date of this Prospectus is December 18th, 1960

An invitation to the farm, Pat and Ted-style

Commission," the prospectus notes. "Commission personnel have not climbed these trees." The price per tree is "Plenty," underwriting discounts "Hardly worth mentioning." "Offered in anticipation of Christmas," the prospectus finishes, "by Pat & Ted Jones: A Partnership."

Squeezed into the family station wagon with his five siblings, Jim McKenzie cranes his neck to look out the window as his dad drives down a long, tree-lined road and into the farmyard. A big haywagon waits there,

Visitor accomodations, courtesy of Ted and Pat

two giant draft horses patiently switching their tails. Somebody hoists Jim up on the wagon, and he sits on one of the bales and asks what the horses' names are, and they are Babe and Nellie, and of *course* he can pet them!

The wagon takes them deep into the pine woods. In a clearing, a big iron cauldron of hot chocolate steams over a fire. A young mother lays a sleepy toddler on a mat inside an 1898 pup tent, scooting a bale of hay in front for instant day care. Jim examines the tipi, framed by heavy branches still rough with bark, then catches sight of a jumbo bakery box, packed with donuts, sitting on top of a bale of hay.

The McKenzies walk into the forest to pick out their Christmas tree, and Jim and his dad drag it out of the woods. Then the kids play, and people talk, and somebody (no doubt Ted) starts a round of Christmas carols. As they sing, it begins to snow. In the soft dusk, the McKenzie kids pile into the station wagon and head home, and everybody falls asleep but their dad.

Years later, Jim will ask Ted why he stopped having those Norman Rockwell tree parties that gave so many kids perfect snow-globe memories.

"How old were you at the time?" Ted asks.

Jim thinks back. Eight? Ten?

"Well, those Christmas trees are about fifty feet tall now!"

Fast forward again, to a panel discussion at a national meeting a few years after Ted's death. Pat is on the panel, sitting right next to Jim as he retells his happy childhood memory for new associates. When he ends by marveling at how generous Ted was, letting them cut down his trees to

Al McKenzie, standing with sons Paul and Jim

make their Christmas special, she bursts out laughing. "That's not why Ted did it. Somebody from the Missouri Conservation Department came and told him he'd planted the trees too close together."

Jim does a doubletake, reassessing his childhood. "I've been telling this story all these years and all I was doing was serving as scab labor?"

She gives one of those shrugs that means, *That was Ted for you.*

"I'm devastated," he says, half teasing, half…devastated. The audience is laughing so hard, the next speaker has to wait for the gales to subside.

§

Ted tried cattle ranching right at the time when the money fell out of the cattle market. Then he tried contour planting, which was a comical struggle because the tractor always wanted to go uphill or downhill, not *along* the hill's contours. Finally, Pat and Ted planted trees along the contour so the tractor had no choice. Then they tried the sod-planting.

In the Eighties, they shift to natural habitat. Ted wants to create a game preserve. Instead of planting crops to harvest and sell, he plants rows of corn at the edge of the woods so quail can feast near shelter. His good friend John Jamieson (no relation to Pat's family) nods with satisfaction. He gave Ted hell early on because the farm was too clean and pristine, shorn of refuge for wildlife. "It needs to be a little scruffier," Jamieson said.

Now it will be.

"You're not leaving much on the ground," Ted complains to the farmer he's paying to help him harvest. Again, he explains that he wants a little extra for wildlife.

On a chalkboard map of the farm, he puts an X wherever he sees a covey of quail. The result is magic: "Ted can take you around the farm and know exactly where and when there will be coveys of quail or deer," marvels Jack Phelan.

Ted keeps careful track, and once they have shot ten birds from a covey, they stop.

He says shooting deer is too easy. Or maybe he is too softhearted. Or maybe it is the look on Pat's face. Nobody in her family hunted, and she would rather plant food for the deer than kill them. One year, she leaves town rather than endure Williamsburg's deer season.

Ted *is* an excellent shot, though. In the Merchant Marine, out on the
tugboat, he watched his comrades fire at a big bird, an albatross or pelican,
and miss every time. "Oh, my God. You're wasting ammunition!" he said.
"Give me the gun." With one shot, he brought the bird down.

Now, with bobwhite quail, he hits his mark again and again—but he
can't stand to eat the birds. He pays to have them cleaned and sends them
to his mother, who deems quail a delicacy. When she dies, he stops hunting
altogether.

Slowly it is becoming clear to Ted, Pat, and all the experts around
them that the future for *their* farm is taking land *out* of farming and
restoring it to prairie instead. Ted plants big bluestem and switchgrass
to hold the soil in place, thwart erosion, and create habitat for the quail.
Pointing to a field with waving grasses as tall as a man, he explains to a
visitor that they are restoring the prairie.

Pat hides a smile. With two species? There is a long way to go until this
land is prairie again. But they have made a start.

16

Who Said Bumblebees Can't Fly?

John Bachmann takes Ted's intuitive ideas and weaponizes them. "At times," he will say, "I think I understood the power of Ted's vision better than he did. As an observer, I could see dimensions of it he might have overlooked."

With that perspective, Bachmann begins to study the metrics. How can they scale what they're doing? For years now, he has studied organizational behavior and marked what makes a company thrive as it grows, not expand like a balloon and pop at reality's first prick.

Like Ted, Bachmann is a strong communicator, Norman Eaker notices. "When they speak it is genuine, insightful, and inspiring. They're both passionate about doing what's right, morally and for the people in the firm."

In company loyalty, Bachmann has inherited an incomparable asset. The other partners feel a debt of gratitude to Ted for opening the ownership of the company to them, and they are determined not to take advantage of his generosity. Rather than suck profit from the company and retire with indifference, they want to make Jones even stronger for those who come after them.

Bachmann needs that kind of support. Soon, he will have to okay a $32 million investment in a satellite network. The hokey videos Ted and Jack Phelan used to make in the company's tv studio, scripted for internal

amusement and motivation, are now joined by polished educational
videos the financial advisors can show their clients. Not long after this
shift, Bachmann will face one of those "bet the firm" decisions: investing
roughly $100 million to convert the computer system.

Edward D. Jones is neither flashy nor fancy, and it lets a lot of trends,
like online investing, pass it by. But in the essentials, the firm keeps up. Has
to, Bachmann reasons. Expansion is now more than an exciting idea. This
is a mass-market business, and they need to hire more financial advisors if
they want to do national advertising and spread the huge costs of investing
in technology across a wider base. Also, they have new competition from
discount brokerages, and the competition from banks and fund companies
is intensifying. To stay, in that overused term, relevant, Jones *has* to be big.

§

Ted is happy to leave the big-picture plans to his successor. He is back to
doing what he loves best: motivating people in person, taking road trips to
check on new advisors and show them how to dress, how to sell, how to
perpetuate the company culture.

Transactions have sped up and increased in complexity, so most branch
offices now have an administrator helping with paperwork, execution
of trades, and routine customer inquiries. Ted, though, has never even
wanted a secretary. He likes to roam the office, when he's in town, and
gather up partners for a spontaneous meeting. When he needs help, he
asks somebody else's secretary. Nobody's going to say no, but the habit's
becoming a bit burdensome. So in 1981, Betty Meyer, John Bachmann's
secretary, is asked to also serve as the secretary Ted doesn't want.

She quickly makes herself indispensable, keeping his calendar
("He had all these commitments and no calendar!") and organizing
his projects. Beneath the bluster is "really a very sweet man," she soon
realizes, impatient with bureaucracy but fond of people. Watching him in
action, she learns that "if you want something, you have to ask for it. And
sometimes you have to demand it. Which, for a shy little person like me, is
a huge lesson!"

She also learns how to invest, because Ted has her keep track of his
portfolio. When she sees that one of his mutual funds earned him more in

one day than she makes all year, she begins investing in mutual funds herself.

Meyer is struck daily by the contrast between her two bosses. "Ted was a country boy," she will say later, "and John was all city. He *loved* to go to New York and deal with the SEC, or go to Washington…." Asked if she gets stressed "working for those two alpha males," she laughs: "I've got three teenagers at home. These guys are a piece of cake." And really, they are. So many high-powered executives accelerate like race cars, rolling right over anybody who gets in their way. These two stay kind.

When Meyer's son, who yearns to be a chef, gets accepted at the Institute of Culinary Education in New York, she thinks, *Oh my God, how am I going to pay for this on a secretary's salary?* She swallows her worries, figuring she will manage somehow, always has. When she mentions the good news, careful to sound calm and upbeat, Ted says casually, "Tell me about this school."

When the first payment comes due, Meyer learns that her son's tuition has already been paid in full.

§

Ted is now able to brush aside the boring stuff and deal directly with people, and it's a joy.

Except when it's not.

In 1980, he makes one of his trips to Hays, Kansas, to see Darrell Seibel. Usually, this is one of his favorite places to visit, but this time, he's nervous.

"Sure is a hot day," Ted says. "How about a drink?"

Seibel brings him a cold drink. Then a second. With the third, unlike Ted, he begins to worry. This isn't thirst-quenching, it's Novocain. Finally Ted says, blurting it like he's breaking up with a girlfriend, "We are getting out of commodities."

Seibel has been hedging cattle, because the banks won't make loans to the ranchers when the price goes down unless they're hedged. He gulps, says okay.

Next Ted visits John Reed, who has been the top commodities trader at Jones every single year and just might quit at this news. Jack Phelan comes along for moral support, but Ted launches into the hard part himself: "John, I hate to tell you this, but our customers have lost money in commodities every year except one, going all the way back to 1936."

A slow smile. "Well, Ted, I was hoping someday somebody would tell me that I had to get out of the commodities business. It's been worrying me for years."

Commodities had seemed like a natural fit for a broker in small Midwestern towns. For Edward, they were part of the full inventory he wanted the firm to offer. But Ted is starting to see commodities as more of a gambling disease, and he wants no part of it.

Doug Hill agrees. He's in Dodge City, the cowboy capital of the world. It seemed like a favor at first, teaching farmers and ranchers how to hedge their prices. "Problem is," he tells Ted, "when reality comes, these guys play in the commodities market rather than hedge their cattle or wheat. I can never convince them to keep the hedge on. And you can't win. If the price winds up higher, they blame you."

Commodities have been one of the firm's profit sources, but when Ted demanded a big-picture accounting of the yield from the *customer's* perspective, it's rarely been a net unrealized gain. He decides that, for their sort of client, the risk is too high.

§

For his ninety-minute commute, Ted hires a driver (who later becomes a Jones financial advisor) so he can talk his thoughts into a cassette recorder. He arrives at the office with a million ideas, and the minute he comes through the door, he tosses the cassette tape to his secretary to transcribe and starts giving orders and suggestions, grabbing anybody in sight to delegate a new project he thought up on the drive. After being nabbed a few times, staffers learn to duck out of sight when he enters the building.

Jim McKenzie learned to duck in hallways years earlier, because every time he ran into Ted, who had known him since he was a kid, Ted would say, "Jimmy, I've got something I'd like you to work on"—and want results immediately. "How have all the mutual funds we have recommended done for the past ten years on the various indexes, compared to all the other mutual funds?" Ted once asked. "Check on that, will you? You can take your time. I won't be back until next week."

§

John Hess, the poor summer intern who addressed all the certificates to the wrong stock exchange, went on to do well in his father's real-estate firm. Then he left, thinking he would seek his fortune in Dallas.

Soon after he and his wife move to Texas, his phone rings. It is Mr. Jones, the man on whose lap he sat as a kid. Eighty-some years old, and he's still recruiting.

"I got your number from your dad," he tells Hess. "Why don't you come back to St. Louis? There's a position here for you."

After his Texas real estate venture fails, Hess makes a trip to St. Louis and stops by Edward D. Jones. Given his experience, he thinks he should be in their real-estate section. Oh, and he wants to be a partner.

Word of this is conveyed to Ted, who exclaims, "We're not going to make this guy a partner! Tell him we will pay him $2,500 a month." One of the other partners murmurs, "They say he's been very successful."

"Well, he's broke now," Ted points out. "He needs a job."

Hess turns on his heel and walks out. Ted follows, carrying a big binder. It contains a computer printout of every salesperson's commission. Ted draws the younger man's attention to two men in North Carolina, one making about $10,000 a month, the other $6,500. "You want to be a partner? Go out into the field and sell, and you *will* become a partner."

"I've never sold anything in my life," Hess says.

"You've sold yourself," Ted reminds him, then walks him down to John Borota's office.

"And who are you?" Borota asks.

"I'm your new hire."

"I do the hiring," Borota counters. Hess turns to Ted, so he can explain—but Ted is already halfway down the hall. He has done what he intended to do: taken Hess (who *will* soon be a partner) right out of his comfort zone.

§

In 1982, *The New York Times* reports that with $11 million in capital, Edward D. Jones & Co. "is a mere one-hundredth the size of Merrill Lynch." The reporter goes on to note that "there are other ways to measure a brokerage firm—like profits. Jones said it recorded a 37.8 percent jump in its earnings last year while gross revenues rose 44.2 percent. Merrill Lynch's earnings, by contrast, were up 1 percent." Jones brokers are paid 42 percent of their commission income, the article continues, "considerably higher than the 13 to 33 percent retained at many discount brokers."

The same year, a Harvard Business School study is released. Its title flips the old taunt on its back: "Who Said Bumblebees Can't Fly?"

§

New avenues continue to open for Jones, especially in investment banking. With Dan Burkhardt, Ted makes calls on John Deere, Walmart, and other corporations around the country. They are following big brokerage houses that have two dozen Harvard interns working on a phonebook-thick proposal crammed with stats and historical references. Dan boils their proposal down to a single sheet of paper and lays out the facts as simply as he can. Ted provides the color commentary.

"Look, you are selling bonds," Dan will begin. "The bond market isn't just institutions on Wall Street. You should consider selling bonds to individual investors all over the country."

Then Ted will chime in: "You don't need Goldman Sachs. You need Edward Jones."

Goldman Sachs is, of course, saying the opposite. When Ted and Dan visit CP National (formerly California Pacific Utilities) in San Francisco, one of the executives repeats what the guys from Goldman Sachs told them: "If you do business with Edward D. Jones, the 'CP' is going to stand for 'cows and pigs'!"

Of all the business and finance stories of the Eighties, one of the most riveting is the explosive growth of Walmart. Edward Jones underwrites many bond issues for the company, and Ted and Dan Burkhardt make several trips to Bentonville, Arkansas, to meet with company executives. Ted comes to know the legendary Sam Walton quite well, and Burkhardt watches the two men with amusement: They are so similar, it's uncanny. Both are happiest in the country; both love small towns and the people who live there. Schooled at the University of Missouri, both started work in the Fifties, and they headed straight for midwestern towns—places that others had overlooked or taken for granted—to find markets for socks and stocks.

At the grand opening of one of the first Sam's Wholesale Clubs in the U.S., a banker takes it upon himself to introduce the two men. He is clearing his throat, readying a formal introduction, when Sam rolls an overflowing shopping cart toward them and calls, "Hey, Ted! The prices on toilet paper are great!"

As usual, Ted is a step ahead of the bankers.

He and Sam are both instinctively frugal; they talk often about how important it is to keep costs low and set the right example. Whenever they meet, they swap stories, outdoing each other with accounts of personal thrift and company-wide cost-savings. Walmart has just begun its Buy American push, and Ted applauds the initiative.

On one of these trips, heading out for a tour of warehouses, Sam mentions that his pickup truck is parked on the far side of the lot; maybe Ted's car is easier to reach?

Ted is driving his Mercedes.

He spends the entire drive to the warehouse explaining how old the Mercedes is, how stripped-down, and how much mileage it has logged. His face is the hue of a ripe tomato. He has lost this one, and they both know it. They remain friends, though, and one day Sam says, "You know, Ted, you and I should get together. Wouldn't it be great if every Walmart had a Jones office in it?"

"That *would* be great," Ted quips, "but I can't afford to buy you right now."

Deep down, everybody knows Ted would love to be in business with Sam Walton—*if* it made sense. And when Walmart opens supercenters, that looks like an opening. What about adding Jones offices only in those supercenters?

It's tempting, but Ted and Bachmann toss it around and decide the gains wouldn't be worth the loss in focus. They will stick with their one-person offices, which are obviously succeeding. "Aerodynamically, Edward

D. Jones & Co. can't possibly work," notes a 1985 article in *Institutional Investor.* "Yet it doesn't just fly—it soars."

The same year, an article about Walton calls him "the richest man in America." After reading the piece, Tom Bartow, then a Jones partner writes to Ted: "It occurred to me that if you had taken the firm public, *you* would be the richest man in America. Thanks for sharing the firm with all of us."

Ted replies with a cross between a checklist and a prose poem:

I am the richest man in America.

I have a wife who loves me in spite of my faults.

I have four dogs. Two love only me. One loves everybody. One loves no one but is still very loyal.

I have a horse I love to ride around the farm, and best of all, she comes to me when I call her.

I have too much to eat and a dry place to sleep.

I enjoy my business.

I love my farm and my home.

I have a few close friends, and money has never been my God.

§

Ted gives sage advice, but he has not withdrawn to a mountaintop, and he doesn't pretend he can stay cool in all situations.

One day Jim McKenzie, now a regional leader, asks him how to handle a financial advisor who's driving him crazy and disrupting meetings.

"You don't have to like everybody in your region," Ted says, "but you do have to give everybody the opportunity to achieve their full potential." Jim nods, lets the advice settle in. A few months later, Ted visits the office of the annoying broker.

When he leaves, he dials McKenzie's office: "Jimmy, I want you to go out there and fire that SOB!"

By now, Jim is calm, and he decides to follow Ted's initial advice instead. The broker goes on to be incredibly successful—and less annoying. Still, it felt good to have Ted share his frustration.

When Jim turns forty, he decides to ask the four wisest people he knows what they wish they'd known when they were forty. One of the four is

Ted, who responds with a deeply personal letter, talking about the darkest hours of his bout with cancer in the Seventies and how he pushed himself past the fear of death. Focus on what matters, he urges. "Most things are not black or white in life; those decisions are easy…. Most things, and questions, and decisions, are in the gray areas. Therein lies the problem."

Ted's confidence buoys Jim, adding a layer of resolve to the optimism his father taught him. A down market? Al McKenzie called it "a bull market in yields." Traffic snarled? "A chance to practice patience." A drenching rain at his tee time? "Good for the subsoil." The insistence on positivity was relentless, sometimes flat annoying. But it was exactly what young people needed to hear to build hope—in themselves, and in life.

The last night of Al's life, he takes part in a Catholic men's discussion group, and the evening's topic is "Prayer: The Preparation for Eternal Life." He goes home afterward, kisses his wife good night, and dies in his sleep.

Jones decides to name its new training center after the man who taught them all how to sell. The decision is unanimous, all the partners rising to their feet except Jim, who is stunned and a little embarrassed, not sure whether he should vote.

At the dedication, Ted says, "For the first twenty years, I called Al 'Mr. McKenzie.'" Because everybody knows Ted was never the formal sort, the measure of respect is obvious. "The outstanding thing about Al McKenzie was his clear perception of what was right and wrong, what was *fair,* and what was moral in our dealings with our customers and each other," Ted continues. "I'm not ashamed to acknowledge that I would not have succeeded in this business had it not been for Al McKenzie's sales training and wise counsel in both my business and personal life."

§

Jack Phelan picks up where Al left off as national sales manager. Jack knows everybody at the firm, remembers their name. Their kids' names. Their *dogs'* names. Ted likes talking about people's dogs too, but when he's handed a problem, he can work himself into a lather. The only time anybody remembers Jack losing his temper was after one of his kids busted their lawn mower for the third time.

Jack's way of helping is to listen, ask the right questions, help people think clearly. He knows the business from the ground up, remembers the days he logged chalking price drops or hikes on the long board. He loved selling, and now he supports all the brokers who are trying to learn its art.

The firm makes tough demands: You must work in a town where you know no one, and before you can open your own office, you have to be able to document making a thousand calls. People's names, ages, occupations, what you presented, how many times you have gone back to see them—all of that on each green index card. A 1986 article in *The Wall Street Journal* describes Jones advisors "opening offices in the kind of places that most brokers visit only if their cars need gas." The communities are small, with efficient grapevines, so a Jones broker has to be above reproach at all times, no careless mistakes.

Yet one new broker after another, they manage to pull it off.

§

Bleachers are set up in the parking lot for Jones's St. Louis headquarters, with big screens, and a band's playing, and everybody's outside waiting to applaud. The ribbon-cutting will be beamed by satellite back to St. Louis from Stoughton, Wisconsin, where a circus elephant is leading the festivities. It is 1986, and Ted, Bachmann, and other partners are opening a new Jones branch office.

The thousandth.

In one decade, the number of offices tripled, just as Bachmann promised they could. Ted's smile is so wide, it's stretching his cheeks, and his face is going to hurt later, because he can't stop grinning. Watching from St. Louis, Darryl Pope nods. Even though Ted's own father raged at him, swearing that he was going to break the firm, Ted never lost faith that his vision could work. This moment must be sweet.

Bachmann gives Ted a little time to savor the triumph. Then he says, "Now let's take it to 10,000."

§

The climb from 1,000 to 10,000 is easier, Bachmann will say later, than it was to get to 1,000. But easy is a relative term. In 1987, the market crashes, and Norman Eaker watches orders come in so fast, the computer system can't get them executed. The market keeps dropping, and there are thousands of orders stuck in the computer.

Ted, with Jack Phelan behind, left, opening office #1000 in 1986.

"Print them," Eaker says, "and sort out the ones for $10,000 or more." They are sorting madly, calling in the big orders, when Bachmann walks in and sees the chaos.

"What the hell is going on here?" he asks.

When they explain, he says only, "What can I do to help?"

Eaker nods to a chair. "Sit down over there, sort the paperwork, and pull out anything over $10,000." They both know that if the market drops again and they have to honor all these orders, the firm will go bankrupt.

Once again, Jones survives.

1 7

Field Work

Ted spends most of the Eighties visiting field offices, firing up (or firing) the troops. He has a method: He pulls into town and stops at a gas station, a grocery store, or a thriving business. Sometimes he just asks if there's an investment advisor in town; other times, he has a little fun, announcing that he's thinking of opening a business in town and needs someone to help him do some investing. If the proprietor doesn't refer him to an Edward Jones office, he worries. If the proprietor knows where the office is, Ted asks if the broker is reliable.

Storing away what he has learned like a chipmunk prepping for winter, he then calls on the broker. "Make a presentation to me," he demands. "Show me the list of people you intend to call on." If the list is not long enough, he grabs a phone book, throws it down on the desk, and says, "Open the book and start calling."

If his victim is a young guy new to the company, Ted walks with him up and down Main Street, standing across the street to watch as he enters every single store or business, meets the owner, and leaves a business card.

"We must kill or cure this fear of making cold calls," Ted reminds the other partners. He likes the reminder one young broker taped to his mirror: "You only get customers by making cold calls."

A less fortunate young man calls a surgeon who is a potential client. Told that the surgeon is in the operating room, the young man politely explains his purpose and asks, "Could you please have him call me?" Listening, Ted drops to his knees and folds his hands in mock prayer. "You were *begging* him to call," he says afterward. "You say, 'This is Ted Jones, please call me' and hang up, so they don't know what the call is about."

§

Ted has a knack for seeing what needs to be changed in somebody's physical set-up. Maybe they need a bigger sign, a first-floor office to save elderly clients the steps, or a nicer location. He is appalled by a guy whose IN and OUT baskets are overflowing, and whose work space is strewn with clutter. "I cleared his desk for him," he reports to the partners.

At an office in Marshalltown, Iowa, Ted rolls up his sleeves again: "We took the coffee cups, sugar, dirty spoons, three or four jars of creamer out of the reception area. IT LOOKED LIKE HELL! DO SALESMEN THINK WE ARE RUNNING A RESTAURANT? DO LAW FIRMS HAVE COFFEE MESS IN THE RECEPTION AREA? PUT THE COFFEE POT IN THE BACK ROOM!"

After shipping a desk to a trainee, Ted kicks himself: "We should have known that [he] would sit at the desk rather than make calls."

"He needs to get old filing cabinets painted; they are good but they are very worn-looking, ragged-looking," Ted writes of another office.

Out in Sterling, Colorado, Mick Hall has too many chairs. Guys hang out in his office, smoke, chat. Mick tells Ted it's becoming a problem, and Ted listens but doesn't reply. He leaves—and returns an hour later pulling a U-Haul trailer. "Give me a hand," he tells Mick. They load all the chairs. "If the guys ask you what happened to your chairs, you tell them your company needed them."

Six months later—to the day—a van from a local furniture store pulls up and unloads the chairs. Somehow Ted has arranged for their storage. With the pattern broken, it's safe for the chairs to return.

Ted likes a space tidy, but not necessarily conventional; he's thrilled when a rep moves into a remodeled jail. "He has a nice, large room for seminars," Ted reports to the home office. "I think it used to be the drunk tank; nevertheless, it will be the seminar room from now on…. The old steel doors are there, the bars are on the window." You can just hear him chuckling: "Of course, with bars on the windows, the customers have to listen to the seminar—they can't get out."

Ted, who cannot match a shirt to a tie, also does quick physical makeovers. "Put glasses on," he tells one young rep. "It makes you look older." Another, he takes to get a haircut. "Clean-cut" is important to Ted, although it can be trumped by community spirit: "While Ron has a full beard," he writes in a memo, "I found out he is a musician and plays in a band all around Corpus Christi every weekend. I think he is a good citizen."

Bob Gay, a skinny guy new to the business, suffers through one of Ted's visits: "What time are you getting in? I'll be at your office at 7:30." And at 7:30 am: "Okay, where are we going?" They make calls, break for lunch, make more calls, and then Ted announces, "I'm going to buy you some clothes. You look like you came out of a carnival." He asks for the nicest store in town, and when they walk in, tells the salesman, "I want this guy to look like a businessman." Bob throws away his plaid suit and builds a career that will last for decades.

Another young broker is wearing a frayed red shirt when Ted visits. At the end of the visit, Ted goes out to his car and surreptitiously whips off his belt. Then he goes back inside and asks where he can buy a belt—he forgot his, and his pants will fall off. The young man escorts him to a store, and while Ted is buying himself a belt he doesn't need, he says, "That's a nice red shirt, but, I don't know, I've always subscribed to the notion that young guys ought to wear white shirts. What's your size?" Quickly, leaving no time for protest, Ted orders him four white shirts.

Of a broker in Bozeman who lacks self-confidence, Ted writes, "I don't know why, because he is a nice-looking guy. He is a kind of dudey dresser, and I told him that. When I got to his office I deliberately took off my tie and left it in the car. (That is something I never do, but I always want to do.) I told him, 'My God, in a town like this, in a casual place like this, what the hell are you wearing a tie for?'"

Even speech matters: When a former preacher has a nervous giggle as he's closing, Ted suggests that he talk like he's giving a eulogy. "The guy made more money in the next hour than he'd made in the past two months," Ted reports, exultant. Of a younger man, he writes with dismay,

"He uses *slang* in talking to his prospects." The poor chap also uses the suggested script word for word, "and it comes out canned, wooden and awkward." He needs something shorter, Ted says. "I think his attention span is short; he tends to waste his energy by going off on all directions…. What to do now? STAY AND SUPPORT FOR THE NEXT 18 MONTHS AND HOPE."

§

Field work is something Ted takes seriously, and he is a combination life coach and drill sergeant, taking time to figure out the root of a problem and how to solve it. His tips are already old-fashioned, but they work. "You will get ahead of the competition if every Wednesday, you and your wife take a farmer and his wife to lunch," he advises one broker.

Before his trips, Rich Malone gives Ted a report on what each broker is selling and how much of it, so Ted can strategize with them about diversifying portfolios—or light a candle under their behinds. When new salespeople are hired, he walks down the line in drill sergeant mode and picks up on small details, learns where people are from, volunteers some detail about that town, asks where their office will be. He carries a three-inch-thick computer printout showing each rep's commission income, and he'll invite a trainee to "cut the deck." The person will pick a broker at random and see huge income, and Ted will say, "That's no good. That guy has only been selling for two years. Find someone who has been at it a lot longer." They leave awed and eager to get to work.

When Ted sees a man filled with nervous energy but struggling to close a sale, he watches closely. "He's like a fisherman," Ted notes. "He keeps his hook in the water, but when they start nibbling on the bait, he jerks the bait out of their mouth. In other words, he gets the inquiry, but as soon as the customer shows some interest, he does not know how to close the sale. He should sit down at his desk, slow down, and teach the customer how the bond works."

Other reps need lessons in spotting quiet money in a small town: a grain bin on a farm; a well-painted home. Driving around, Ted asks, "Who owns that drugstore there? What about that Chevrolet dealer? Let's go see him." He asks Charlie March, a broker in Fulton, Missouri, what his approach is to people living in mobile homes.

"I never stop at mobile homes," the broker replies.

"That's a big mistake, Charlie. You want to knock on every door. If somebody's rude, just say, 'I want to thank you and appreciate you giving me your time. If I can ever be of service, please stop by and see me.' Give them your business card, and then leave."

So Charlie wades through tall grass, passing a very large dog on a very heavy chain, to reach the home of a burly guy who tells Charlie, in no uncertain terms, to get off his porch. Charlie musters the gracious reply Ted suggested, then turns tail.

Six or seven years later, a man walks into Charlie's office to open an account and asks if Charlie remembers him. "I gave you such a hard time, and you had such a gentlemanly approach about it. I thought I would come by and do some business, because I've inherited about $600,000 and I'd like to invest it."

§

Jim Weddle has only been running his office for a year and a half when his first trainee, Bob Campbell, joins him. That Monday morning, they see a panicked teletype come through from another investment advisor: "Ted's in my office!" What direction will Ted head next, everyone along the teletype line is wondering. The next two bulletins make it clear that Ted is traveling a straight line toward Weddle. Who is a nervous wreck. Campbell can't understand why this is such a big deal. Finally, Weddle calls the last place Ted lighted and asks if he's gone yet. The office administrator says, "You need to talk to Randy right now!" Turns out Ted has just found out that the trainee in that office was not making the calls—and fired him on the spot.

Weddle is processing this news when he hears Ted at his door.

"Jim, tell me about your ten best clients," Ted says without much preamble. Then: "Tell me about ten prospective clients and what you know about them." Weddle knows enough to please Ted, who turns next to Campbell. After dictating a 30-second elevator speech, he opens a phone book, and tells the trainee to start calling. "Let's step out," Ted tells Weddle. "Bob's going to be busy for a while. Tell me how I can help you."

"Well, I'd love to introduce you to the editor of the newspaper, but I can't get my foot in the door," Weddle says. "The fellow who runs the biggest bank in town has been telling people the only good investment is a CD. And there's a CPA who does the taxes for all the individuals I want to do business with, and I haven't even met him."

After giving the editor a long, solid interview, Ted chats with the bank president about farm stuff, and by the end of the conversation has him saying, "Yeah, diversification is a good thing." When they leave, Ted asks Weddle the layout of the CPA's office and the name of the receptionist. He strides in, greets her by name, calls out that he needs to see the CPA and walks right past her, turning in the right direction for his office. After asking a few questions and listening closely to the answers, he says, "Jim here offers IRAs. Some of your clients would probably benefit from that." And the man says, "Yes, they would."

As they walk out, Ted says, "We need to go check on Bob." They hear his booming radio voice from the door, still making calls. So Ted heads off to the next office—and Weddle gets on the teletype to warn them.

§

Ted keeps a "worry list" of anybody he's afraid might not make it, and you can hear the relief in his voice when he says he's taking somebody off that list, they're doing great.

"I spent too much time being interviewed by his newspaper, didn't have enough time for Fred," he writes, disappointed and determined to return soon. After visiting a man who seems sensitive, convinced that people in the firm don't like him, Ted writes, "I tried to get over to him that we do love him, and I think it would help if Jim Goodknight would find some excuse to pat [him] on the back."

Enthusiasm comes easily to Ted; praise does not. He knows when people need it, but he delegates. A man is funny and engaging, "but he is different from most of our men," Ted writes. "I think he needs a lot of patting on the back. I have asked Jack Phelan to be sure to congratulate him."

Basically, Ted is investing in people. "He will be successful," he writes of a man in Iowa. "Just how successful—I don't think I can measure that yet." Instead of focusing on the bottom line, he pays attention to the human element that can shoot it up or down.

Of a rep in Iowa who is always complaining, never optimistic, Ted writes, "I've tried to analyze [his] problem…. It just seems to me that he really is not willing to work very hard or try ideas." Laziness and pessimism are inconceivable to Ted, who gives the man a few *more* ideas to try but admits he might "just remain in the state he is in at this time, which is one of negativism. I believe if we can get [him] turned around he could make an excellent broker for us." Ted is doing his best but says, "It is a difficult thing to try to convince a fellow to work harder. I tried to use a little psychology on him. I kept pointing out that he was near the bottom," even though the guy was making far more than he'd made as the manager of a filling station and convenience store. "I told him with his good looks and his brains he ought to be making $100,000 a year." Learning that the rep grew up on a ranch, Ted said, "For godsakes, it ought to be duck soup for you to get in your car and go out and see these ranch people."

After learning that a young broker has emptied his savings account getting started, so "if his check doesn't come in exactly on time, he can't make his house payment," Ted has a $1,000 check mailed to the man as a no-interest loan, so he can keep a little reserve. "People will succeed if we expect them to be loyal to this firm," he remarks. "When they need us is when they start out."

Loyalty, for Ted, is the backbone of the firm, and it must bend in both directions. When a group of Jones brokers is being recruited by Hilliard Lyons, Bob Gay is having private doubts and trying to make a decision. Ted comes up to him, somehow knowing, and puts his arm around Bob's neck and says only, "Have you about got it straightened out yet?" Bob meets his eyes and says, "Yes, Ted, I think I have." Ted says "Good!" and that's the end of it.

§

Ted may not have kids of his own, but he has a father's instincts. Of a young couple who have bought a small brick home in the nicest part of Dyersburg, Tennessee, he writes, "Their house cost $45,000; I think they can swing it." When he invites a young man to bring his fiancée to dinner, the young man says he can't; she lives in Hawaii. "How he met a girl in Hawaii I don't know," Ted writes to the partners, still puzzling over it.

People's personal happiness matters to him, in a fond way and also as shrewd business. When he learns from the grapevine that a young man who is doing well does not want to raise a family in the town where he opened his office, Ted says, "Let's tell him *now* that he can move to any other town." Another young man "*could* succeed, but his very young wife is not supportive."

Ted has a traditionalist's faith in marriage to settle somebody down. "OK—he has met a girl; now he likes the town," he jots in a report. "I wish he would get married; he would do even better," he says of another young man. "You're single and twenty-five," Ted tells a third. "I want you to meet with every minister and every priest in this town and ask him for a date with a nice girl in his parish."

The recipe he gives Tom Hissink for success as a financial advisor is "One, get married and have kids. Two, buy a house and a nice car and get yourself into debt. I guarantee that you will work and make good money." They're eating lunch at a deli when Ted shares this advice, and at the next table is an eye-catching young woman. Ted strikes up a conversation and introduces her to Tom. When they leave, Ted orders the cashier to find out all about her. (Alas, the next day the cashier reports that she is married.)

When Ted calls on yet another bachelor and sees "a whole paper sack full of medication on his desk," he says briskly, "Go home and start taking care of yourself." The guy is a bachelor and has walking pneumonia, which Ted informs him can be serious. "Where is your mother located?" Kansas City. "Go back there this weekend and have her give you some chicken soup and put you to bed." When the young man says he wants to make it to the end of his month, Ted replies, "You can't sell securities in the cemetery. Go take care of your health."

Once a broker is wed, Ted does his best to support the marriage. Driving in to the St. Louis office from Williamsburg, Ted stops at Tom Miltenberger's office. Tom is out, but his wife, who works as his administrative assistant, is in the office.

"Hi, Susan," Ted says. "How are you doing? You need anything?"

They have just moved into a new house, so Susan quips, "I need a washer and dryer."

Ted finds Tom and says, "C'mon, we're gonna go make some money." They make call after call. Tom comes home that evening and says, "Holy *cow!* Ted had me working hard today. What did you say to him?"

She thinks a minute, remembers the tossed-off line. Tom groans. "Next time, say you need a toaster."

§

A guy in Kansas slides right off the worry list when, after performing abysmally in the training class, he makes a big sale that brings his monthly total to $4,500. Ted congratulates him and takes him out to lunch, and when they drive around afterward, the young man shows so much familiarity with the town that Ted is sure he's not faking. "I think he has been going door to door," Ted writes happily. "[He] came to us immediately after getting divorced. I think he was probably all mixed up; his lifestyle was all mixed up. I think all of that has been straightened out. I remember the first time I met him he told me that he wanted to come to Kansas City because that is where his ex-wife lived and he was hoping to put that back together. I asked him about his ex-wife, and he said she got married two weeks ago. So I think that stage of his life is behind him and maybe mentally and psychologically he is making a fresh start."

Up in Mount Pleasant, Michigan, Rich Miller is young and broke, and in his first month working for Jones, Ted shows up without warning. Luckily, Rich has an eleven o'clock appointment all lined up—until the woman, whose name is Eva, calls to cancel. She has broken her foot.

Ted takes Rich to McDonald's for lunch. At the counter, Ted says, "My wallet's back in my briefcase," so Rich pulls bills from his thin wallet and buys them both lunch. "Let's go take some lunch to Eva," Ted suggests. "She's probably having a hard time getting around."

Rich pulls out *more* of his scant cash and buys a burger, fries, and a Coke for Eva. When they knock, she invites them inside, touched by the thoughtfulness. As they chat, Ted talks with enthusiasm about an investment, and Eva confides that she has a $42,000 CD coming due.

As they leave, Ted tells Rich, "Well, son, that $42,000 order I just got you should pay for lunch."

§

If somebody proves Ted wrong, he doesn't necessarily admit it outright, but he becomes that person's biggest supporter—which sends an even stronger signal than a few compliments.

The times he really goes the extra mile are when he senses someone is good and decent but struggling for no fault of their own. A middle-aged broker who lost both legs in an explosion "is making calls, has guts and determination," so Ted outlines all sorts of possibilities for him and tells the partners to be patient. In Savannah, Ted spends extra time—"I'm going to give it all I've got"— going with a Black rep to call on lawyers, bankers, and newspapers, learning in the process.

A single mother who "arrived in town dead broke" but has already worked hard enough to afford a couple of purebred Arabian horses wins Ted's admiration—especially when he learns that she was raised on a sheep ranch and, as a young girl, herded the sheep and then stayed with them until they bedded down for the night. She "knows how to work," he says, suggesting they send her on as many trips as possible, because she is isolated in North Dakota.

He notices weak spots, too. "[This broker] can no more handle this town than the man in the moon," he writes. "We made a mistake putting him here. This is a large, sophisticated town, and we haven't put a man in, we've *put a boy in*. He looks to me like he will work, and he's a nice kind of a kid, but he is a kid and his wife is a kid, and they cannot handle this town." Fire him? Nope. "I think we would be doing a disservice to this young man if we let him go. My recommendation is to put him in a small country town where he has a chance of succeeding. [And] I think we've got to pay for the move."

When a rep who is "extremely cocky, and sometimes perhaps overbearing about success" buys a flashy, expensive home, Ted warns him that he might alienate the townspeople and encourages him to project a different image.

In place of praise, Ted issues challenges. Contests and promotions spark up the selling; he offers a frozen Rhode Island Red chicken if you sell so many bonds and threatens a live chicken if you don't sell enough. When Jim McKenzie enters his first sales contest and he's halfway to goal, feeling pretty confident, Ted tells him that if he meets *twice* the goal, Ted will send him and his wife to the Lake of the Ozarks for the weekend.

Though generous with rewards, Ted never hesitates to pluck somebody from their comfort zone—and Jim McKenzie winds up profoundly grateful for the challenge. His father, the famous Al McKenzie, taught just about everybody at Jones, including Ted, how to sell. When Jim interviews for a job, he reminds Ted of his father's huge list of clients and says, "I was thinking maybe I could help him." Ted gets up and walks away from his desk.

About thirty minutes later, he returns. "You're still here?"

"Yes, Mr. Jones."

"But I thought you said you wanted to be in the city and work with your father?"

"I said I wanted to be a Jones broker. It could be in the city or in the country."

"Oh," Ted says, sitting back down. He leans forward. "If you stay in the city, you'll just be 'Al's boy, what's his name again?' But if you leave, you will develop your own self-worth."

§

On a surprise visit, Ted finds Jim Harrod out, so he goes next door and chats with the people at the barber shop. By the time Jim returns to the office, Ted is ready to say goodbye. All the barber shop folks knew and respected Jim, and that was all Ted needed to hear.

Harrod went to that barber from then on, even though his wife winced at the cut every time.

"What are you gonna do when you close up?" Ted asks Charlie March just before noon on a Saturday. Afraid Ted will suggest putting out a trout line, Charlie hastily says he has to go home and mow the yard.

"How long will it take?"

"Three hours at least."

"And what would it cost to get it mowed and trimmed the way your wife would like it?"

"At least $25."

"And what's your mower and trimmer worth?"

Where is this going, Charlie wonders. "Maybe $125."

Ted reaches into his pocket and pulls out $125. "I'd like to buy your mower and trimmer. Now, find somebody to mow your lawn. How many phone calls can you make in an hour? Could you make $25 in that hour?"

"Uh…sure."

"Good. Each time your yard needs mowing, you owe me three hours of phone calls."

§

Ted's memos back to the management committee are frank and often cranky.

"When salesmen have asked St. Louis for a business card with their picture on it, St. Louis clerks say it can't be done. THIS IS BUREAUCRACY AT ITS WORST!"

He is "shocked at the waste of time and money that our new salespeople are spending on advertising." To the rep mailing out 250 full-page letters every month, he says, "Stop! No one reads this garbage! Stick to the basics—shake hands with people." To the partners, he writes, "Is this really the year to be having the summer meetings in very plush, expensive places?"

He never uses profanity with the reps, but he uses it freely to get the partners' attention. "The SOB should not be sent to another meeting— HE HAS NOT BEEN MAKING THE CALLS!"

"Who had our man in Sterling, Colorado, train in his home town?" The guy will get zero calling experience, Ted figures, because he already knows everybody. "Who is putting older men in retirement towns and large cities?" You never let somebody work in the town where they plan to retire, he reasons. They will retire themselves early. Besides, he is not sure older brokers will have the hunger and physical energy to interject themselves into the larger, more competitive towns.

Convinced of the value of his field trips, Ted decides the other partners should pitch in themselves and do some of this intensive training and mentoring—without racking up a lot of airfare. He rattles off possible assignments, making it clear just how closely he pays attention to their lives: "Bachmann in northern Wisconsin where he vacations, Ron Lemonds in Nevada and northern California where he has relatives, Ron Larimore in Colorado where he skis, Pete Key in Florida where he vacations."

The brokers can't be allowed to lose momentum, Ted concludes. "It's very hard to re-start a cold motor."

§

Women have not won easy acceptance as financial advisors. The first woman to buy a seat on the New York Stock Exchange did so in 1967—and she remained the only woman for more than a decade, working amid more than 1,300 men.

No one could live with Pat Jones and think of women as unintelligent or insipid, so Ted is more open than most. Still, he is wary. When Barb Gilman becomes one of the company's first female financial advisors, he visits her office in Stephenville, Texas, several times, checking to make sure she is making the calls, putting in the requisite effort. Once, they are talking when several downtown attorneys and businesspeople pay Gilman a surprise visit—to ask if she will run for mayor. "In six months, you know more people in Stephenville than we do," one says, "and we were born here."

Gilman thanks them and explains that she has a business to establish, so she won't have time for anything else. When they leave, Ted is silent for a minute.

"Wow," he says finally. "Well handled."

Later, he drafts Gilman for one of his field trips. It's nervewracking, seven days cooped up in the car with her boss, but she wouldn't trade the experience—or all the stories she hears, many of which she promises to take to her grave. The only rough patch comes when they arrive at the office of a man Ted knows he needs to fire.

They get out of the car, Gilman reluctantly coming along for the execution. As they walk in, Ted says, "I'll show you where the bathroom is, Barbara." The loo is tucked behind a stairway, and once they are out of earshot, Ted whispers, "You fire him."

"What?" she snaps. "It's your name on the door!"

"Exactly. You fire him."

She does it, arranges the logistics, and refuses to speak to Ted for several miles. Later, it dawns on her that this was a test.

Soon after, she is put in charge of the training department.

§

Ted terrified salespeople by showing up unannounced, asking for their stack of green cards, and picking people at random for them to call on, now. But he is protective, too. One day he listens over the cubicle wall as John Beuerlein, a young intern at the time, makes fun of a salesman for asking what he thinks is a silly question. Ted is quick to round the wall and explain, about an inch from Beuerlein's nose, "This firm has MBAs, CPAs, investment bankers, traders, accountants, every kind of professional you could hope to find in an investment firm, but the highest calling is sitting across the desk from a client helping them solve a financial problem. You don't get that, you're not worth a plug nickel to me!"

The lesson—or, as Beuerlein will think of it, "near-death experience"—lasts for forty-two years.

As tough and demanding as Ted is, though, he also manages to convey the importance of taking life lightly. "Never take yourself too seriously," he warns Don Bolin. "You're not gonna be right 100 percent of the time." Perfectionism is a lousy excuse to avoid a risk, a chance, an experiment that just might work.

18

Meeting of the Minds

Back in 1974, Ted and John Bachmann began reading Peter Drucker's books, starting with *Management: Tasks, Responsibilities, Practices*. Both felt a shock of recognition: A transparent overlay of this philosophy would align perfectly with Jones. Taking the book a chapter at a time, they invite anybody else who's interested to join a weekly discussion of these ideas.

A few years later, they were in Chicago, and they heard Drucker talk about the structure of business in the next century. He described a "confederation of highly autonomous, entrepreneurial units geographically dispersed, bound together by a strong central core of values and services." Ted nudged John and whispered, "He's talking about us."

In 1980, they met with clients from Humana and mentioned some of Drucker's books. "We don't read Drucker," a top Humana executive replied.

Ted and John looked up, stunned.

"We go see him," the man continued.

So they, too, decided to go see Peter Drucker.

§

The relationship begins in the Eighties. Drucker pronounces Ted a genius. He has identified a market no one knew existed: the serious, conservative, long-term investors living in small towns across America. And he has done so right underneath the eyes of his competition. He saw what Drucker calls "a market in contemplation." Which, Drucker informs him, "is about the hardest thing a businessman can do."

Most people have one stroke of genius, he adds. Ted had two. Not only did he find the market, but he figured out the distribution system.

Ted shrugs off the praise. Focusing on serious, long-term investors came naturally to him. His father was a fine trader, buying and selling, making money off of each trade. "If I have to be in the business of trading stocks, I'm gonna sell this place," Ted once told Doug Hill. "I want people to hold them over time. The people who buy and trade don't make money over time; they *lose* money. But they don't ever admit it."

Even Edward said, "Put the good stocks in your bottom drawer and forget about them." The rest is a game. And you must have both the inclination to play and the ability to lose.

§

By 1981, Ted and Bachmann are testing the idea of expanding into metropolitan areas (Bachmann is for it, Ted against) on Drucker. They lay their opinions in front of him like they're in couples counseling. Bachmann points to Kansas City, where they already have offices, as proof of urban potential. Ted insists that "Kansas City is different."

Agreeing with Bachmann, Drucker keeps asking Ted, "Where are you going to put your next offices?" Ted replies with an allusion to Wee Willie Keeler, a ball player who hit the ball wherever no fielders waited.

Jones will do better where there's competition, Drucker insists, because then people will have a context in which to evaluate and compare them to other firms.

Ted goes back to Wee Willie: "He hit 'em where they ain't."

Both men dig in, and because they genuinely like each other a lot, it's as much fun as baseball to watch them argue.

"Ted, you are going to fill up every small town in the country," Drucker warns. "At some point, you have to go in the cities."

"I don't want to."

"Your clients can tell the difference between you and a big wirehouse," Drucker assures him. "And there are also serious, long-term investors living in cities. Now, they may live in the Empire State Building, but they are just as conservative as your rural clients, and you should be serving them, too."

By now, everyone else in the room has leaned back to watch. Finally, Drucker says, "What do the facts tell you?"

"We just *know*," Ted says.

"Why not get the facts?"

Ted grudgingly orders an analysis, and it shows that business ramps up faster and becomes profitable sooner in the larger towns. The closest big city is Chicago, so Ted decides to sneak up on it, starting in the suburbs. The offices do *better* than the small town offices. After a close look at the numbers, Ted steps aside and lets the future unfold.

§

In 1986, Bachmann gives Weddle his year-end review, and Weddle thanks him and rises to leave.

"There's one more thing, Jim. Why don't you sit down again?"

Weddle clutches.

"You're aware that we consult with Peter Drucker?" Bachmann begins.

"Of course. I studied Drucker in grad school."

"Well, Peter wants to be a client of the firm as well as a consultant."

"Wow," Weddle says. Talk about a vote of confidence. "Who's going to be his advisor?"

"You are."

Bachmann has already arranged for Weddle to be licensed in California, so there's no wiggling out of this terrifying responsibility. What if he loses the firm its most important consultant? Weddle gathers himself and calls Drucker, hearing what will become a familiar greeting in his thick Austrian accent. Soon Weddle is seated in the Druckers' living room reviewing a fascinating array of assets—including a world-class collection of Japanese art, some of it on loan to museums. Like many of Weddle's clients, though, the management guru has records piled in big boxes, and it takes several hours to do an inventory. When they finish, Weddle says, "I'd like to take you and Doris to dinner."

"Absolutely not," Drucker says, his tone so firm that Weddle worries he has offended him. "Doris has fixed meatloaf."

And so they sit at the Druckers' kitchen table and eat meatloaf. And the relationship thrives for years.

§

Ted and Drucker continue to wrangle. "The places to be are the Evanstons," Drucker says, and Ted groans. It is no longer possible to be successful at the scale of Edward D. Jones and remain anonymous, Drucker points out. When they talk about building a new headquarters, he teases that Ted should "build a moat around it and fill it with cow manure, so that anybody who went in there would have cow manure on his boots."

"Good idea," Ted replies, pointing out the only down side: Cow manure is expensive.

Drucker does understand where Ted is coming from. He's always seen a distinct difference between the Goldman Sachs customers and the people he knows. But in the Forties and Fifties, a healthy amount of money was spread across small towns—and now their downtowns are economically stressed.

"Ted—how do I put it? Ted never really got over the feeling that he was a small-town boy in the big city," Drucker tells another Jones partner. As a niche strategy, small town offices have been fine, and they are definitely Ted's comfort zone. But as a defensive strategy, the model is now inadequate. "Your market is not geography but people."

The idea of defining the market any way *but* geographically throws Ted. His heart remains with small town America, where he finds it easy to feel connected to the earth. To chat with strangers; to make friends and feel the warmth of being known. The clients in those small towns do the kind of hard, honest work that has steadied him and given his life direction. They deal plainly and shun pretense. They share his beliefs and his values.

But so do a lot of people in *big* towns, Drucker points out, and Ted comes to accept the shift, and the possibilities for expansion widen.

By 1993, two-thirds of the firm's branch offices are in the suburbs of the nation's largest cities. Returning to Jones for more consulting in 2002, Drucker tells the partners, "You are now the largest securities retailer in the country for the middle class…. You are learning that the market is much richer than you imagined. You have not saturated the market. You have scratched the surface."

The company will be faced with balancing decisions, Drucker adds, and "there are turbulent years ahead." Then he calms those words: "You do your best in bad years. You hear less from your competition, and your values stand out so clearly." Besides, he points out, "your competitors have not shown any sign of understanding what you are doing"—and even if they did fully grasp the Jones philosophy, "it would be too much like hard work."

In 2008, the *Harvard Business Review* writes: "Jones does not define its archetypal customer by net worth or income. Nor does it use demographics, profession, or spending habits. Rather, the definition is psychographic: the company's customers are long-term investors who have a conservative investment philosophy and are uncomfortable making serious financial decisions without the support of a trusted advisor."

This is a definition Ted would have liked quite well—once he made his peace with all those new offices in metro area suburbs. It is "one of the great tributes to Ted that he forgave me," Drucker says. What is now obvious is that these suburbs often function as small towns themselves.

Without that moat of cow manure.

19
———

The Merry Prankster

When a real estate agent comes calling, Ted walks him down by the pond and confides that he's been trying to train the catfish. Not realizing that the fish will swarm anytime they expect food, the guy watches, eyes wide, while Ted shrills "Whoo Fish!" to "call" them, and they all swim over and leap into the air. "Throw a stick," Ted suggests. "Sometimes they'll bring it back." So the guy hunts around the brush, finally finds the right stick and tosses it into the pond. He is crestfallen when the fish don't retrieve it.

§

Once, Ted rents a bus to take his sister Ann's family, along with Pat and the Willcoxsons, to Watkins Mill and a Civil War fort in Kansas. They reach the mill at nine in the morning and are informed that it will not open for another hour. Dismayed, Ted takes the historic site interpreter aside. "I'm Preacher Jones," he says, "and this is part of my congregation."

They are allowed in.

On road trips, Ted and Dave Clapp always assume new identities, often traveling as Baptist missionaries on their way to a convention. They like to see how far they can take it.

Once Ted and Bill Murphy stop at a Howard Johnson's, and by the time they leave, Ted has the waitress convinced that he's a professional water skier from Cypress Gardens in Florida. They laugh all the way to Fulton.

For big company meetings, Ted drafts Jack Phelan as his straight man, and they make videos, do Bartles & James commercials, play Laurel and Hardy, whatever. For the new satellite system, they show up in space suits and talk about setting up the satellites.

Along with the pranks go the props. Training young advisors, Ted suggests they pull out a box of cake mix and set it on the table, not saying a word. When the client finally asks what in heck the cake mix is for, you list off all the ingredients in a cake made from scratch, then ask how easy it will be for that cake to come out perfect. The client's brow will furrow, thinking of all the variables that can ruin a cake. Then talk about how you end up with clouds of flour and broken eggshells dripping goo on the counter and dirty beaters, and sometimes you get a good cake, and sometimes you don't. Ted taps the Betty Crocker box to illustrate: "It's all here, everything you need in all the right proportions." The cake mix is a mutual fund, measured for you, pre-sifted, with results you can count on.

Ted can pluck a clue from a particular situation and use it to weave a tale, spin a yarn, stitch up a moral his listener will remember. A loaf of bread—what it costs, what it used to cost—becomes a way to talk about inflation and why you need investments and income streams that grow.

Ted's sport in the Army was boxing, and he uses it to advantage, standing at the mic at company meetings wearing two giant red boxing gloves. One says Handshaking, and the other says Phone Calls. Resplendent in a polka-dotted tie, Ted demonstrates this one-two punch:

"You shake hands with them. Three weeks later, you call on the phone"—Wham! "Three weeks after that, you go see 'em again"—Pow! It's as hokey as can be, even in these more innocent times— but it sticks in people's minds.

And so do the chickens. When Dan Burkhardt is developing a bond

Ted, giving the old one-two punch!

underwriting for the Providence Gas Company in Rhode Island, Ted says, "The only thing I know about Rhode Island is that they have a chicken named after them."

Turns out that's all he needs to know. They build an entire marketing campaign around the Rhode Island Red chicken. Ted even snags one from a neighbor and poses for photos threatening the poor critter with an ax.

The closing dinner for the offering is at the Racquet Club in Ladue, not Ted's usual scene, and Dan asks the serving staff to bring out a big silver-domed tray with a plump chicken under the lid. It's the final flourish.

§

One of Ted's props is personal. When he travels to New York, he trades a regular handkerchief for a bright red bandanna and, while in Manhattan, will pull it slowly from his pocket to mop his brow. He wants to be seen as a farmer, not only because that is his comfort zone, but because he knows it will make the city folk underestimate him.

After a meeting in the nation's capital, Ted tells one of the Jones brokers, "These people think we're a bunch of country hicks." Then he grins. "Don't ever tell them any different."

At the Noonday Club, Edward's friends relay the rumors they hear, characterizing Jones as "a bunch of mutual fund salesmen working out of the trunks of their cars" and calling the company "the laughingstock of St. Louis." Steaming, Edward tells Jack Phelan. When Jack relays the slur, Ted laughs in delight. "We're sneaking up on the whole bunch."

§

The other reason Ted portrays himself as a country boy is that he loves a good story, and he knows that if *he's* the story, people will remember him, and therefore Edward D. Jones & Co. The stuffed shirts at the SEC will talk about this guy who came in with a red bandanna and wiped his brow saying he had to catch the bus back to St. Louis.

Besides, Ted hates to be bored. A little role-playing makes things more interesting.

Don Boschert, a broker in St. Charles, calls Ted "the Columbo of the securities industry." He pulls out the bandanna, lets people think he's clueless and rumpled and out of his depth. "But he always, always, has them outfoxed."

On a trip to the American Funds headquarters, for example, Ted visits the company's service center. As soon as he sees somebody off the phone, Ted approaches and introduces himself.

"Of course, Mr. Jones," the woman replies.

"I was wondering—I didn't have time to check the market this morning—if I give you my American account number, could you run a quick report?"

Out of the printer tumbles the report, a cascade of at least sixty pages on continuous-feed paper that folds back and forth like ribbon candy. The woman looks uncertain—has she somehow screwed up the Print command? But Ted looks like a cat who has dined on a flock of canaries. He had made his point.

§

Jack Cahill is interested in working for Jones. "If you and your wife will come to St. Louis at your own expense," Ted says, "I will interview you." Cahill makes the mistake of thanking "Mr. Jones," who snaps, "You want to talk to me or my dad?"

The Cahills drive to St. Louis from North Platte, Nebraska. Walking up the steps to the office, they see an unprepossessing guy standing on the steps. "Are you Jack Cahill? I'm Ted Jones." Jack is taken off to be grilled, and Ann is told, more gently, how hard it is to start a new business from scratch. They want to make sure she will be supportive.

Rejoined, they are taken to lunch—at McDonald's. Ted explains that the last step will be one of those multiple-choice psychological exams. "It takes us two weeks to get these back," he says. "It will tell us if you're a good fit."

Two weeks go by. Cahill brings his lunch in a sack every day, terrified of missing Ted's phone call. He wants to be polite, not too pushy. A few more days go by. Finally he musters the courage to call: "I really want to work for you," he blurts. "Did the test come back?"

Ted chuckles. "Jack, you could have had the job two weeks ago. We never even send those tests in, because it costs $25 to process them." A pause. "We would have never called you back. You have to *ask* for the orders. Don't forget that."

Cahill winds up a general partner, and he is brought to St. Louis. The real estate market is upside down, and his house in Nebraska isn't selling. He and his wife take a deep breath and buy a new house in St. Louis anyway. Then the bank calls and says, "We are in an unusual cash flow position. We have to delay closing on your house."

The home builder explodes—"Absolutely not!"

Upset, Cahill confides in his colleagues—and word reaches Ted. Loud fast footsteps in the hall, then a booming "Cahill!" Ted is standing in front of his desk, a stuffed manila folder under his arm. "Let's go to lunch."

This time, it's not McDonald's. "Let's go to the M.A.C.," Ted suggests.

Good food and the club's overstuffed masculine luxury ease Cahill's worries. He listens as Ted tells stories. Then Ted leans forward. "Jack, are you having some trouble with your loan?"

Cahill gives an abbreviated version.

"Well, they're right across the street. Let's go see them."

Ted tells the bank's receptionist, "We have a serious problem. We need to meet the bankers on the Edward D. Jones account right away." They all file into a conference room. And Ted starts telling the story of the Carthage Marble Company, a family investment—walking around the room, making grand, sweeping gestures. He winds up at the window, leans against the sill, and does a triple take. Dropping to his knees, he looks underneath the sill and says, "My God, your *bank* is built out of Carthage marble! What do you think Carthage Marble is worth?"

At this point he opens the mystery folder, takes out a big ledger, and reads off the appraisal of $13 million. He asks if they think that sounds right. Politely, they say they're sure it is. Like a skilled defense attorney, Ted puts his hand on Cahill's shoulder and says, "Gentlemen, Jack Cahill was doing a great job for us, and I asked him to give up his business and move to St. Louis. I said 'Yes, it's a good time to buy a home.'" He slams the ledger book down. "Now he is in danger of losing his *house*! I am pledging the Carthage Marble Company against his loan."

The bankers stammer that they will make sure the loan goes through.

"I would expect nothing less," Ted says and strides from the room. He marches right into the elevator and stares at its back wall. Right behind him, Cahill sees the bright red suffusing Ted's neck and the tips of his ears. This means he's either angry or happy, but which?

As soon as the doors close, Ted throws back his head and laughs. "Those bankers!" By the time they reach the car, Cahill is emotionally exhausted. "Wasn't it interesting that the bank was made of Carthage marble?" he asks, mustering small talk.

The corners of Ted's lips twitch. "I have no idea what kind of marble that was."

§

People who loved Ted worry about retelling the tales and pranks that have become lore. They are told so often and with such relish, people might forget how serious and smart he was, underneath the schtick.

On the other hand, the stories and pranks are a big part of who he was.

Almost as big as the circus.

§

On a trip to Switzerland, Jack and Shirley Phelan see a poster for Circus Nock, which is playing in town that night. They make the mistake of mentioning this to Ted. "That was the end of that," Jack will laugh later. "Boy, we were going to the circus."

He should have seen it coming; how many times had he and Ted snuck out of work and gone to the circus? Pictures of circus elephants hang in the Jones farmhouse. Every summer, when Circus Flora opens, Ted buys tickets for all the Jones associates in St. Louis—especially their kids.

Does he miss having children of his own? Does Pat? They never talk about it. Once, when asked about kids, Ted nods toward Jack Phelan (who has six children at the time) and quips, "That's Phelan's department." But instead of avoiding the world of family because they don't have children, Ted and Pat embrace it, Ted holding father-son campouts, Pat rushing to welcome schoolbuses full of kids to the farm.

And when the Phelans have their seventh child and name him Edward David, his namesake tears up. From then on, little Teddy is the first person he asks about every time he sees Jack.

§

The Great Circus Parade is one of the most colorful bits of Milwaukee's past. Thirty times, beginning in 1963, horse-drawn English circus wagons, calliope wagons, and ponderously dignified elephants paraded down East Wisconsin Avenue, just as nineteenth-century circuses would have paraded through town to capture every potential circus-goer's imagination.

One year, Ted—a generous donor to the Circus World Museum in Baraboo, Wisconsin—is asked to be the parade's grand marshal. He will ride the circus train—half a mile of railroad flatcars stuffed with lions and tigers (caged), clowns (unfettered), costumes and props and happy music— from the museum to Milwaukee for the parade.

He brings his good friend John Jamieson, and they linger over breakfast and arrive just in time to board. They expect assigned seats, but it's first-come, first-served, and all the seats are taken. So they perch on a bench outside the train's restroom.

Nothing dampens Ted's spirits. This is an *opportunity*. He holds a cup aloft, securing donations from everyone who enters the loo. In a lull between visits, he starts laughing, thinking about "the image of the stockbroker—great brass doors, you know, and all these magnificent structures housing all this magnificent wealth…."

His impromptu pay toilet raises a significant sum for the museum— more than the legendary Ernest Borgnine ever did as the chief parade clown. Ted owes the Baraboo, though. He once insisted that the museum director accept his donation check in front of the Edward Jones office in Baraboo—and bring an elephant.

The circus makes a withdrawal in the 1980s.

§

"Wanna go to the circus with me?" Ted asks Bill Broderick, a Jones investment banker, in 1986. "Pat doesn't want to go."

Bill has zero desire to go to a circus, but he figures a trip with Ted Jones could never be a waste of time. He thinks back to the year he joined the firm, 1982, with the Dow down to 750 and all his friends convinced he was crazy to go into the investment business.

"Well, at least A.G. Edwards is a good firm," they said.

"Er…I'm going to work for Edward *Jones*," he replied. *And I have not lost my mind*, he told himself. The firm was solid and profitable, and Ted Jones had his own view of the world: colored by strong opinions not necessarily compatible with anyone else's, but with more common sense than most people. Four years have borne out his assessment. But he's about to see another side of Ted altogether.

They fly to Milwaukee for the Great Circus Parade, checking into a nice hotel (for once) so they can watch the parade from the hotel's bleachers rather than take their chances among the thousands who are spending half the night on the street just to make sure they will have a spot where they can see the parade.

The two men share a room, both clad in their regulation Brooks Brothers pajamas. The next morning, Ted is up like a shot, instantly alert, eager for the day to begin. When the old circus wagons creak past and he can see the tigers through the bars and hear the bronze bells of the Ringling Brothers bell wagon chime, he's as elated as an eight-year-old. Then comes the Marine Corps Marching Band, which is *spectacular*. Best of all are the elephants, high-stepping down the street.

He has, of course, seen this countless times. It never grows old.

§

After a board meeting of the Carthage Marble Company, Ted plans to take several of the Jones brokers in that part of Missouri out to eat. Just before noon, he bounds into Jim Goodknight's office and says, elated as a groupie shown backstage, "You'll never guess what I saw on my way over!"

"Yeah?"

He spaces the words for effect: "I…saw…an…elephant."

Goodknight snorts. "Was he pink?"

Miffed, Ted insists on proving it. And so they drive off to see the elephant, who is with yet more elephants, grazing in a field in Carthage. The Tarzan Zerbini Circus has come to town.

Much later, an article from a circus newsletter shows up in Goodknight's mail. It's all about the Tarzan Zerbini Circus of southwest Missouri. Ted has just found out that Carthage is the circus's winter headquarters.

§

What *is* it about circuses? Eli Jones, in his wanderlust, was drawn to the bright colors and wound up buying a share of a circus in Mexico City. Edward grabbed the same brass ring, maybe to fill in some of the cheerfulness and childishness his early years lacked. Or was it because the high, frantic energy matched his own ambition? He planned to buy an entire circus someday. While his kids rode the Shetland ponies he would later purchase, he chatted with Sidney Rink, who was training his jumping mules in St. Louis but in his younger days had trained elephants. In one choice gig, Sidney wore a swallow-tail coat and a silk top hat and, with grand and sweeping gestures, told the circus's story.

Rink had a firm but gentle hand and an uncanny ability to sense an animal's feelings and direct their behavior. It is said that he once borrowed $35 from Edward for an urgent trip to D.C. The "Miller Bros. 101 Wild West Show and Circus" had gone bankrupt, and unpaid workers were picketing, their outrage at boiling point. The bankruptcy receiver wanted Rink to cross the picket line and bring out the animals, the only remaining asset of any value. Hidden in the back of a truck, he made it onto the circus grounds unnoticed. Inside, he lined up the elephants in the way they had long practiced. Each twined their trunk around the tail of the elephant in front of them, and Rink quickly showed their leader, Old Modou, how to swing a heavy chain from side to side. Climbing atop Old Modou, Rink guided the elephants outside, the chain swinging in such a wide arc that the roustabouts scattered.

Ted inherits pictures of Sidney Rink, and he proudly donates them to the Circus World Museum. His miniature circus wagons will find a home at Westminster College, where they circle the interior of the library and add enough festivity to cheer up anybody grinding through a textbook. Circus books go to friends, though quite a few still line the shelves of the Prairie Fork visitor's center.

Even if his father and grandfather had not gone a little crazy over circuses, Ted might have found his way there all by himself. Inside the closed circle of a circus, everything is the biggest, the tallest, the best—the kind of hyperbole that would have appealed to the storyteller in Ted. The magic of a circus materializing, its striped tents rising in some bare parking lot—the circus is the original pop-up. All is festive and carefree, dramatic and daring and exaggerated. Life sails right over the top, where Ted likes it. He watches everything, gobsmacked by the bareback riders or giggling at the clowns. Mixed in with the marvels are dreams—to fly! To *soar*. To twist your body into a knot, eat fire, hurl a knife with unerring precision, or whisper a tiger through a hoop. There is something of the Wild West in any circus—the swagger, the animals, the shattering of mundane rules.

Ted also likes the brightly painted horses and grindingly cheerful, repetitive melodies of carousels, a word he mispronounces on purpose because he feels sure it should be kuh-ROW-sels. That, after all, is how it is spelled. Ted's mind lands on stuff like this. His opinions are as strong as Pat's, but playful as well as political. Jazz makes him happy, and ragtime, and polkas, and any chance to belt out a song. Every time Circus Flora opens in St. Louis, he reserves the whole tent one night for Jones associates and their families. And to open the thousandth Edward D. Jones branch office, he invites a circus to the ceremony. The most solemn witness to Ted's triumph is the elephant, who arrives blinged out for the occasion, a braided headpiece on his forehead and a spangled necklace beneath his trunk.

§

As much as Ted loves circuses, he hates ceremonial occasions, stiff banquets full of speechifying, and formal parties with rigid rules of etiquette. He's been known to get up and leave a long restaurant dinner halfway through, and once he has his secretary send out menus ahead of a restaurant dinner party so people can pre-order. Patsy might enjoy sipping a glass of wine and taking time for conversation, but Ted wants the ordeal over as quickly as possible. The savored ritual of studying the menu and lingering, toying with a decision, means nothing to him. Food is swell, but the trappings can make it tedious.

At a regional meeting at Sun Mountain Lodge, high in the Cascade Mountains, Ted gets antsy when people linger to mingle and drink at the end of the banquet. "Anybody want to step outside under the stars for a singalong?" And there they are, standing on a mountaintop singing old sailing songs and show tunes. When people pause to catch their breath, Ted embroiders a tale about where he first heard the next song…

Even at meetings that are salespeople only, no spouses, Ted starts piano singalongs. He likes the energy of it, the camaraderie. The brokers get into the spirit and write "Shine On Edward Jones." Ted is likely to climb up on top of a table to sing—just as he will to make a point at work, if he's feeling short and afraid nobody's listening.

Bob Ciapciak, whom Ted has nicknamed Chapstick, comes down to the hotel lobby early—Edward Jones people are notoriously early arrivers, he has noticed—for a meeting in Huntsville, Alabama. Already there, Ted nods toward a piano. "Do you play?" Ciapciak does not. "It's time to learn the company song," Ted announces when several more brokers join them. "Of course, you learned it in training. Who plays the piano?"

Ted puts on his dancing shoes with Marie Downey (head of Personnel) at the first Founders Day in 1983.

A man raises his hand slowly, like a kid who's not sure he knows the answer but has to save himself somehow. Ted gives him an old song to use as melody and makes up the company song (which does not as yet exist) on the spot, belting it out over the laughter. Hotel staffers gather to listen to these crazy guests who have taken over the atrium.

More than one photo is taken of Ted, his head tilted back, his face red, belting out a song. Anticipating demand, Jim McKenzie rushes to find a piano tuner, paying "heart surgeon rates," the day before a meeting at Ben Homan's house. "The guy can sing," Ben marvels afterward. "He knew more remote ditties, army songs, second and third verses.... It was after midnight when we finally ran out of gas."

After a regional meeting in Grand Island, Nebraska, everyone heads for the parking lot—and Ted, who will later be described, incredulously, as "stone cold sober," decides he wants to dance. He starts his old diesel Mercedes, opens the door so the radio's tunes fill the air, and twirls Kathy McKenzie around the asphalt dance floor.

Ted never flirts or plays favorites—except to always pick a woman petite enough that when he twirls her, his hand can reach over her head.

In a vineyard high in the hills above San Francisco, there is an unusually gorgeous wine-tasting party. As the chairlift takes the guests up, they can hear the strains of live music, and when they reach the top, they can see the misty blue of the ocean. Everybody's spirits lift—and so do the wine glasses. Soon they're all singing, dancing, and in bursts of enthusiasm, falling down and laughing all the harder. The next morning, Harley Catlin chuckles. "I can't believe Ted got that drunk."

"What are you talking about?" someone said. "He doesn't drink at these things. He hadn't had a drop all night."

Ted—who made it a point to nurse a ginger ale with a twist of lime at any company function—was just having fun.

On some of its 240-mile route across Missouri, America's longest bike path—the Katy Trail—is sandwiched between America's longest river, the Missouri, and the limestone bluffs at the edge of the river valley.

When not running close to the Missouri River, the trail traverses remnants of bottomland forest of oak, sycamore, cottonwood and river birch. The trail also passes thousands of acres of Missouri corn and soybean fields, and barns and farmhouses that were built from trees harvested nearby more than 100 years ago.

In addition to providing a scenic window on rural Missouri, Ted wanted to bring new visitors and life to the small towns along the route of the old Katy railroad. This is Clinton, the westernmost town on the Katy, about 70 miles from Kansas City.

Just across the Missouri River from St. Louis is the largest town directly on the trail, St. Charles. This statue of Lewis and Clark stands between the trail and (in this photo) the flooding Missouri River.

Cooper's Landing is on the trail near Columbia. It offers campsites and other amenities—including a beautiful view of sunsets over the Missouri.

There are 26 trailheads and two remaining restored depots, like this one in Boonville, along the Katy. The trailheads are generally on the sites of old railroad stops and provide information on the local area and its history.

The landscape is part of the allure of the Katy Trail but the small communities along the way tell their own story. The Peers Store (with prairie in full bloom in June) is one of the remaining original structures along the route that were built in 1896 for the arrival of the Katy railroad. Several grain elevators like these still stand along the trail.

These scenes from Prairie Fork Conservation Area illustrate the diversity of habitat—aquatic, wetland, prairie and forest—available for study and enjoyment on this 700+ acres in the middle of Missouri. Serious scientific research is being done on this place that was a worn-out and eroded farm when it was acquired by Ted's father in the 1930s.

Crow Pond at Prairie Fork is today (top photo) the site of conservation education programs and of many Eagle Scout projects. In the photo above, Ted and Pat survey Crow Pond in the 1980s and envision what it might become. It was one of the first ponds built on the farm to solve erosion problems in the 1950s.

The prairies at Prairie Fork. The farm that Ted and Pat loved and worked tirelessly on for decades was given to the University of Missouri and the Missouri Department of Conservation by Pat in 1997. Today visitors and students can study and enjoy its hundreds of acres of native plants, similar to ones that would have been found here in the 1800s.

People Magazine chose Pat as a 2007 "Hero Among Us" and named her the "Prairie Godmother". This photo of Pat with blooming monarda—or bee balm—accompanied the article.

This liatris or blazing star, stands above a field of coreopsis in mid-summer at Prairie Fork.

Ted, after a 1988 Katy Trail hearing, on the steps of the Missouri Capitol. He not only provided the funding but the will and the inspiration to push the Katy Trail forward, long before its success was assured.

This was the scene on a blustery April 29, 1990, when hundreds of people crowded the trail in Rocheport and watched as Governor John Ashcroft cut the ribbon on what would become America's longest rail to trail project.

At the opening of the trail, Governor Ashcroft, who was instrumental in the trail's creation, presented Ted with the first Governor's Medal for Distinguished Resource Stewardship. The medal recognized those who care for things that "don't belong only to us". Ted passed away only a few months later, after a long battle with cancer.

Fourteen years after the Katy opened—while continuing to support and encourage Missouri conservation causes she and Ted believed in—Pat was present at the dedication of Missouri State Park's Edward D. and Pat Jones Confluence Point State Park. Shown here are Pat and Jamie Coe as they return from Confluence Point.

Pat at 85! Out on the prairie helping with a winter burn, which was done every few years to eliminate invasive plant species and establish native prairie plants.

Jamie Coe with Pat in the Gator (below)

With border collie Angus, named after her Scottish grandfather, Pat inspects the prairie in mid-summer.

Ted with Peter Drucker in the 1980s. Drucker was one of the pre-eminent management consultants and authors of the 20th century. He advised dozens of companies globally and wrote more than 30 books. Drucker said of Ted, "He enjoyed people. He gloried in their success. He worked hard to make them succeed."

WAL*MART

WAL-MART STORES, INC
CORPORATE OFFICES
BENTONVILLE, ARKANSAS 72712

Sam M. Walton
Chairman and Chief Executive Officer
(501) 273-4210

July 25, 1985

Mr. Edward D. Jones, Jr.
Senior Partner
Edward D. Jones and Company
201 Progress Parkway
Maryland Heights, MO 63043

Dear Ted:

It was good hearing from you recently by phone. Also, I appreciate the letter you wrote me and the article you sent concerning your very fine company. I meant every word I said when I indicated that I felt you and your management team were one of the best examples ever of our free enterprise system and folks working together with common objectives. Congratulations to you all. Best wishes for your continued good health and success. Come see us when you are down this way.

Very truly yours,

Sam

Sam Walton

SW/wpt/0722/73

Despite the accolades of Ted's business career, he and Pat were recognized equally for achievements like this award presented at Tree Farm Day at the University of Missouri in 1983—for "outstanding accomplishments in tree farm management."

A note from Sam Walton. Sam and Ted became acquainted in the 1980s. They both loved small towns and rural America, and recognized an opportunity to bring products and services to these previously overlooked places.

WELCOME "Learn, Get Dirty and Have Fun!!" Pat Jones 2003

Serious conservation research is being done at Prairie Fork today, but Pat's mantra of "Learn, Get Dirty and Have Fun!!" is a constant reminder of what she believed. Pat beams with a group of visitors at the Soil Shed. The Shed is used for education and instruction about the importance of healthy soil to the environment.

In her Gator with a group of Edward Jones associates out for a tour and a tree planting—and some conservation inspiration.

Whether it's a simple hike in the woods, searching for and studying the aquatic life in ponds or coloring images of what you found there, Prairie Fork is being used today as Ted and Pat hoped it would—to instruct and educate visitors about the complex web of life that is needed for a healthy planet.

This photo illustrates why the Missouri River, entering the Mississippi from the right, is called "the Big Muddy." Before Missouri State Parks created the Ted and Pat Jones Confluence Point State Park in 2004, the only way to reach the confluence was by boat. Today visitors can walk to the place where America's two longest rivers meet. Ted's dream was that the trail would one day reach from one side of Missouri to the other. Missouri State Parks and others continue to work to make that dream a reality by extending the Trail from its current stopping point about 12 miles west of the confluence to the state park named for Ted and Pat.

20

—

Want to Split That Burger?

People notice a boss. They notice the physical and psychological aura of success. Edward Jones walks into a room and people immediately know he owned the company. But while his father is at the M.A.C. having a manicure, Ted is walking into a barbershop saying, "Give me the works." He keeps some version of his military crewcut most of his life, and for decades wears Clark Kent glasses, the frames dark against his ruddy cheeks. His favorite shoes are Hush Puppies, suede lace-ups far comfier than any wingtip. His shirt's nearly always ballooning up, desperate to escape from his pants. Friends speak fondly of his "horse blanket sport coats."

Ted's wardrobe quickly becomes a source of gentle fun. The white socks he wears with dress shoes. The highwater pants. The short-sleeved shirts, usually in a windowpane plaid that matches neither pants nor tie. A colleague teases him into buying a pair of bell-bottom jeans, but they have to be hemmed so high, the bell disappears. Ted is destined to stay in straight-leg trousers, full at the top and straight down, "like clown pants," another friend says.

He does take *care* of his wardrobe, such as it is. His favorite dry cleaner is run by a man called Raspberry, and Raspberry also makes and sells a barbecue sauce Ted considers the finest in the Mississippi Valley. He buys it in quantity whenever he needs a jacket dry-cleaned.

Alas, Raspberry can't keep him from rumpling. Tim Rupp remembers his first sight of his boss: A blue Mercedes pulled up outside his office in Rolla, Missouri, and "out of one door stepped a five-foot-four man wearing seersucker pants that looked like they'd been slept in and a powder blue oxford button-down that looked pretty wrinkled, too."

One day a man in blue jeans, a flannel shirt, and a cap approaches broker Jerry Woodin, smiling. "You're doing great," the man says.

"Oh, my God," Woodin realizes, "it's Ted Jones." The managing partner thought he'd stop by on his way to a draft horse sale.

"This is the guy I'm working for?" Ed Steck asks himself. The man behind the voice is short, and he's wearing a peach striped shirt, a patterned tie, and black-and-white checked pants—with the corner of a red bandanna sticking out of a back pocket.

But then Steck watches Ted go down the line, asking each student in the Series 7 cram course where they came from. He has a story to share about each place, a bit of its history he has learned, a quirky landmark in that town. People begin to relax. And so does Steck.

Another day, Ted comes to work in his "visit with the bank" suit, then leans forward and pulls the collar back to show Jim McKenzie how frayed it is. "I don't want them to think we're making too much money here." He has arranged, at a time when the firm does not need to borrow money, to borrow money if needed. They are headed to the bank to discuss the contingency plan.

"You want the firm to look *that* poor?" Jim teases.

Dead silence. Ted is not amused; probably because that is exactly what he's after.

§

On a trip to San Francisco, Ted and John Borota have a few hours to kill. "Let's go to Brooks Brothers," Ted says. "I need a new sport coat." While he fingers jacket fabrics, Borota wanders off. The next time he looks up, Ted is in front of a mirror in the corner of the store, tugging an alligator belt through his pants' loops.

Borota walks over. "That looks real nice," he says. "How much is it?"

Embarrassed, Ted confides the price, then blurts how tired he is of not having a good belt that fits. He unfastens the belt, then glares at Borota: "If you tell anybody I spent $80 on this belt, I'll call you a liar!"

At a weekend house party at the Joneses, one of many. In the chatter, a guest mentions that she is planning a shopping trip to New York. Ted's head comes up. "Will you bring me back some Brooks Brothers pajamas? The kind with a drawstring on the pants. But I just want the top."

"Gladly," she says, "but why don't you want the bottom, too? I'll get you the whole set."

Ted chuckles. "Did you ever try to tie a string around an orange?"

§

While visiting New York, Ted receives a call from Webster Tilton, brother-in-law to Gussie Busch, the beer magnate who outlasted Ted's grandpa. Tilton is in the city visiting friends, and because he knows Ted's dad, he invites Ted to join them for a Broadway play.

Ted strides down the long theater aisle in his summer seersucker suit and a pair of yellow argyle socks.

Tilton's niece distracts him from the New York stares by complimenting his excellent taste in socks. Thanking her, he confides that he seldom wears this pair, because he is afraid they will shrink in the wash.

A few weeks later, Ted receives a package from Hammacher Schlemmer: a sock stretcher, accompanied by a note from the niece assuring him that if he washes his socks in cold water and then places them on the stretcher, they will be just fine.

When the firm commissions a commemorative portrait of Ted Jones, people blink to see him posed in a distinguished sport coat, its cut and cloth finer than anything they've ever seen him wear.

This is because the jacket does not exist. The artist painted it on.

§

Ted and Pat are well-matched even in their disdain for matchy clothes. Once Ted invites people to dinner at the farmhouse, and it is a nicer than usual sort of dinner. One of the wives is in the kitchen helping Pat prepare hors d'oeuvres. "I can finish up if you want to go get dressed," the woman says. "It's probably time to get ready."

Pat blinks, not understanding. "I am ready."

When she and Ted sign up for a cruise and she is told she will need a floor-length gown, she sews it herself.

When Ursula and Edward plan a gala dinner at Bellerive Country Club to celebrate their golden wedding anniversary, Ursula tells her daughter Martha, "Oh my God, take Pat out and get her a dress. It's my fiftieth wedding anniversary." Knowing Pat, she might show up in L.L. Bean.

Martha picks out a dress at Montaldo's and has it sent to the farm, and Pat wears that dress to Edward Jones functions for years.

She could easily live without a mirror. She will go to Crane's General Store to "drop off the mail, come in hair flying," says Megan Dudley, a waitress at the adjacent Marlene's restaurant. "Some days I'm not sure she's even brushed it." Pat wears her work clothes for the farm, her mud-splattered boots, and she never bothers with makeup or jewelry. "Is that poor woman okay?" people murmur if they do not know who she is. "Does she have a place to sleep?"

For Al McKenzie's retirement party, Pat drives in from the country. National sales managers for mutual funds have flown in for the occasion, as have Jones partners and financial advisors from all over the country. The women are wearing cocktail dresses. Pat is not wearing The Dress, but she is pretty dressed up by her standards: nice white jeans with decorative brass studs, paired with a good jacket.

Al's son Jim catches sight of Pat standing alone, thumbs hooked in the pockets of those jeans. Behind her shimmers a Pointillist canvas of sequins and sparkling jewels, and he sees her stiff posture and white jeans and thinks fondly, "She needs to get back to her country life."

§

Another reason for their simple wardrobes is the famous Jones frugality. Much as he adores food, for example, Ted is hardly a foodie. One day, he invites Dan Burkhardt to come back to the farm with him. They will have a simple supper, he says, a hearty soup. With a twinkle in those cornflower blue eyes, Ted confides that he likes to add a dollop of brandy.

Burkhardt straightens his tie. He's envisioning a silver tureen, the sort of serving piece Ted's father meant when he reminisced about a downtown restaurant that served the best turtle soup in St. Louis, and how the waiter would very precisely add a dollop of sherry to the tureen....

They reach the farm. Pat must be away. Ted opens a jumbo can of Campbell's beef barley soup. He heats it and, with great ceremony, adds a shot of brandy to the pot.

Dinner is served.

As for lunch with Ted, it could be a comedy skit. He hates booths, will only eat at tables. After the main course, he always wants the waiter to read off the entire list of pies—and then he always orders apple. With the pie, he asks for "about an inch of black coffee to kill the sweet—not enough to pay for." He says this straight-faced and unabashed, looking the waiter in the eye. The waiter blinks, then brings him half a cup of coffee, gratis.

In Ames, Iowa, Ted invites a broker out to his car and pops the trunk. There's a cooler with various lunch meats; another with pop. "Make yourself a sandwich," he invites the guy, who's been decorating his office and his life with displays of affluence. "This is how we travel."

When Bill Broderick forgets to get their parking ticket validated at a restaurant and reaches for a couple of singles in his wallet, Ted looks at him aghast. "What are you doing?" Broderick explains. "Back up!" Ted orders.

Waiting in line at Wendy's, he asks Bob Campbell if he wants to split a cheeseburger.

"I think I can eat one on my own," Bob replies dryly.

§

McDonald's is Ted's favorite lunchtime destination. One day he takes an entire training class there, everybody crisp and hopeful in their business suits, and asks, "You know why I brought you guys here? Because it's clean, the people are courteous, and the menu is predictable. If you want quiche, go somewhere else."

Visiting Dave Clapp, Ted leans against the door-jamb and says, "Say, I notice it's about dinner time. Do you want to grab a quick bite to eat?" Chuffed at the idea of going out to eat with the firm's managing partner,

Clapp says yes eagerly—and finds himself sitting across from Ted in a hard, slick orange plastic booth. Afterward, he does some research and learns that Ted's father bought the company that makes the wax paper that sandwich is wrapped in. "Ted just wants to make sure they're still using his paper!"

Ted does love hearing the stories of Midwest Packaging Materials. During World War II, the company made the wax-paper bags used to package bread. One day, the phone rang: "I'd like some wax paper, please." It was a man's voice.

"What size bags?"

"I'd like it cut in squares, not bags."

"Er…okay. How many squares?"

"I need a truckful. My name is Ray Kroc."

The connection is cool, but there were many other reasons Ted liked McDonald's: speed, efficiency, a reliable cheeseburger, a simple demonstration of frugality.

"Yeah, the Joneses owned the wax paper company," Doug Hill will remark later, "but also, it was a cheap lunch that sent a signal. Your culture is not something written on the wall. Your culture is something you *practice*."

A classic example: Ted tells Bill Hauk, "Call the president of Mercantile Bank—they never call on us—and tell him we'd like to have lunch." The president shows up, trim and neat in a well-tailored suit, and they all climb into Ted's car, and he drives across I-270 to McDonald's. Bill wonders if the man has ever *been* in a McDonald's. His suspicion is confirmed when the banker orders—"a medium-rare burger."

They take their greasy sacks of lunch to Creve Coeur Park and sit on a bench to eat. As he crumples his bag, Bill realizes that this was Ted's version of statecraft, putting the other power player at a slight disadvantage, refusing to cater to his dining customs.

Once, the joke almost gets reversed. On a company trip, the brokers cook up a scheme to meet at an upscale supper club and then have the waiter bring out a Big Mac for Ted. Alas, Ted and Patsy change their minds at the last minute and stay home to harvest tomatoes, and the joke is foiled.

§

A shy extrovert who loves circuses and company singalongs but dreads cocktail party schmoozing, Ted contains contradictions. One of the sharpest is his ability to be both frugal and lavishly generous. Jim Goodknight, who has had some wonderful meals with him that *weren't* cheap, begins to realize that Ted isn't miserly; "he just wants every dollar to count. There's a whole lot more to it than the money."

When food is left over from a conference, for example, he wants it taken to a nearby shelter for men who are homeless. The hotel refuses, citing rules. Ted is frustrated beyond words. When he has people out to the farm and tons of food and beer are left over, he sends a truck to fetch some Catholic seminarians from a nearby monastery. They feast, and by the time they pile back into the truck, they are tipsy, well-fed, and singing at the top of their lungs.

§

Ted goes to a travel agent to book a big trip for himself and Patsy. After meeting him, the dubious travel agent calls the firm to verify the existence of a Ted Jones. He does not look the part.

Planning a trip to Japan, he tells a travel agent, "I want to stay in the Japanese hotel for the average person. I don't want a big, fancy hotel." The first place they book is *still* too fancy, so once he's in Japan, he finds himself a different one. When the company's travel coordinator wangles a shockingly low price for a room in a small-town hotel in Texas, Ted concedes that it's a great deal but reports, "I got 'em to throw in breakfast."

When Peter Scott has to book accommodations in Cleburne, Texas for Ted, he finds him a motel room and is nervous that it won't be nice enough. Sure enough, when Peter arrives to pick him up, Ted launches into a tirade about having to move to a different room. Over Peter's flustered apology, he says, "The room you had booked cost $10 more, and I didn't want to spend the money."

On a business trip in southern Missouri, Ted breaks a shoestring. No problem: He finds a shoe store in downtown Joplin. To his shock, the store has no shoestrings for sale. He finds a two-pack for 49 cents at a Ben Franklin dimestore and tells the manager he only needs one. He's willing to pay 30 cents for one, but he doesn't want to pay for a shoestring he doesn't need. When the manager informs Ted that the pack cannot be split, Ted goes back to the shoe store and offers to sell them the other shoestring. "I have something I don't need," he says, "but you obviously do."

At tax time, Ted brings all his documents to his accountant in an old striped cardboard suitcase, the kind you can buy at a dimestore. Again, he may be making a point.

§

People who hear a few of these stories envision Ted Jones in a dressing gown and nightcap, waiting for the Ghost of Christmas Past. They couldn't be more wrong. Quietly, with utmost secrecy, he gives loans to his associates, helps them through crises, makes sure their kids can get to college.

He gives David Crane, son of the owner of his favorite store in Williamsburg, the Edward Jones scholarship to go to Westminster College.

As an anonymous donor, he helps form a private foundation to create summer conservation jobs for college-bound Black kids. Working with the Fulton chapter of the NAACP, the foundation selects the kids, buys them uniforms, provides transportation, and pays them a salary to work two summers at the Whetstone Creek Wildlife Management Area. He gives steadily to environmental causes, community causes, anything he knows will make a difference, not just an impression.

It is a way of *living* that Ted is trying to demonstrate. Avoiding waste. Investing carefully. Seeing through the shimmering luxury goods that suck up cash and give back hardly anything. A Buddhist monk paying close attention to every grain of rice he swallows—that is Ted with money. Mindful, careful, appreciative. But always willing to let it be turned into something far more valuable.

2 1

On the Road Again
(and Again, and Again)

"This is the hometown of Calamity Jane," Ted announces in Princeton, Missouri. Mention just about any small town across the middle swath of the country, and he can tell you something quirky in its history or describe a cool landmark. This internal database endears him to new hires who grew up in these towns. But God help you if you don't know your own history.

In Kearney, Nebraska, Jim McKenzie takes Ted to the Cattleman's Mining Company restaurant. Glancing around appreciatively, Ted recognizes the photographs on the wall, taken by a pioneer photographer a century earlier. "What do you mean you don't know him?" he asks McKenzie. "This is your town! Don't you know the history of your town?" In McCook, Nebraska, he tells the Jones broker's client about the guy who first brought a certain breed of cattle there, and the client grins. "That was my grandfather!"

Ted reads a ton of local and national history along with his nonfiction spy thrillers, westerns, animal books, and circus books. He knows the stories braided across the country. Even when he's flying, he can look down and recognize something that clicks with a tale he's heard, a wondrous bit of nature, a momentous event. The Oregon Trail? He is as familiar with its route and hazards as the settlers who made its first ruts with their wagon wheels. Even Japanese culture became an interest after his year there during the Occupation. Riding a tram through the Missouri Botanical

Garden in a sudden rainstorm, Ted is seated toward the back with Patsy and a visiting financial advisor. As they near the Japanese garden, Ted starts singing a Japanese war song—in Japanese. (Today, he might be tossed off the tram, but he means it as appreciation.) And when he finally persuades Rich Malone to take a company trip to Hong Kong, he personally shepherds him around the city, regaling him with all the history.

Back home, Ted visits Darrell Seibel in Hays, Kansas, whenever he can find an excuse, and they go to historic forts and march up and down the parade grounds together, in step. Ted likes the sound of their thumping feet against the wooden sidewalks. He also likes thinking about Buffalo Bill coming through Hays, and General George Custer, and William F. Cody....

Bill Borgstadt takes a lot of trips with Ted, and on several occasions, Ted makes him stop the car. Bill never has a clue where they're going or why. Once, they scale a barbed wire fence—in their business suits—and climb a hill, so Ted can show his friend the ruts that the pioneer wagons made, still engraved in the prairie.

If you're driving with Ted and pass a historical marker, you will have to make a U-turn and go back. "You may never be here again," Ted will point out, giving the words solemn weight.

On their frequent road trips, he refuses to let anybody drive back by the same route. "You will never learn anything if you go home over the same road that you left on," Ted says. "You always have to alter the route."

§

When he doesn't have a traveling companion to share the sight-seeing, Ted documents his observations carefully. In Wibaux, Montana, he writes, "I am right now looking at a monument of Pierre Wibaux, who was a rancher here and came over from France. He was a contemporary of Theodore Roosevelt...." Looking at a bronze of Wibaux, Ted does the math: the guy died at sixty years of age. A point of interest: "He ran a ranch with 85,000 head of cattle."

The same afternoon, Ted visits the Marquis de Mores chateau, home of a Frenchman who married a banker's daughter. Her wedding present from Daddy was $3 million, "and looks to me like this Frenchman came out here and spent the money," Ted remarks. "The home is a reminder of how these people lived," just as his farmhouse is a reminder of how he and Pat live.

More to his taste than the Frenchman's chateau is Theodore Roosevelt's Maltese Cross ranch building, a log structure he describes as "seven of my steps long and four of my steps wide." The cowboys climbed a ladder straight up to the loft, where they slept.

§

Always preferring to be outdoors, Ted urges regional-meeting campouts at Roaring Rivers State Park in Cassville, Missouri. Then he drives down to cook breakfast for his sleepy financial advisors—bacon, eggs, hashbrowns, and cowboy coffee. "Who's interested in driving down to the Pea Ridge battlefield?" he asks after breakfast. It is the site of the most pivotal Civil War battle west of the Mississippi, and Ted never tires of the place.

"I'm sure the rookies all thought they would ride around the battlefield, look at some markers, and leave," Jim Goodknight says later, chuckling at how "Ted took them on a twelve-mile march over the whole battlefield so he could show them *everything*."

Unaware of these excursions, Rich Lawson, an advisor from Warrensburg, Missouri, who is also interested in military history, decides to stop at Pea Ridge on his way to Roaring Rivers. He enters the visitor's center, where big picture windows overlook the battle site. In front of the center window, a crowd has gathered around a man who is recounting the bloody climax of the battle. "That guy sure knows what he's talking about," Rich thinks, listening from a distance. "Well, obviously, they give talks there every day."

The crowd clears, and Rich recognizes his boss standing at the window. He was the one giving the lecture.

§

Once Ted gets stranded in a blizzard and has to bide his time for three hours in the Davis Bros. Store in Readsville, Missouri. Most people would shop, chat about the snowstorm, munch a candy bar. Ted researches the store's history, going all the way back to 1917, when it was opened by a twenty-two-year-old whose father sold molasses by the barrel in Indian territory and loaded wagons with dry salt bacon. He learns how young Riley Davis bought fifty cases of eggs a day—even more than Ted bought for his schoolboy business venture. He imagines the inventory: the wool and the hides, the cured ham and bacon, lard, fur, ginseng and mayapple and sassafras roots. Once he's safely home again, he writes it all up, just because it's interesting.

§

One of the seldom acknowledged joys of travel is the pranks it makes possible. Checking into a little hotel, Ted hands over his credit card. The clerk reads "Edward D. Jones" and says, "You know what? There's a company in town called Edward D. Jones!" And Ted says, "Really? Do you know what they do?"

She doesn't, so he trudges away disappointed.

With his family, Ted plans Mystery Trips, renting a small bus. The dry run is taking his niece, Martha Key Altvater, who teaches history, to Eureka Springs and the Wilson's Creek battlefield. Then, in 1986, he piles everybody in an RV bus and drives them all over Missouri, stopping at Watkins Mill, Fort Scott, Excelsior Springs…. Another trip is, of course, up to Baraboo for the circus.

When the various nieces, nephews, and siblings meet at the bus, it's always empty—no chilled beverages, no snacks. Neither Ted nor Pat has remembered to stock refreshments. But Ted *always* remembers to bring song sheets so they can have a sing-along. He stands in the front of the bus with the tour-guide's mic. Or they take over a Holiday Inn bar in some small town and sing like they're supposed to be there.

"You enjoy it," Martha says later, half laughing, "because *he's* enjoying it so much."

§

Ted never grumbles about his ninety-minutes-each-way commute or his frequent road trips. He likes motion, and he likes cars. There are so many trips he wants to take. Insatiably curious, he drives out to Utah to research the farm's genealogy, and that opens other possibilities. His farm was settled by Captain Anderson from Virginia. He could go to a courthouse in Virginia and look up the Andersons....

Early in his married life, he drives a Buick Riviera; then he moves on to Mercedes, liking the diesel version you can plug in on arctic nights. One morning, he's having trouble getting the car started, and John Martin comes over to the farm to give him a hand. It's the Sixties, and Mercedes still make a lot of noise and blow a lot of smoke when they start. Finally, the engine turns over, and Ted says fondly, "Listen to her purr."

Still, he buys his Mercedes stripped down, worships them, and drives them into the ground. When he decides this particular German automotive brand has gotten too expensive, he startles everyone who knows him by switching to a lower-priced Audi.

Pat isn't nearly as interested in cars. She has a little Datsun pickup truck, and for some time, a Chevy Corvair. Once she parks it and leaves the windows open, and when she returns, the car is vibrating and buzzing, dozens of bees ricocheting off the walls and swarming above the steering wheel. She has parked over a nest.

When the first Prius comes off the line, she trades in her little Honda Civic immediately. Whenever she encounters another Prius driver, she asks, "What kind of mileage you getting?" Meanwhile, she takes swipes at anybody—politicians, environmentalists, *anybody*—who drives a gas guzzler and ought to know better.

One day, John Beuerlein picks Pat up in his new BMW. She eyes it warily.

"I had to have a ride worthy of you," he teases, trying to forestall any preaching.

The flattery washes right off. "What are the emissions?" she demands. "How many miles a gallon?"

22

Finding the Right People

In 1967, Doug Hill flies from Homer, New York over the winter holidays for an interview. He checks into a motel and spends all evening shining his shoes. The next morning, he puts on his best—well, his only—suit. He arrives half an hour early for his 9 am interview and sees the office already crowded with people eager to see their broker in the Board Room. Ha! He has found himself the right business.

Forty-five minutes later, he notices a man in a three-piece gray suit, light glinting off a watch fob on a chain, and says to himself, "That man owns this company."

Jean Burnett, the switchboard operator, interrupts Hill's train of thought: "Young man, what are you doing here?" When he explains, she says, "Let me take you back to the Gold Room." Dazzled by the name, he follows her eagerly—and finds himself in a room with a metal desk and two folding chairs. The brass doorknob is the closest thing to gold.

He waits another forty-five minutes. Then a man strides in, body tilted forward, arms pumping. The janitor, maybe? A lot of physical energy there. He's wearing Hush Puppies, khakis, and a blue shirt—pretty nice, for a janitor. He looks around, as though he can't even see Hill. "I'm supposed to be interviewing somebody for a sales position."

"Oh, my gosh, are you Mr. Jones?" Hill says.

Ted looks him up and down. "You're interviewing for a sales position?

You're awful young. You should be interviewing for a clerk's job."

Hill assures the older man that he is aware of his age, and there's nothing he can do about that, but he knows he can make it in this business.

Ted leaves and Jack Phelan comes in, then the real Mr. Jones, then Jack again. Worn down, Hill blurts, "Mr. Phelan, if I have to work for you for nothing to prove I can make it in this business, I'll do it."

"That's interesting," Jack says, and leaves again. Hill looks out the window and sees him walking down the street with Ted, no doubt going to lunch. Forty minutes pass.

Upon his return, Ted says, "Didn't anyone come in and tell you to go to lunch?" But he makes no apology. Finally Hill is dismissed; they cannot make a decision yet, but they will call him.

That's the most chicken crap way of getting rid of somebody I've ever seen, Hill thinks. He flies home. The day before Christmas, the phone call comes: Edward D. Jones & Co. would like to hire him.

Phone in one hand, Hill punches the air in glee. Out of the corner of his eye, he sees his mom beaming and realizes he's going to have to tell her that he offered to work for nothing.

The caller waits a beat. "And we're even going to pay you."

§

In his last year of law school, Larry Sobol sees an Edward Jones ad on the placement board. His undergraduate degree was in business, and he's intrigued enough to apply. When he shows up for his interview, he is guided to a small room. A man walks in, and they stare at each other. The man has on Hush Puppies and a sport coat and slacks that don't come close to matching. "Are you the person interested in the legal job?" he says finally, and when Sobol nods, he starts firing questions. Not the sort of questions you'd ask in a law interview, though. A municipal bond prospectus is lying on the desk, and Ted throws it to Sobol and says, "Pretend you're a salesman. How would you talk to me about this?"

Sobol shrugs to himself, thinking, *This is strange, but it's probably as good a test as anything.* He starts talking about tax savings, winging it. He gets the job.

§

Charlie Van Dyke, Ted's young neighbor in Williamsburg, works in human resources. He comes to his mentor for advice about how to hire the right person.

"You can't," Ted says, blunt as ever. "We learned that a long time ago. You hire them, and you work closely with them, and you get rid of them quickly."

On an earlier occasion, he asked Charlie, "What business do you think I'm in?"

Charlie's obvious guess was wrong. "I'm in the salesman business," Ted corrected him. "My job is to find the right people for the offices. People ask me, 'How did the market do today?' and I have no idea. Other people keep tabs on that."

So how does he find so many of the right people if hiring the right people is impossible? With grilling and gut instinct up front, hawk's-eye oversight, and ruthless action when a hire is not working out. Ted cannot abide laziness, passivity, waste of money, a dissolute lack of discipline, or, above all, dishonesty in any form. He does not trust slick, and he can spot a phony in a second. He has an uncanny read of human behavior, especially when it comes to what motivates people to succeed.

He invites a young guy who wanted to work for Jones to come out to the farm. They are entertaining, and Ted is "outside somewhere," Pat says. The young man finds him sitting on a tree stump with his knees spread, elbows on knees, tartar sauce from a fish sandwich dripping onto the ground. Ted doesn't bother with small talk, just asks, "How much money do you want to make?"

More than ambition is at play, though. Ted is adept at identifying the traits and qualities that will make for a successful Jones broker—which is ironic, given that he never wanted to be one himself. On the other hand, maybe that's why he cherishes uniqueness, preferring people who are a little offbeat. He likes to joke and play, though he doesn't trust people who only want to clown around. And he despises fancy rhetoric. "Don't tell me about potential," he says, "tell me about performance." He will hire former lawyers, postal service employees, high school principals, or jazz trombonists—anybody he senses can do the job.

"You don't have to be the smartest person to run this place," Ted tells

Darryl Pope. "Hire smart people. Get them to work for you."

Also, keep them feeling good about themselves. When Pope takes the test for the New York Stock Exchange, he's worried sick to hear the results. Ted calls him in and gives a long, slow preamble, letting him suffer a bit, then says, "I want to know how you cheated." Pope goes pale, protests that he didn't—then realizes this is Ted's way of saying he did well.

§

In 1976, Jim Weddle is working on an MBA at Washington University, intending to become a research analyst. He hears a presentation by Mort Brown, who is responsible for hiring analysts at Jones, and approaches him when they break for cookies. The business model sounds cool, Weddle says, confiding that he hopes to become a research analyst.

"We are looking for a couple of individuals to work in our research department," Brown confides, so the next morning, Weddle puts on his suit and tie—he owns one of each—and drives to the Jones office. He explains his errand to the receptionist and winds up talking to John Bachmann.

Weddle did his undergraduate work at DePauw University, and his accolades are noted on the résumé he hands Bachmann. After a quick glance, Bachmann says, "I'm sorry, Jim, but in our firm, we only hire people with degrees from reputable universities."

After a few stunned seconds, Weddle takes a chance: "The only person who could have an opinion like that is one who graduated from Wabash College."

And Bachmann cracks up.

Their alma maters, both small schools in Indiana, have a football rivalry that dates back to 1890.

Still chuckling, Bachmann says, "When can you start?"

So Weddle adds a thirty-hour work week to his fulltime graduate work. He loves the fast pace, the intellectual challenge. He loved the idea of working with individual investors who really need your help, in locations that are convenient for those clients. But turns out he loathes being a research analyst. He can *do* the heavy duty number-crunching, but there is nowhere near enough human interaction to suit his personality.

Luckily, his cubicle is next to Jack Phelan's, and he listens all day to those kind, funny, thoroughly professional phone calls. One day, Weddle stands outside Phelan's cube and waits for him to get off the phone.

"I'd like to become a registered representative," Weddle blurts. They talk a while, and then Phelan smiles. "Good. You're hired."

"I need to finish my degree, though," Weddle says, thrown by the fast result.

"Fine. Keep working in research, finish your degree, and in your spare time, study for Series 7 and 63," the federal and state qualifying exams for registration.

Weddle goes home and tells Stacey, his new wife, that he'd better stop wasting the hours between midnight and 5 a.m. They both think it's worth the sacrifice. They have only been married a few months. In December, money is so tight, Weddle listens enviously to his fulltime colleagues talking about the holiday bonus. One day, Darryl Pope, a high-up partner he has never actually spoken with, comes to his cubicle.

"Yes, Mr. Pope?"

"First, it's Darryl. Second, you're going to want to open this."

In the outstretched envelope is a week's salary as bonus.

"But I'm just an intern," Weddle stammers.

"You're doing a good job supporting the branches," Pope said, "and Ted appreciates what you're doing."

Weddle will stay for the next forty-two years—and wind up the managing partner.

§

Some of Ted's opinions are idiosyncratic, like rolling his eyes over anybody who reads the sports page and not the important parts of the paper. He has a soft spot for anyone who has done military service or grown up working hard on a farm. Of one young man, he writes, "I am convinced that he will go up and down the fruit tree sections of the state and call on farmers."

Watching some of the people Ted hires, Jim Goodknight shakes his head, not sure what the man is thinking. But nearly always, it turns out that he's right. He seems to have an instinctive ability to tell if someone is blowing smoke. He takes in guys who were rebels as kids; people whose parents had no money; women, more and more of them, as he sees that they can cut it.

The Jones way is not to steal brokers; Ted wants to find them early and train them, soak them in the company's culture, treat them so fairly that they will stay loyal. He sets up rooms at the training center—a kitchen table, a dentist's office, a pharmacy, a wooden screen door with a doorbell. (Do you knock or ring the bell? How far back do you stand? How long do you wait?) Young people learn how to talk to a stranger about what is more deeply personal than a love affair: their money.

Along the way, of course, Ted loses some of the people in whom he has invested time and energy. His method takes a lot more work up front. But the people who stay are pure gold. They know he has high expectations, and they don't want to let him down. The main times Jones loses a broker are when a guy is going through a divorce, strapped for cash, and a competitor makes an offer too tough to refuse. In the back office, there is hardly any turnover.

Always recruiting, Ted writes the home office after granting an interview, "This woman from the newspaper would make an excellent saleswoman. I tried to recruit her, get Joy to have her come in to see you."

When he sees Mary Beth Heying, who works for Jones in marketing, he asks her, "Hey, are you any relation to that Heying insurance agency in Wentzville?" He often passes the office, tucked into an old, dark blue Victorian house, on his way to work. When Mary Beth says that's her husband, she senses the wheels turning behind his eyes. "When is he coming to work for us?" Ted asks, faux casual.

Bill Christensen's father and brother are already working there when he joins the firm, and there are family dynasties like the Seibels. Today the patriarch Darrell Seibel is still in Hays, Kansas, sixty years after starting his career as a Jones financial advisor. Seibel family members—fourteen in all—have served Edward Jones clients as branch administrators, financial advisors, regional leaders, general partners, and home office associates.

Ted was the owner's son, Jack Phelan is a relative, Pete Key is Ted's brother-in-law, and so is Bill Lloyd, who married Pat's sister. "In all seriousness," Ted says one day, "I don't think you should keep people out just because they happen to be related (of course, I am a prime example)."

Family member or not, Ted believes everyone needs to prove they are willing and able to do the work. He adds a practical caveat: "You should judge people as individuals, but when you hire them don't put them with their relatives."

Because he is always looking, always recruiting, Ted knows what that looks like. One day he warns his buddy, John Jamieson, "I was just over at the Gingham Café, and I saw that State Farm fellow over there having lunch with one of your boys. I'd imagine he's trying to hire him." That was exactly what he was trying to do.

§

What are firing offenses? Abject laziness, for one. Ted wants his reps to be out of the office at least two full days a week, making calls. If he thinks they're shirking, he assigns someone in St. Louis to call them every hour on the hour on Tuesdays and Thursdays. "If we find him in the office, we have to fire him," he insists in case after case. "This is his only chance of making it."

When a man "is not doing the work…has very bad call reluctance," Ted writes, "I am disgusted with him. He has a very nice office and a system. He should have neither…. Fire him in two months if he is in the office when you call, as per his office hours."

The word "ruthless" almost fits, though he is careful to give people a solid chance before he takes swift action. He is rooting for them, but their fate is their own call. "You're good, and you're smart, and I want you to succeed—or I'll help you find another job," he says. He will wait to be shown.

"We have to put [this new broker] on the worry list," he writes. "I think we should watch him for the next two months and see how he does. I am hoping that he will make it. I think there is a possibility that he will."

If not, Ted says goodbye. He advises the reps to do the same if they are having trouble with an administrative assistant. "Possibly all of our salespeople should be taught that when you hire an employee, if they don't work out at the end of the first month, let them go." Two-month ultimatums never work, he warns: Usually, the salesman starts looking for a job with another firm the day after the ultimatum.

Ted keeps the firings calm: "It's no crime to fail in this business as a salesman," he will say. "Maybe you're not cut out for it." Only arrogance reddens his face with rage. One day, after a man presses him repeatedly for extra commission, Ted asks politely, "May I use your phone?" He calls the operator and says, "Would you get me [the managing partner] at Stifel Nicolaus?" When the man comes on the line, Ted introduces himself and says, "I'm sitting here with a fellow, and I think he'd make a good addition for you. Why don't you talk to him?" Ted hands the broker the phone and walks out.

His strong opinions would give today's HR experts a coronary. "His appearance was *Miami Vice,*" he writes. "Why wasn't this man let go a year ago?"

Vice or immorality combine in the next category of firing offenses— and it doesn't matter how much money the person is making for the firm. Any sign of dishonesty or disloyalty is fatal. When a top producer makes an outside agreement with an insurance company, cutting Jones out of the commission, Ted meets with the partners. They go around the room stating their opinions, and everybody thinks that after the guy's abject apology, he should be given another chance. "Interesting. It's almost unanimous," Ted says. Then he slams the table with his hand. "If this man stays in this organization, I leave. Open your *eyes*. He deliberately tried to cheat us. Can you name one time when anybody in this organization has tried to cheat HIM?" The final decision is not majority rule: "Over my dead body does he stay."

"If you were on the team, you were on the team, and he would chew his arm off for you," Bob Gregory says. "But he didn't believe in dishonesty at all."

Nor did he tolerate fakery or pretentiousness.

"It caused him real pain," Darryl Pope says, "when he came to like you and saw that you were someone who was able and excited and energetic and then found out that was just a show."

23

Weekends in the Country

In the early days, a Jones company trip to the farm meant a lone woman in a dress, coat, and galoshes, then men in hats, jackets, trousers too nice for a farm, and their sturdiest (not very) boots, all of them perched on a horse-drawn wagon looking a little uncertain. Over time, though, the farm weaves itself into the life of the firm.

Money can seems abstract—capital letter abbreviations on an exchange—even though what it provides is the stuff of people's lives. On the farm, everything under that pale pink sunrise—the roosters crowing in clear air, the clean sweat, the pine woods and splashy creek—is grounded, and it is easy to think concretely. For one client, dividends might be seed money; for another, a house, or tuition, or cancer treatment, or rehab, or the rescue of a racehorse whose broken health needs mending.

Associates who have known only pavement and streetlights come out to the Jones farm and leave changed. They begin to talk about "the farm" as though they, too, are a part of it. Dinners and meetings often feel different in that rural peace; the conversations more real, the laughter freer, debates managed without rancor.

Young brokers traipse after Ted, who wears them out as he strides through tall, wet grass. Many a work relationship deepens after a meal at the farm. When Jim Goodknight becomes a partner in the firm, Ted invites him out for an impromptu dinner and doesn't even bother to call Patsy; he knows she will open their home to anyone. When the two men show up, it's raining so hard, the ground is sloppy. Pat appears, face smudged, clothes and boots mud-spattered. "I was out planting trees," she reports, beaming. Quickly, she throws together dinner, nipping out to her garden to cut stalks of fresh asparagus. It is so tender and perfect, nothing else on the menu matters. Jim leaves the farm already fond of Pat. His affection only increases when, at a company meeting held on the farm, she walks up clutching a black woolly caterpillar, showing people the wide stripe running down his back. To these experts who think constantly about the future, she explains that this stripe predicts a harsh winter.

Doug Hill drives down to the Lake of the Ozarks after work on summer Fridays, so Ted will often say, "Doug, you goin' to the lake this weekend? Why don't you stop by the farm on the way down?"

Hill sighs; he'd rather just get to the lake. But he knows Ted has something on his mind. He'll make the two of them an old-fashioned—just one because he knows Hill is driving—and then say in no uncertain terms what he does and does not like. Direct mail, for example: waste of time and money. He'll pick up a roll of stamps and say, "Why don't you just throw these in the trash can?"

It's not mentoring—it's not that gentle. One Friday evening, Ted says Hill is too tough on people, and it's all Hill can do to bite back the retort, "I just watched what you did to me!" But Hill—who will later rise to managing partner—can tell he's being readied.

The setting for these sessions is no doubt deliberate: It is private at the farm, and low-key, with none of the formality Ted detests. When Ron Lemonds is invited to bring his wife out to the farm, he buys her a new dress and puts on his best suit. Pat answers the door with a bandanna tied around her hair, and Ted comes around the corner wearing his hunting clothes.

§

Dave Heald, national marketing and sales manager for the Putnam Group of Mutual Funds, flies down from Boston for a meeting in the old barn on Ted's farm. He arrives the day before, bringing fresh lobsters and clams on ice. That evening he's in the farmhouse kitchen making a chowder base, and Ted sticks his head in: "Can I help?"

Dave has him stir the onions. Ted pours himself a drink and starts stirring, and pretty soon he's singing at the top of his lungs. He stirs those onions for a solid hour, and they never burn. Amused, Dave lets him keep going till he runs out of air. Dave remembers one of the first times he met Ted. They were going to do a joint presentation at the Missouri Livestock Auction.

"You ever been to a live auction?" Ted asked, and Heald said no. "Well, you mind getting cow dung on your shoes?"

§

Jones reps are coming in from another part of the country, and they will drive out to the farm after lunch. Ted asks Barbara Webb what time she's planning on being there.

"Around 11:30," she says.

His brow furrows. "I think you should be here earlier."

Gladly, she says, what time?

"I think you should be here by 6:30."

So she sets her alarm to ring before dawn and makes it out to the farm just before 6:30. Ted is assembling something for the event and asks, a little dubiously, if she thinks she could bring him a tool from the barn.

"I grew up on a farm," she calls over her shoulder. When she slides open the barn doors, there have to be at least ten thousand mud daubers inside. But she finds the right tool and brings it back.

"No problem?" Ted asks.

"No problem at all, Ted, glad to do it."

She has passed what she now realizes was a test.

§

Ted will only hunt quail, but he welcomes friends to hunt deer on his property. When Doug Hill resists moving to St. Louis to be partner because he will miss the hunting and fishing, Ted says, "Oh, Doug, I've got a farm—you can hunt there." From then on, at the start of every deer season, he calls Doug and asks, "Are you coming out?"

When a group comes out to hunt, they sleep in a tent or in the

This photo, from a Montana gallery, was displayed in Ted's office for years.

sheepherder's wagon, one of Ted's proudest finds. An old horse-drawn wagon, it is wooden, but its original canvas cover has been replaced with metal, which has kept it in good shape. The metal roof is curved, like a quonset hut, and has a little smokestack; underneath its shelter is a stove, a kitchenette, and a bed. For Ted, it probably conjures his earliest memory, riding in that horse-drawn milk wagon.

He hangs out with his guests at the deer camp in the evenings, then goes home to his comfy bed. Early the next morning, he is back, showered and shaved, to fix them cowboy coffee, which means building a fire, boiling water, pouring in coffee grounds, letting them boil, then breaking an egg into the pot. As the egg cooks and sinks, it collects all the coffee grounds and settles them on the bottom of the pot.

One of the deer camps is for a group of men from the New York Stock Exchange. Ted has D-Boy Garner act as their guide, and after the hunt, D-Boy helps Ted set up a big tent and cook lobster and steak in the woods. "First time I ever had *that*," D-Boy says happily. But the next morning, when Ted pours him a mug of cowboy coffee blacker than oil, D-Boy takes a sip and feels his eyes flash lightning. Surreptitiously, he knocks his cup over. Ted offers to refill it. "Nah," D-Boy says hurriedly, "two sips of that are enough to wake you up!"

§

One day an investment rep from the city climbs on a horse at the farm, pretending he can ride, and the horse darts ahead, the guy hanging onto his mane for dear life. When the others catch up, he has straightened in the saddle. "I just had to test the horse," he says with a shrug, saving face.

When top executives from a big utility company in Las Vegas come to St. Louis and drive out to the farm, it's part of a first-class weekend planned by Jones staffers. They charter a very comfortable, well-appointed bus for the ninety-minute drive out to the farm. After the sweet tang of barbecue and some of Ted's most engaging stories, the execs are contented, utterly relaxed, and ready to climb back on the bus. Before they can board, two of Ted's dogs dart past. Some visiting curs have invaded their territory, and the snarling and snapping escalate fast. Without bothering to say a word, Ted goes over to a hydrant and turns a power hose on the dogs—spraying several of his high-powered guests in the process.

Years later, right in the middle of the formal Q&A session for a Canadian regional leaders conference, Gunner, the little Jack Russell terrier, leaps onto the stage and lies down, dead center, for a nap. On another occasion, Jones associates are meeting around the guesthouse conference table when Gunner jumps up on somebody's lap—and then walks from lap to lap all around the table. Pat ignores the look of horror on one woman's face. "Dogs are dogs," she says, her eyes crinkling, dimples deep.

Doug Hill brings a group of Jones regional leaders and their spouses out to the farm. The group splits along gender lines, the men playing horseshoes and the women excited about a nature hike. Pat is eager to take them, and Hill decides to leave the horseshoes and come along.

They are walking, the women asking questions about flowers and trees. Pat stops mid-reply to point: "If you look up in that tree, you'll see a deer stand."

One of the women tilts her head back and squints, frowning. "But Pat," she says, "how do they get up there?"

Fighting to keep a straight face, Pat shoots Hill a look that says, *Seriously?* Then she calmly explains what a deer stand is.

§

In their time at the farm, Jones people come to know Pat as well as Ted—and to realize that rural life is not a monotonous idyll devoid of drama. One day there's a dead bobcat in the creek. Another day, chatting on the screened-in porch—amid turtle shells, animal skins, bright feathers, the skull of a skunk or a fox—Pat holds up a finger to shush someone. A possum is creeping closer. With a scrabble of toenails, the dog who's been dozing at her feet tears off on a chase. The possum immediately lies down and plays dead—for so long that the watchers wonder if its little heart has stopped. Finally, with an air of brushing itself off, the possum stands, looks around to see if the coast is clear, and walks away, leaving Pat laughing. She prefers this to any soap opera.

Another day, visitors notice a black snake, his four feet stretched along the baseboard. "Aren't you a handsome fellow?" Pat says to the snake. And then, to the visitors: "We haven't had anyone in the guesthouse for weeks—he must have been trapped there all this time. I bet he's thirsty. Let's carry him out to the birdbath and give him a drink." The snake extends his head toward the water, and they watch his throat ripple as he drinks. Quenched, he wriggles off into a patch of woods.

The drama ratchets up when a large group comes out at the farm. "Get Jack Phelan away from the house," somebody hisses to Jim McKenzie, explaining that there's a snake in there, and he's terrified of snakes. Dutifully, Jim distracts Jack long enough for the snake to be removed. Later, he murmurs to Pat, "I hear there was a snake in the house?"

Pat shrugs. "If you live in the country, you either have snakes or mice."

Ted, the World War II veteran who was one of the first to occupy Japan, is almost as scared of snakes as Jack is. But Pat swims alongside water snakes in the pond and secretly allows black snakes to overwinter in the basement. One year, a friend counts fourteen snakes down there. If one ventures upstairs, Pat just opens the door and gently sweeps it outside with a broom. She is never bitten. Once, she is stung by hornets, but she quickly defends them: "Not their fault. I mowed over their nest."

2 4

—

The Glue Will Hold

When friends visit the Joneses at the cocktail hour, there's a crackling fire
and ragtime music playing. Pat has a glass of red wine, and Ted drinks
bourbon over ice that he crushes with great showmanship, taking a cube in
each hand and clapping them together.

They have a lot of simple fun.

Ted, Pat, and Pat's brother Truman have a ritual contest to see who
can hold a pitcher of water straight out for the longest time. (Pat always
wins.) Over at the Willcoxsons' house, Ted teaches Susan, who is fifteen
and embarrassed, how to swing dance, spinning and twirling her until she
is relaxed and laughing. Because he loves ragtime so much, they always put
on the soundtrack from *The Sting*, and the kids sit lined up on the couch,
and Ted conducts with a baton.

There are camping trips, weeklong float trips on the Current or the
Meramec, backpacking trips in Montana, weekends in the Ozarks in a
secluded spot where they have to ring a bell when they reach the river, so
the guy who lives in the little house will come out and row them across.

Another camping trip—this one with their neighbor Jean Y. Smith,
who teaches in the health and physical education department at the
university—is to The Lost 1,400 Acres. The land is rough, grooved
with creeks, hilly, its forest scraggly. The story is that during the Great
Depression, a man from Kansas City bought the place sight unseen. He

traveled here, took one look, went home to Kansas City and committed suicide.

Ted can appreciate a good story, but they all hope this one's hyperbole. The land *is* rough, though. They ride horseback through the woods, set up camp at Cow Creek, grill their dinner, and sleep on the sandbar.

§

Pat's cheerful loathing of the kitchen is by now obvious to everyone.

After a funeral for one of the Jones reps, Ted asks her if people can come back to the farm. "Sure," she says, and once they're home, she starts piling what they have to eat on the counter, assessing the possibilities. Looking at their leftover ham, Ted frowns. "Is this all the ham we have? We'll have to get some more."

"This is all the ham we've got," Patsy replies, "and when it's gone, we're going to stop eating."

Though she hates to cook, she loves to eat healthy food. On a company trip to California, she and Ted meet the Phelans for breakfast in an elegant, sun-drenched hotel restaurant. Pat roots around in her giant purse and pulls out a zip-locked bag of granola.

She will do the same years later, on a trip with Barbara Webb for the fifth anniversary of the Tempe campus. Webb stops by Pat's room so they can go downstairs for breakfast before the celebration. With only a hint of apology, Pat explains that she brought her own and pulls out little bags of granola and maybe chia or flax. As they head to the celebration, Webb mutters to herself, "If I'd known she was going to eat seeds, I would've ordered room service!"

She now has real sympathy for Ted, who is under orders to avoid sweets. When he and John Martin stop on the drive back from Kirksville, Ted buys a cupcake. As they pull up to the farm, he hands John the wrapper: "You better take this. Don't let Patsy see it."

John Borota is just a trainee, first week on the job, when Ted invites him on a road trip to Hays, Kansas. At least three times, they get off the highway, at Ted's suggestion, for a cup of coffee and a sweet roll. When they return to the farm, Pat asks a single question: "Ted, were you eating sweet rolls while you were on the road?"

Eyes as wide as a choir boy's, Ted says, "No, Patsy, not a one." Borota might be young, but he's smart enough to keep his mouth shut.

§

Even when they travel abroad, Pat and Ted pull it off with no muss or fuss. When they go to China, for example, they carry suitcases so narrow they could double as briefcases, and every evening, after walking along the Great Wall or seeing pandas, they squirt some Joy dishwashing soap into the sink and wash their underwear and socks.

Visiting the Great Wall in the 1980s

They travel to Austria. They take a mail boat up through the Aleutian Islands. In 1982, they spend three weeks in England, where Ted hopes to do genealogical research. He starts looking up Joneses and is soon vanquished. "Do you know how many *Joneses* there were?" he will demand of friends when he returns, and they will hide smiles and wonder why he was surprised. For Ted, the highlight of the trip turns out to be an excursion to a port in the North Sea, because he gets to go out on a tugboat.

The year of the England trip, Ted and Pat also spend a solid week whitewater rafting with a few Jones brokers on the Salmon River. Torrents of water rush over the sides of the raft as they are swept through narrow gorges, but Ted stays calm. "Your turn to bail," he teases financial advisor Sherl Prawl every time they get a serious drenching.

Mainly, though, Ted and Patsy like staying home, and they will make any excuse to do so. They turn down a trip to Africa with Ted's sister because it is asparagus season. They turn down an invitation to fly on a supersonic jet because Pat's tomatoes are coming in. Ted turns down a company trip to Africa—the first reward trip to venture so far. AIDS is just becoming known, and he's just read that one out of ten people in Africa have AIDS. He is enough of a hypochondriac to bail. Pat is furious. This is her kind of travel: sleeping in tents, observing animals in the wild, driving through the savanna with its wide, iconic trees…. Years later, she convinces him to go.

Many of the opportunities dangled before the Joneses, though, are less compelling. Once, they beg off because Ted is busy making a master plan for a Japanese garden. Usually, though, he lays the blame on Patsy when he declines. It eventually dawns on their friends and family that he wants to stay home just as much as she does.

Urged to join an elite country club, Ted laughs and shakes his head. "Look, I live on a farm. My wife doesn't play tennis, and I don't play golf. They don't *want* someone like me—I'm not contributing to their revenue flow!" As gregarious as he is, he remains private, with zero interest in fraternizing with wealthy business leaders. Though few see it, he has a thoughtful, introspective side.

The sort of social life he and Patsy like best is riding on horseback to visit the Van Dykes or the Willcoxsons. On chilly evenings, the three couples sit outside drinking warm wine. At some point, Ted will invariably climb up on the picnic table and regale them with song. Pat never stops him. She has heard all her husband's songs, stories, and jokes many times, and she knows he stretches them like taffy, filling in with gesture and emphasis. But she never once rolls her eyes.

She has, as Ted's future successor, John Bachmann, puts it, "the grace and patience which are required to live with a person with the character and the enthusiasms of Ted."

§

Ted is just as patient with Patsy, but he's a little more meddlesome, with all sorts of ideas for her. For some reason, he is determined to get her interested in beekeeping, and he buys her all the accoutrements. After a tactful length of time, she gives away the beekeeping stuff, bestowing it upon a man who sets up hives for farmers in return for jars of honey.

Next, Ted buys her a greenhouse. The first year, she grows enough tomatoes to feed Callaway County. Once she has given away the five hundred tomatoes, she gives away the greenhouse, too. It's too steamy in there. She wants to be *outside*, with her vegetable beds and her bright fields of sunflowers. Inside a greenhouse, she cannot hear her horses whinny, and there is no breeze to ruffle her bangs.

Ted shows up at work with a bunch of tomato plants and walks around the office asking who wants one.

Every Election Day, it is common knowledge that he will leave work early, racing home to cancel Pat's vote. Their politics remain very different, and neither one is budging. When Pat begins to hold forth in front of company, Ted might say, "Patsy, go pick some gooseberries, let's have a gooseberry pie." She will shrug good-naturedly and goes off to pick the gooseberries, but at the next opening in the conversation, she will again hold forth. She is not an easy woman to lead.

Pat's nephew, Truman Young Jr., puzzles over the relationship, especially when he hears Ted say, around other people, "Hey, Patsy, get me a beer." Truman knows his aunt well enough to realize that she is just playing along; that the minute their guests have gone home, she will toss back, "Get your own beer." This, he decides, is "a happy marriage in which Ted only seems to be the boss."

Truman's cousin, Melissa Curry, comes to the same conclusion. Her Uncle Ted is "a blustery kind of guy," she says, and on family visits, everything is done the way he wants it done, which initially raises her hackles. If he puts on jazz records, everybody has to dance. Then Melissa notices that Pat does *not* have to dance. Everybody else gets bullied into it, and Pat lets Ted do his thing and watches serenely, because he knows better than to drag *her* into a jitterbug.

Subtract their political parties, dig a little deeper, and these two care about the same things. They make no attempt to nag, convert, or in any way change each other. If someone asks a question that falls into Pat's bailiwick, Ted steps back to give her the floor. They have always known instinctively—and necessarily, because both are strong-willed—how to give each other freedom. Pat brings Ted back to earth. He makes it possible for her to live exactly as she chooses. They do whatever they can to make life better for each other.

"Ted thinks the world of his Patsy," Jim Zerr knows. He has helped them farm their land for a few years, and he can see it plainly, just by the way Ted talks about her. When somebody at Jones presents Ted with a

T-shirt that says "No. 1," he bursts out laughing. "Well, I'm going to have to fight my wife over this one."

In late middle age, they flee to separate beds to get a good night's sleep. They are frank about their comfort, seeing no need for coy pretense. Their marriage has never struck anyone as soppily romantic, with awkward public displays or a crackling electricity flashing between them. They are far too restrained—Pat too Scottish, Ted too matter-of-fact—for such nonsense. They know the marital glue will hold.

§

Edward D. Jones Sr. dies in 1982. Folded into his wallet is a yellowed, crumbling piece of paper: a bill for his mother's funeral. She died at his birth; he never knew her. But she carried him into life, and he carried this last remnant of her presence with him all the years of his life.

§

Pat's sixtieth birthday falls during hunting season. "Are you coming out?" Ted asks in his ritual call to Doug Hill. "Sure," says Doug. "I've got some steaks for you from Annie Gunn's."

"That's good," Ted says, "because it's Pat's sixtieth birthday."

"What have you got for her?" Doug asks, already dreading the answer. "Have you got a cake or anything?"

No, he does not. Now, he realizes he should have. "Um, Doug, why don't you drive to Columbia and pick up a cake for us?"

So here is Doug, clad in hunting clothes, standing at a bakery counter asking, "Can you write Happy 60th Birthday Pat?" He buys lots of candles.

Just before their outdoor supper, a cold November rain begins to fall. Moving fast, they collapse the cots, kick the sleeping bags out of the way, and shove the picnic table inside the tent. They will be able to grill under its awning. Dinner's fun, everybody loosened by the change of scene. When they have finished their steaks, Ted calmly takes credit, asking, "Hey, Doug, what did you do with my cake?"

The sixty candles nearly burn the tent down, but Pat loves every minute.

§

A year later, in 1986, Hilda Young dies. She has outlived her husband by forty-four years, and she has conserved more than nine hundred acres of Meramec Valley woodland.

Pat, her brother, and her two sisters inherit that land. Pat turns around and hands her one-fourth share of the land to the state of Missouri, making it possible for the Department of Natural Resources to purchase the rest of the vast, pristine parcel her mother assembled. It will be called the Young Conservation Area.

In 1988, Ted and Pat remodel, opening up the house and letting it breathe. Ever practical, they build a small guest house first and move into it while the big house is under siege, consumed in a din of saws and hammers. Ever the historian, Ted has "Edward Jones Sr. bought this land in 1933" chiseled into granite over the wood stove. "Edward Jones Jr. built this house in 1987" is engraved below. And on the other side: "James Callaway Anderson, b. 1792 near Leesville VA, settled this land Dec. 18, 1832."

There are a few squabbles. Ted fancies gold fixtures in the main house's bathroom. Pat...doesn't. They work through these differences, and their home ends up more spacious but still rustic, with a great big fireplace. In the mud room are farm jackets and every kind of boot you might need, lined up like soldiers. A picture of circus elephants catches the eye, then a painting of a prairie sky at night, then one of a cowboy with his dog. There are bursts of color and interest: the Japanese prints and sake jars Ted has collected, Pat's pottery collection, a cool Swedish chair, and the handwoven Southwestern rugs they have bought over the years, letting them get muddy without thought of future value. Best of all, Ted finally has a garage for his beloved car. He shows it off like a ringmaster, grandly sweeping a hand toward its wonders.

He doesn't yet know what a short time he will have to enjoy it.

2 5
——

The Great Katy Fight

On a trip up to Baraboo to visit a Jones office (and, natch, see the circus), Ted rides a bit of Wisconsin's 23-mile Sparta-to-Elroy trail, the nation's first rail trail. What a great idea for Missouri! He met Pat cycling through its scenery. Now, because they live close to the river, they know exactly how the Missouri-Kansas-Texas railroad (K-T for short, then Katy) winds through Missouri. And in recent years, they have watched the little Petticoat Junction towns dry up, businesses closing, people moving away, as the railroads fell out of use.

The idea of converting the Katy to a trail bubbles like a pot of pasta that's about to foam and spill over. Ted can't stop thinking about it. A 1983 amendment to the 1968 National Trails System Act gives states leeway to turn the old railway corridors into trails people can hike or cycle. In 1986, the Missouri River floods so badly that the damage seals the decision: The railroad is pulling out altogether.

Darwin Hindman, a lawyer (and future five-term mayor) in Columbia, Missouri, loves the outdoors and the idea of trails criss-crossing neighborhoods and connecting towns. He forms an all-volunteer coalition to turn the old Katy railway into a trail, and signatures pour in from young cyclists and environmentalists.

Even the president of the railroad likes the idea of a trail, with its echo of Lewis and Clark. The Missouri Department of Natural Resources

Ted, Pat and Darwin Hindman, Ted's wingman in the Katy Trail fight.

knows all about the National Trail Systems Act and would be delighted to create a long, winding trail, meanwhile preserving the land for future railroad use if necessary. But to even begin, the state must apply for a Certificate of Interim Trail Use—and to do that, DNR needs the governor's consent.

The Hindmans used to live in Mexico, Missouri, and they know the Edward Jones broker there, John Minor. When he mentions Ted's interest in bike trails, nature, and Missouri's landscape, Hindman asks for an introduction. He wants to bring somebody with business expertise when he meets with Missouri Governor John Ashcroft on September 4, 1986.

Before Hindman has finished asking, Ted agrees.

They slide about ten thousand signatures across the governor's desk and begin to make arguments for a rails-to-trails conversion in Missouri. Out of the blue, Ted tells the governor that he's so excited about the idea, he will give the state $100,000 for the trail. Hindman looks up sharply. He *will?*

The governor looks impressed. But he is also impressed by the lobbying strength of agricultural interests that have come out against the trail, and he refuses to dismiss the farmers' concerns lightly. Ashcroft knows the Katy is "not just an ordinary set of tracks. It mirrors Lewis and Clark's progress up the Missouri River." That route is part of not only Missouri's heritage but the entire *nation's* heritage. A trail could be "a teaching tool as well as a tourist destination."

But the legislators will have to agree.

Ted gives double what he offered, $200,000, to the Conservation Federation of Missouri to speed the purchase of the right-of-way. But he has a heck of a time persuading the state to accept his gift. The farmers—

the very people he has long admired and emulated—are adamantly opposed. State legislators are therefore nervous.

Instead of getting riled up, Ted just shakes his head and says sadly, "They don't understand yet." He keeps talking, as persuasively as he can.

The opposition mounts. Ted is declared a Communist. Insults fly. This must be the way Theodore Roosevelt felt when opponents to his plan to protect the Grand Canyon called it "a fiendish and diabolical scheme." Like that Teddy, though, Ted is hard to discourage. He warms to the fight.

Around this time, Dan Burkhardt arranges a hunting trip at the farm. Sam Walton and his brother Bud—who cofounded Walmart with him—both love hunting, especially upland and waterfowl. Sam can't make the trip to Ted's farm, so Bud is coming in his stead to hunt quail. He brings his dogs, who leap between the truck bed and cab for the entire drive to Missouri. At dinner, Ted gives a pumped-up talk about starting the Katy Trail. The next morning, as they're getting ready to go hunt, he asks D-Boy Garner what he thought of the talk.

"It was a good speech," D-Boy says grudgingly. What *he* will remember is how well his dog and Ted's little Brittany performed the next day, responding to voice commands when they were forty feet out and impressing the hell out of Bud.

When the weekend's fun is over, Ted returns to the fight, dogged as his spaniel. Harry Willcoxson accompanies him on some of his trips up and down the proposed trail, and they talk to farmers along the way, trying to set their minds at rest. "No, there are not going to be Harleys on the trail." "Yes, this would be a *good* thing for the region."

Ted writes the governor on September 15, 1986: "I stayed at the hearings from 7:30 pm until the last dog was dead at 12:30 am on Thursday morning." He acknowledges valid concerns from the trail's opponents: hunters trespassing, hikers and bikers leaving trash behind. But you don't need a bike trail for that, he adds: "My farm is along State 'D' in eastern Callaway County, 10 miles north of the MKT trail at Portland, Missouri. I have picked up, on one occasion, over 300 beer and soft drink cans on my 1 ½ miles of road frontage."

He assures the governor that state ownership of the trail will alleviate such problems and suggests big signs: FINE FOR HUNTING.

CONFISCATION OF FIREARMS. MOTORIZED VEHICLES
PROHIBITED. "Governor, I know you will be damned if you do and
damned if you don't on this Rails to Trails proposal," Ted continues. "My
gift to the State has no strings attached. I would hope that if the Rails
to Trails does not go through my gift go to the Missouri Conservation
Department."

By now, Ashcroft's children have seen
a "body" hanging from a tree with a sign
around its neck that reads "Governor
Ashcroft." The air is heavy with resentment,
and there are significant arguments on
both sides. But a trail, he feels sure, is in the
public's best interest.

And Ted Jones is a man with "a
capacity to persist."

Town after town after town, Ted talks
himself hoarse. On a piece of hog wire
stretched across the trail, he sees a huge

Signs like this were displayed
along the railroad, expressing the
sentiment of many.

sign: "NO TO ASHCROFT'S ALLEY!" One farmer places a large
wooden gate across the tracks with a child's bicycle tied to it, as though a
bicyclist died trying to get across. Another parks not one but three mobile
homes on the tracks, creating, in Jim Denny's words, "a helluva blockade."

Denny is the first director of the Katy Trail, but as there is no trail yet,
he, too, spends a lot of time driving around with Ted, talking to people
and going to town meetings. People start off madder than the hornets
whose nest Pat crushed. Both Denny and Ted stay easy: "I think your
problem's with those folks in Jeff City, sitting there in their mahogany
playpens," one might say. Counting on Missouri friendliness and civility,
they usually reach a place where they can at least all talk calmly.

Why are the farmers still so upset? They rattle off a litany of worries:
City people will come and get rowdy, steal stuff, make noise, trash the trail,
frighten or maim livestock, pee on the crops. Hindman's group asks the
state legislature to pay for fencing along the trail wherever the landowners
request it. The trail is rerouted to avoid inconveniencing a business. Water
drainage problems are fixed, gratis, by the state parks construction crew.

When the farmers still won't budge, Ted asks someone from the conservation department what the sticking point is.

"They're worried there won't be bathrooms along the route and—"

"How much would it cost to put privies up and down the trail?" Ted asks wearily. The conservation agent hazards a guess.

"Done."

§

John Sam Williamson says all that talk of farmers being scared of petty stuff is deliberate exaggeration. His farm, a large holding in McBaine, has been in his family for six generations. He is not opposed to the idea of a trail; what angers him is the *way* this is being handled.

"We have two miles of the Katy Trail on our farm—it cuts the farm right in half," he says. "And we *own* the land under the trail. The railroad had an easement—my grandfather gave them that right-of-way for a dollar in 1892." The land beneath the tracks was still his grandfather's, Williamson points out, and the easements were to be used for a railroad, no other purpose.

Most of these easements are only fifty feet wide; this is not a debate over land or money. It is a debate over principle.

Williamson thinks about the railroad stretching from McBaine to St. Louis in 1904, and how his grandparents rode a buggy to the train station and took a train for the first time in their lives to see the St. Louis World's Fair. Later, his grandfather had lumber brought in on the railroad to build a tobacco barn, and they used the railroad to ship cattle to market, and his dad helped load wheat onto the train as a teenager. "The railroad was a wonderful thing," Williamson says. "It was an *asset*." Maybe the Katy Trail will be an asset, too. But somebody should have asked the farmers to whom the land reverted when the railroad left. "We were completely ignored as landowners; it's like we weren't even there."

Williamson and Ted talk this through cordially, though neither budges. At least Ted isn't one of the folks accusing the farmers of being scared of urban roustabouts or thieves on bicycle. And he is "just kind of a regular fellow," Williamson tells his wife, smiling over Ted's plain clothes and his way of standing in the back of a meeting, cocking his head, and putting a hand to his ear because he's hard of hearing. Obviously, he's done well with his company; after all, the Williamsons have money invested with a Jones broker in Columbia. But he doesn't seem as…refined…as Williamson would expect from the head of such a big company. He's down to earth.

Finally, it's a point in his favor.

§

The Katy Trail will become a reality "over my dead body!" Sen. Richard Webster thunders.

"That's acceptable," Ted replies.

When he's not talking to farmers, he walks the halls at the state capitol. He and Darwin Hindman tag team, calling on as many legislators as they can and attending meetings in the evenings.

Hindman's wife, Axie, remembers pulling up to one of those meetings and seeing Ted in a ball cap, directing parking. He's all in, enjoying every minute of the fight, throwing every ounce of ability and leverage he can muster toward a cause he believes in. Still, the meetings get so angry, she's afraid they'll turn violent. When Darwin and Ted go on their own, she worries until her husband is safely home.

Ted and Pat at an event to support creation of the trail in 1988

Pat doesn't worry. She knows Ted's tenacity, and even though he's short and middle-aged, she can't imagine anyone overpowering him. If he wants this trail to happen, it will.

By now, the Katy Trail controversy is dominating Missouri headlines. An editorial in the *St. Louis Post-Dispatch* reminds readers that "if things go as planned, St. Louisans could park near the old Katy tracks at St. Charles, mount their bicycles and pedal to Sedalia on the western side of the state…. Right now this is only a dream, several years from completion. Much must be done before Missourians can have one of the finest hiking and biking trails in the country."

And the first thing that must be done has a deadline rapidly approaching. The state legislature holds the fate of the trail in its hands. If they do not appropriate enough funds in their 1987 budget, the trail will be dead. The Interstate Commerce Commission is going to issue a certificate of abandonment, and the state will have only six months to reach an agreement with the railroad, so by the next legislative session, it will be too late.

Sen. Jay Nixon, future governor of Missouri and a Boy Scout of a guy, athletic and outdoorsy, pushes his colleagues as hard as he can toward the trail.

The budget appropriation is approved, winning by a single vote, after midnight, on the last day of the session.

§

The legislative win is not a clear and definitive victory. The year before, two hundred landowners filed suit in the Montgomery County circuit court, saying this was an unconstitutional "taking" of their property and therefore illegal under the Fifth Amendment. The suit has been transferred to federal court and assigned to a judge. So now everybody has to freeze in place—like a giant game of statues—until the judge hands down a verdict.

The judge affirms the constitutionality of the Rails to Trails Act—but does not address the way in which the land was taken. The landowners appeal the decision and lose again. They decide to take their case all the way to the U.S. Supreme Court. After holding fish fries and barbecues to raise the money, they find themselves an attorney who has been admitted to the U.S. Supreme Court bar and can argue their case.

Meanwhile, as soon as the appellate court supports the original ruling, Ted stuns many of the trail's opponents into silence by donating $2 million to build the trail.

He leads up to the decision with his usual flair. Legislators have scheduled a meeting, open to the public, to discuss the proposed trail. An inside source tells Ted they plan to invite him and tell him he's a great guy, then apologize that the state doesn't have any money, so this trail just can't happen.

Ted picks up the phone, calls everyone he knows in the area, and asks them to attend.

The meeting opens. The legislators begin to compliment Ted, telling him what a great conservationist he is and what a shame it is that they can't take this land. Ted then goes around the room, asking each legislator in turn, by name, "If you had the money, would you take the land?" Each one answers with assurance, "Well of course I would, if we had the money." Ted's witnesses are in place, listening. He pauses for effect. "Okay," he says. "You have the money."

He gives the $2 million to the Conservation Federation of Missouri, which will distribute the funds as needed, preserving a flexibility that would be lost if the state held the funds.

All the wrangling over details and logistics…stops.

"I wish we had somebody like Ted Jones on *our* side," Williamson grumbles to the *St. Louis Post-Dispatch*.

The Missouri case has reached the nation's highest court, as have several other states' rails-to-trails battles. The justices say they will hear only one, selecting a case from Vermont that is very similar to Missouri's.

The Williamsons and several other farmers fly to DC to hear the case argued in a big, echoey courtroom. All those in the gallery are admonished to remain silent. The justices walk in, and Williamson notices that each one has someone behind them to hold their chair and slide it in once they have arranged their robes. Some of them are quite elderly. A green light on the podium means the attorney can continue speaking; yellow warns him that he has one more minute; red means stop right now, no matter what. The justices can interrupt at any point, so the attorney has to be on his toes.

Once again, the Rails to Trails project is ruled constitutional—the vote is unanimous. But this time, several justices issue a concurring opinion that the landowners are entitled to compensation. The tone is "like they're stomping their feet," Williamson thinks, a little miffed. Later, he will explain, "We weren't necessarily *wanting* compensation." The possibility had been mentioned already, but the farmers were fighting for principle.

Now, though, the justices are saying "we should have gone to the U.S. Court of Claims already."

When they do so, they find that to determine compensation, each tract of land must be appraised—yet another delay.

The final Supreme Court ruling comes down in February 1990. Ted rushes home with two bottles of wine. ("He doesn't even drink wine," Pat will chuckle later.) The governor gives his consent to build two pilot projects, and the state parks staffers jolt into action, gearing up the construction crew and pushing hard to get two pilot sections of the trail done by spring.

DNR sends Ted regular reports. The 156-foot Rocheport Bridge cost $23,000. Materials used for the first five miles of the trail: 8,440 tons of aggregate. The crushed limestone will fill in the tracks, packed hard so it's a smooth, flat surface for both hikers and cyclists.

Because these are railroad towns, they are set about ten miles apart, which is perfect, an hour's bike ride. One day there will be twenty-eight trailheads, with parking spaces at each. Businesses in the little towns will be able to serve food and drink, rent out bikes, sell gifts.

In two months, a chunk of railway is turned into the beginning of the Katy Trail.

§

The Katy, Pat decides, has been the hardest Ted has ever fought for anything. She never had any doubt that he would get it done. But it stings a little that he poured so much of himself into the fight—because they now know it will be his last. At one of his regular check-ups in Kansas City, the doctor has confirmed his suspicions: The cancer is back.

Ted does not make a big deal of the diagnosis and will not

Ted along a stretch of trail, newly converted from the railbed

let Pat make a big deal of it, either. She studies a newspaper photo: Ted coming down the capitol steps, reporters with their mics thrust toward his face, people behind him holding signs like "I want to open a Bed & Breakfast on the Trail in Rocheport" and "Southern Boone county Votes for the Katy Trail!" He's clad in a navy blazer with a touch of his dad, a white pocket hankie, and under the jacket, a checked shirt open at the neck. He is sick by now, but the ruddy complexion belies it. Head tilted down toward the mic closest to him, he prepares to speak his mind.

He would not have changed a thing, she realizes, not even if he'd known all along that he was dying.

On April 16, 1990, a meeting about the Katy is held at the farm. Ted wants to surface the original two hundred miles of the trail, then acquire a section from Sedalia to Windsor and surface that, then surface the section from Windsor to Pleasant Hill, then acquire a Rock Island section from St. Albans to Windsor and leave it as primitive trail.

By summer 1990, the Katy Trail's first nine-mile stretch, between Rocheport and McBaine, is drawing a hundred people every weekend day.

§

Ted pulls back from the wind, snuggling deeper into the soft hood of his blue sweatshirt. A green jacket that looks like it might be Pat's is buttoned over the hoodie for extra warmth. Every few minutes he coughs—the kind of cough that is half stifled and clearly painful. When he is introduced and the crowd applauds, he barely stands, using both hands to wave down the applause and sitting again quickly. Watching, friends in the crowd feel their hearts tighten and wonder if he will make it through the dedication ceremony. But then Darwin Hindman begins the story of how Ted built his business, and the old spark lights in Ted's eyes. He listens intently, and when Hindman moves to his fight for the Katy Trail, all the hard work and original thinking "and lots of money, by the way," he laughs hard, and the pall of illness dissolves.

Called to the mic, he rises easily and strides in his quick, purposeful way, body leaning forward as though forging a headwind. The award is a Spike Man, spikes from the Katy railroad welded into a heroic little man by an artist from Columbia, Missouri. Spike Man was the theme for the first Katy fun festival, and Ted remembers it well—he helped park cars there, too. He accepts the award and fake-drops it, joking because it is heavy.

"I also want to recognize Pat Jones," the speaker continues. "Where is Pat? Stand up, Pat! Pat, where are you?" Ted has spotted his wife and is gesturing encouragement, circling his finger to direct her up to the mic. She ignores him.

He sighs and takes the mic. "I particularly want my wife to come up. You said earlier I was sitting next to my wife, and I'm not married to Mrs. Ashcroft, and I want to get things straight before I get in trouble!"

Pat grins and, rather than come onstage, walks over to take the seat next to Ted's empty one. But when they present the real prize—two bikes, both cobalt blue, water bottles fastened to the frame—she does walk up to the stage, and through the speakers, people hear her murmur a delighted, "Oh, *my!*"

As soon as Ted reclaims the mic, though, she is off the stage like a shot.

Ted brings up four Boy Scouts, introducing them as his friends. While they stand there, tickled but shy, he dives straight into his prepared remarks. This, he reminds the crowd, "is the longest continuous 200-mile hiking and bicycling trail" in the nation, and it's in Missouri. "Now, you know, Texas is first in goats. They have got more goats than any state. California is first in the Mediterranean fruit fly. We're first in the trail, and we're gonna be first in a lot of other things, and education's the most important."

The last presentation to Ted is pure mischief: "Since you aren't known for tooting your own horn, here's a horn to go with your new bicycle." Ow-WOO-gah! Ted accepts the horn with appropriate solemnity and then, in classic married-guy style, promptly hands it to Pat. Laughing, she tucks it into her capacious purse. There is another pained cough from Ted, a wide smile pasted on fast to cover it. When they introduce Governor John Ashcroft, though, Ted shoots to his feet like a fit twenty-year-old.

Ashcroft speaks of his dream to make sure every Missourian can reach their fullest potential, saying, "This trail is part of that effort." He describes the towering limestone bluffs on one side of this first five-mile stretch, the pictographs carved into their surface, the Missouri River flowing along the other side of the trail. Then he quotes *Lonesome Dove*: "All America lies at the end of the wilderness road, and our past is not a dead past but still lives in us. Our forefathers had civilization inside themselves and the wild on the outside. We live in the civilization they created, but within us, the wilderness lingers. And what they dreamed, we live, and what they lived, we dream."

Now, he finishes, Missourians will be able to live the past dreams of the pioneers who walked this trail. Hikers and cyclists will see the sights that greeted Lewis and Clark.

That was long before the steel tracks were laid, before the trains screeched to a halt, before Ted Jones shamed and cajoled Missourians into restoring the trail—and the spirit of exploration. Ashcroft slips a ribbon around Ted's neck, weighted by "the first medallion ever struck to honor those who, through their efforts, preserve the natural beauty and history and heritage of the State of Missouri."

Ted Jones has just received the first Governor's Award for Distinguished Resource Stewardship, acknowledging his willingness to care for "things that don't belong only to us," Ashcroft tells the crowd. "The environment is something that we borrow from our children."

And the trail is a legacy.

As Pat once told a friend, "We didn't have any kids, so we decided to adopt the State of Missouri."

§

After the dedication, the governor asks Ted if he can stay a little longer. Doug Hill offers to give Ted a ride back to the house so Pat can go on back and start the celebration. So Hill is standing there listening when the governor approaches and profusely apologizes to Ted for all he had to go through to get the Katy Trail built.

On the drive back, Hill is still incredulous. "I can't believe I witnessed this with my own eyes," he says. "That's one of the nicest things I can envision any governor doing."

"Yeah," Ted agrees, "it *was* kind of nice." They reach the farm, and Doug can hear the ragtime music floating from the back yard. Instead of heading straight back to the party, though, Ted grabs Hill's arm. "Doug, stop. Doug! Look at those bikes!"

Hill stands on the side porch, staring at the new blue bikes.

"You're not looking hard enough," Ted says. "Look harder."

Finally Hill exclaims, "Ted, what am I *looking* for?"

"Those," says Ted, "are the most expensive bikes you're ever going to see."

Ted, with his newly awarded medal, and Pat at the opening of the trail

26

——

The Cancer's Return

"I want to leave you something," Ted says again, pestering his lifelong friend.

Willcoxson, still a string bean, well over six feet tall and lean, bends close. In a husky voice, he tells the Dutchman not to worry about it.

"No, really, I want to do this," Ted insists, making a production out of it. His eyes twinkle as he builds to the climax. Finally he announces, as grandly as he can between coughs, "Harry, I'm leaving you my wardrobe."

§

After he beat melanoma in the Seventies, Ted was healthy for almost two decades. Now the cancer is back and moving at light speed, shooting through his lymph system to his lungs. With a cold chill, friends remember the back pain he's been mentioning, and how he's always looking for a good chiropractor.

"I never smoked. You tell them," Ted urges Jack Phelan. "You make sure that you tell everybody I never smoked." It's a point of pride: He has done nothing to cause the early death that is now inevitable.

Ted considers himself Christian, though he's quick to point out that "most of the wars of the world have been the result of organized religion." His secretary, Betty Meyer, can tell he also hates the way religions become big businesses "and take money from poor people and tell them they will go to heaven if they give more." Yet she has heard him quote phrases from an Egyptian tomb—"something about Thebes"—with unmistakable reverence. "He knows his own God his own way," she realizes.

There's a goodness about Ted, the sort that people associate with devout faith, and he has a fierce sense of right and wrong. Stricter than most, his moral code hinges on neither the hope of heaven nor the fear of hell. My religion, he once told Jack, is "looking across beautiful fields, taking walks in the countryside, and knowing there had to be an almighty creator." Intricacies of dogma do not interest him.

Pat has no interest in formal religion either; hardly anyone in her family did. Once her grandfather suggested they go to church and she looked up, startled. Turned out he had designed the building and wanted to check on the sound.

And so, without formal religion to cling to, Ted and Pat take the news the way they take most things: with a practical stoicism.

Ted jokes to keep everybody *else* from feeling sad. "Based on your credit rating and my health," he teases during a negotiation, "this will have to be a cash-only deal. No checks." He grumbles to Bill Hauk that he's not going to live long enough to collect Social Security; he'll be dead right at sixty-five.

Ted has *never* made heavy weather of any disappointment, struggle, or hardship, his friends realize now. "He just accepted life as it was," says Bill Broderick. "He kept the hard things to himself."

After lunch at Marlene's with Bob Ciapciak and a few other guys, he says, "You know, fellas, everybody wants to get to heaven, but nobody wants to take the first train." *He loves life*, Ciapciak thinks sadly. *He loves people. He is in no hurry to give it up. But he's accepting it.*

§

When the time comes for the annual partners meeting, Ted gives his final address. He has the famous boxing gloves with him, and he tosses them out to the audience. "People ask me what I will miss the most," he says. He has to stop to cough, but his voice is firm and clear. "What I will miss the most are the fights."

In the audience, Jim McKenzie cringes. Shouldn't he mention his wife, or his loyal colleagues, or the farm? The whole room has gone quiet. But as the startle fades and people start to grin, Jim thinks back on all those fights—all the times Ted protested unfair practices, fighting regulations that put Jones, the underdog who operated by altogether different rules, at a disadvantage. All the way along, he has fought stubborn opponents who were resisting change, from his father opposing Ted's version of expansion to the farmers opposing the Katy Trail. He's saying "Stand up for what you believe."

Next comes the follow-up question: "What do you want us to remember you for?"

Disingenuous, Ted acts surprised, though he has been thinking about his legacy for months now. "That's a good question," he says, pacing the stage. Then he brightens. "Geez, if I could be remembered for just one thing? I guess I'd like to be remembered as the most successful communist in the country."

The silence lasts longer, broken by a few murmurs: *"Did he just say 'communist'?"* The guy who asked the question summons the nerve to say, "You're going to have to help us with that one. Here we are, squarely in the middle of the free enterprise system…."

"Well, think about it," Ted says. "What does pure communism stand for? Pure communism suggests that the people who create the value that is the organization should own the value that they create. The Communists had it right. They just executed the people instead of the plan."

The laughter starts out nervous, then builds.

Later, after Ted's death, John Beuerlein will ask Pat if it bothered her that he said what he'd miss most were "the fights," instead of her or the farm, the horses, the firm.

"Not at all," she will say calmly. "That's who Ted was. He was the kind of guy who could see things as they were, yet have the vision to see how they might be in a more perfect world—and the courage to try to close the gap." Then she will grin. "And if it involved a fight, all the better!"

§

Soon Ted cannot manage trips to the office. He settles in at home on the farm. When Bud Morgan calls from his Jones office and asks Ted what he's doing, Ted says, "Well, I'm sitting here on the porch swing just swingin'.

I've got this phone without a cord…." Still that sense of wonder and enthusiasm, canceling self-pity.

So many Jones associates want to see him, talk with him, listen to him, say goodbye if they can bear it—that a schedule is needed so they can sign up to come two and three at a time, not have twelve people descend upon the farm at once.

When Jean Burnett visits, Ted calls out, "Hey, Patsy, are you cooking us anything to eat? Are we going to get anything to eat around here?" Not once does he mention his illness. They talk about everything else under the sun.

Bob Gregory is nervous to go. He has never felt nervous talking to Ted before, but now he is dying, right in front of everyone. Ted spots the shyness right away. "Feel my arm," he tells Bob, holding it up. "Feel these bumps!" The cancer has spread all over his body. Touching it, talking about it, closes that awkward distance. Ted turns the conversation toward Gregory's life, refusing to let him get down.

On another visit (they have gotten easier) Ted asks a favor, his expression as serious as a man asking to borrow money: "You know, next time you pull in, I'd appreciate it if you'd kind of toot the horn. You know, you might catch Patsy and me in the sack."

When Barb Gilman, one of the company's first female financial advisors, comes to see Ted, they take a walk around the farm's circular driveway, her arm tucked through his.

Gilman tells Ted they have an idea: The communications team is going to set up a video camera in the guesthouse, and if Ted can't sleep or he has a minute free, he can spontaneously record his memories and thoughts.

"Nope."

"What do you mean *nope*?" she says. "It wasn't a true-false question! You can't take all this history to the grave with you. That's just not fair."

Ted has always known how to bait somebody; she has laughed about it herself. "He'll get you strung out on a string and then cut it. I swear it's his hobby." He does the same thing this time, waiting just long enough that Gilman is ready to strangle him. And then he says, "I'll do it on one condition. You come out and ask me questions."

"*Fine,*" she says. "Why didn't you just say so?"

They make quite a few tapes this way. One day Gilman drives with him to the duck blind, so they can take some video footage there. Ted gives her one of his straw hats—nobody else is gonna get melanoma if he can help it—and they sit by the river and talk.

She finds herself grateful the Katy Trail was such a battle; she's convinced it kept Ted alive longer. "Trail's done," he announces on one visit, his tone satisfied.

"No, it isn't," she tries to protest, buying time. But the hurdles had been crossed, and they both know it.

Later, she is inside the farmhouse when the phone rings. Nobody else is near, so she answers—and it's Sam Walton. Ted wrote to tell him about the cancer. Now Sam is calling to tell Ted that he has cancer, too.

§

At another videotaping session, they are waiting to resume, and Ted, coughing and clearly in pain, asks Steve Clement, head of video production for the firm, where he grew up. When Clement says he was a military brat, Ted's face lights up, and he begins to talk about all the places he was stationed in Japan during the Occupation, about "big palaces, beautiful castles," and the former Japanese cavalry camp barracks where they used the stables as a motor pool, and the time they "loaded the whole outfit on freight cars" and traveled across the country.

The phone rings. "City jail," Ted answers cheerfully.

In his healthy years, he was full of schtick, and while the jaded might roll their eyes, he was so genuinely amused that the fun was contagious. His jokes and stories could have seemed trivial, little bursts of showmanship to break the monotony and make a message stick. But now? When you are dying, and your body is weak and in pain, and you are still cracking jokes and telling funny stories, it is not trivial. It is a stance toward life, a brave and selfless generosity that wants to relax people into shared laughter, not trade misery for pity.

When Tim Rupp phones from his Jones office in Rolla, he and Ted talk more than twenty minutes, Ted stopping periodically to cough and Rupp fights back tears as he realizes how sick his mentor is. Ted does not go into detail. "How are things going for you, Tim?" he asks, with such genuine interest that Tim finds himself opening up about his own concerns.

"You've got the ability," Ted assures him, and when they hang up, Rupp is feeling confident again, pumped up—until it hits him, what Ted has done. He has turned a sympathy call into yet another way to get a young broker back on track.

Graham Holloway, a top executive with American Funds, flies in to see Ted one last time. "Ted, where are we going to eat?" he asks, keeping things upbeat.

"We are going to go up to Kingdom City to the McDonalds," Ted replies without hesitation, "and we are going to have a cheeseburger. My doctor told me not to eat so many cheeseburgers, but from here on I'm going to eat all I can!"

Jim Hamilton, a senior vice president with the Federated Securities Corporation, wants to meet Ted before he dies. Barb Gilman drives him out to the farm. "Ten minutes after hello," she will recall, "Ted handed him paper and pencil and said, 'Now, I've got $7 million here. How should we set this up for Patsy?'"

Moving away to let them speak in private, Gilman chats with Pat, and when she hears *her* coughing, teases that it is sympathy. Pat just smiles. Months later—after Ted is gone—she will have a benign tumor removed from her lung. She is not about to bother while Ted is so sick.

Watching the two of them, Gilman thinks about how tightly their lives have been braided, how they have been friends to the core. Ted has made it possible for Pat to live the simple, earthy life she dreamed of, doing just about everything she wants to do and hardly anything she does not want to do. A line in Toni Morrison's *Beloved* captures Pat's gift to Ted: "She is a friend of my mind. She gather me, man. The pieces I am, she gather them and give them back to me in all the right order."

§

Dave Heald, from Putnam, flies from New England to spend some time with Ted. As usual, he brings lobster and fish. Knowing Pat's culinary disaffection, he will broil the fish himself. First, he makes lobster bisque and popovers—but he can't work their new oven, so the popovers are flat. "That's good!" Ted says, sinking his teeth into the dense, unpopped popover. "I'll have another."

Later, sitting by the fire, they have a drink. And what does Ted talk about? His reps. "Dave, you better make sure our guys get out and make their calls, or they're not going to make any money," he frets. "*They have to make the calls.*"

§

Jim McKenzie remembers a letter Ted wrote after his first bout with cancer, thanking everyone who wished him well: "My health seems to have improved, at least I don't have the very bad cough that I had. I have had ten radiation treatments to my chest. They are painless and take about ten minutes. My last treatment was around December 15. The doctor looks me over once a month with X-ray. While there is no cure, my form of melanoma, which has moved to my chest, seems to be on hold. Those who know me, know I have never smoked or even chewed." And then he segues into his famous Body Buyer story:

Calling on a customer who ran a funeral home in Centralia, Illinois, Ted mentioned that he needed a good strong box to hold oats for his horses. The guy said he had just the thing, an Army body-shipping box left over from World War II. Ted stowed it in the back of his Ford station wagon, leaving the tailgate down. Then he called on another customer, a doctor who presented him with a round cardboard box, hatbox-size, wearily explaining that his patients had given him not one, not two, but twelve fruitcakes. Ted thanked him and went to an investment club meeting. When he emerged, the car was ice cold, an arctic wind rushing through the open back, and the engine would not start.

The garage mechanic saw the body box and asked if Ted was an undertaker. Nope, Ted said, and they chatted a while, until the guy couldn't stand it any longer. "If you're not an undertaker, what are you doing with a body?" That gleam came into Ted's eyes. "I am a body buyer," he announced, and then he leaned close and gave a few gory details about how the poor guy was hit by a train. Ted jerked his thumb toward the round box in the front seat, then nodded toward the box in back. "Decapitated."

By now the guys in the shop had all gathered around to listen, jaws hanging open. Ted drove away laughing so hard, tears streamed from his eyes.

It seems an odd story to append. But Jim sees exactly what Ted is doing. After giving a few frank details in an upbeat way, he "then diverts away from himself and tells the body buyer story to make you happy. Instead of saying, 'Woe is me,' he injects humor into other people's lives. And what's in there, too, is Ted telling you what he did in a day as a financial advisor"—multiple client calls, conversations, meetings.

Goofy stories are his favorite way to teach.

§

The original plan was for Ted to eventually move from home to someplace where he would have round-the-clock nursing care, so he didn't burden Patsy. The cancer moves too fast. "He's not going *anywhere*," his doctor says firmly—except to the hospital. He will spend his last few months there, away from his beloved farm.

"Can he leave, can I take him out for a ride?" one of the partners, Roger Thomas, asks.

"He might die in your car," the doctor says, "but if he wants to go, get him out of here."

So they roll Ted's wheelchair out to the parking lot and lift him into the truck, Ted still wearing his hospital gown with the back flaps open. His IV goes in the bed of the truck, the tube threaded through to the front. Ted wants to go to the Katy Trail. They drive to the trailhead, park, and sit there a long time, watching people go by. Oblivious to their audience, the cyclists and walkers are chatting and laughing, the usual stresses smoothed from their faces. If somebody happens to glance up at the men in the truck, Ted calls out, asks if they are enjoying themselves. They so clearly are.

Soon Ted is too weak for such jaunts. But when Doug Hill and his wife come to the hospital to visit, Ted climbs out of bed, and the three walk the hall together, Ted joking as usual.

"It's so nice to see you in such great spirits," Vicki Hill says.

"Oh, I feel good," Ted tells her. "I'm going to die, and I know I'm going to die, but right now, I feel good. You folks are here, and I can't tell you how much I appreciate you coming here to see me."

Jim Zerr, who worked with Ted on the North Callaway fire station and helped him farm, visits too. Ted is sitting up in bed, and they talk a bit, just chatting about the weather and the land. When Ted says, "Jim, I've gotta lie down," it hits hard. All Jim can think of is Ted, ruddy-cheeked and strong, belting out "Shine On Harvest Moon" at one of their parties. This just isn't right.

Rodger Riney hears the news and drives to the hospital in Columbia to see Ted one last time. More than twenty years later, he will still tear up, his voice breaking, when he thinks back to this last visit. Ted is in bed, though, pale against the sheets, barely able to talk. He tries to lift his hand for emphasis, and it takes all his effort and energy just to lift it a few inches. "Rodger," he says with effort, "keep your overhead down."

A few weeks later, word goes out that Ted does not want visitors now; he wants people to remember him the way he was. But a few old friends still show up, like D-Boy Garner, who has been shoeing the Joneses' horses for years. D-Boy visits about two days before Ted dies and finds him slowed way down, yet still talkative. Taking care not to overtire him, D-Boy rises to leave. Ted says, "You promise me one thing. Will you take care of Patsy?"

Ted asks for Betty Meyer, and she rushes to the hospital. His liver is failing, and his skin is a bright saffron color. She kisses his forehead lightly, just as she kissed her father's when he was dying, and Ted, looking over at Pat, teases, "That's the first kiss I've ever gotten from Betty!"

When Pat is out of earshot, Ted tells Betty, "I'm going to give you some extra money. I want you to take care of Pat after I'm gone."

§

Ted dies on October 3, 1990, just eight years after his father's death. The news is broadcast and headlined across the nation. "The man credited with the success of Edward D. Jones & Co. is dead," a Channel Five anchor announces solemnly. Channel Two takes a different angle: "Conservationists and outdoor enthusiasts are mourning the death today of Edward Jones."

All Edward Jones offices are closed that Friday. The flags outside the Edward Jones headquarters are flown at half mast for the rest of the month.

Ted has arranged to give his body to the University of Kansas medical center. He wants no marker, no commemoration. But he has planned every detail of his memorial service, calling Betty Meyer to tell her he wants tuna salad and chicken salad and a Dixieland jazz band, and he doesn't want anyone to be sad. The service must be held at the farm. A poem must be read aloud: "The Galley Slave" by Rudyard Kipling.

The poem spills over with a man's love of a ship and his shipmates: "*It was merry in the galley, for we revelled now and then—/If they wore us down like cattle, faith, we fought and loved like men!*" That steady drumbeat continues to the climax: "*But to-day I leave the galley and another takes my place;/ There's my name upon the deck-beam—let it stand a little space.*" And then comes the end:

It may be that Fate will give me life and leave to row once more—
Set some strong man free for fighting as I take awhile his oar.
But to-day I leave the galley. Shall I curse her service then?
God be thanked! Whate'er comes after, I have lived and toiled with Men!

A minister speaks, more because he was a friend of Ted's than to invoke a specific deity. Columbia's five-term mayor, Darwin Hindman, also speaks, because he knows better than anyone what Ted did to make the Katy Trail happen.

The memorial celebration is small on purpose; had notice gone out publicly, the crowd would have been ten times as large. Only a handful of people from the firm are included, alongside neighbors and friends—Ted's usual mix of business executives and blacksmiths, teachers and farmers. Nobody feels up to a sing-along, but they share stories and laugh, just as Ted hoped, and there is music of course, Dixieland jazz and ragtime.

The only thing better would've been an elephant.

§

Years pass before anyone can bring themselves to clean out Ted's office.

The company culture remains intact far longer.

In 2001, a front-page article in *The Wall Street Journal* is headlined "For Edward D. Jones, Avoiding the Internet Is a Secret to Success: Folksy Stock Firm Skipped E-Trading and Dot-Coms; It's Looking Into E-Mail; Handwritten Notes to Clients." (Although Ted might have quibbled over the postage cost of those notes.) Under John Bachmann's leadership, the company manages to avoid the perils of online trading and the inevitable pop of the dot-com bubble.

"Jones's culture is key to its success," Harvard business professor

Michael Porter tells the *Journal*. "It is a case study of a business that doesn't try to be all things to all people." Nor does it get carried away by greed or false promises. In the midst of the exuberant internet stock craze, the reporter found the Jones management team in Alaska, meeting for five days in a windowless basement room at a Best Western.

John Hess says he learned "that integrity is the only important thing in your life, and if you lose your integrity, you're pretty much out of business." He has drummed the same message into his children.

"Put your family first and be honest" is what Bill Christensen can still hear Ted saying. That emphasis on family was what led Jim Goodknight to the Goodknight Plan, a way to ease off a hyperbusy schedule and concentrate on what matters most. "Ted taught us all to have balance in our lives," he says. "You can't work twelve, fifteen hours every day and make the job the only important thing in your life. It's awfully easy to just work. But you do it at the expense of your family and your community."

People who remember Ted still marvel at how different he really was. The way he would stop and give you his time. How genuine his affection felt. He liked to say he was "a farmer who had to take a job off the farm to make ends meet." He happened to be the head of a brokerage firm, but he didn't define himself by Edward Jones.

And yet.

§

The year before Ted died, Edward D. Jones & Co. outperformed Merrill Lynch by 33 percent and A.G. Edwards by 31 percent.

That same year, *Fortune* published an article about Edward D. Jones & Co. that would have tickled both him and his friend Sam: the headline was "The Walmart of Wall Street." The subject was the firm's exponential growth.

By the time Ted stepped aside, a company with a single, traditional office had expanded to 300 branch offices in small towns across the country. By 2020, the firm had more than 15,000 branch offices and nearly 20,000 advisors.

27
———

Going on Alone

D-Boy Garner notices that Pat is quieter after Ted's death, a little hesitant to speak. But she is still Pat, not a mournful ghost. Her expression remains calm, her conversation far-ranging. She does not weep in public; she will not ask others to bear, even for a minute, her loss.

She stops lighting the big, crackling fire in the living room and contents herself with the potbellied wood stove. Susan Willcoxson suspects the big fireplace reminds her too much of Ted. Even that, Pat will not admit. The height of her demonstrative grief? Her stark and simple answer when Betty Meyer asks how she is: "I really miss him."

The firm commissions an oil portrait of Ted, and it is presented to Pat at a company event. When she goes home that evening, she immediately removes a painting from the wall and lifts the portrait of Ted to hang in its place. "Now you are here," she says, "and you can watch and see everything."

§

As her life unbraids from Ted's, Pat comes into her own. He was a force of nature, and for forty years, she gladly stepped back, letting that energy accelerate unchecked. Much as she loved sports, there was nothing competitive in the way Pat Jones loved.

But now, she steps forward.

First, she decides she might as well have some fun. She treats herself
to a cross-country train ride, America's version of the Orient Express. She
takes her sister-in-law on a boat trip in the Amazon. When she is ready to
settle again, she puts in another pond—in a spot where Ted never wanted
one. He liked a close-mowed lawn; she lets it grow a little, leaving it "long
around the ears" so the wavy blades provide habitat for her precious bugs.

Many of Ted's habits, though, are now hers. When there is a Jones
night at the circus, she invites David Crane to bring his kids, insisting,
"They need to see this." The Cranes find themselves seated with Pat in
the front row, and after the circus, she takes them backstage to meet all the
performers.

One of Pat's first projects is to write a check fat enough to win her
a place on the board of directors at William Woods College. It's an all-
female college, and the women on the board generally have afternoon tea
at their meetings—tiny sandwiches, delicate pastries, fragrant milky tea….

Pat shows up dressed—well, like Pat. "What's on the agenda?" she
asks. "Let's get to work!"

One of the other women has a friend whose husband works at Edward
D. Jones. "Is Pat Jones kind of eccentric?" she asks, describing the initial
encounter. "We weren't quite prepared for that!"

The Jones company remains part of the farm, encouraged to bring
associates out just as often. Pat feels responsible for keeping that relationship
strong. Every spring and fall, groups come once a week, and she gives a little
talk, answering questions about the farm or Ted or life in general. After a
catered lunch, people go for a walk around the pond, then each guest takes
a turn with a shovel and plants a tree, watering it in and mulching it over.
Sometimes it's a bit comical, when a female associate has shown up in high
heels or the ground is too hard for the most swaggering volunteer to break.
But it always ends with a satisfied group picture, everybody standing with
Pat in front of the tree. White oak, Kentucky coffee tree, bur oak, dogwood,
ironwood, redbud, bald Cypress… the diversity increases every year.

Various partners take turns "interviewing" Pat. Jim McKenzie comes
often. "What's the attraction of living on a farm?" he asks to start her off.
"There are trees all over the place, but you call this a farm," he teases.
"What's the story there?"

Sitting under shade trees on a warm spring day, listening to Pat's lively answers, Jim can't think of anywhere he'd rather be. After one session, she points out an oak tree and reminds him that he threw his jacket over the top of that tree when it was waist high. She remembers more than most people, even the tiny details that mean more to someone else than they possibly could to her.

When he speaks to Jones groups around the country, he's often asked, "Did Ted and Pat have any children?" He has a ready answer: "Some would say Ted and Pat did not have any children. Some would say they had more than three thousand." One day it occurs to him that maybe he's taking a liberty; maybe Pat would rather he answered differently? Suddenly nervous, he tells her what he's been saying.

She nods, pleased. That's exactly right. First, the whole company, and then, the whole state.

§

One golden September afternoon, a group of branch office administrators comes out to the farm. Away from the usual blur of ringing phones and urgent paperwork, they climb onto horse-drawn wagons, roll past the prairie's red-tinged bluestem and blue-violet asters. Back at the house, a big white tent is set up outside, and a trio strums, fiddles, and plucks country tunes. The guests, here to be thanked for their ceaseless contributions, pose for pictures outside, where bales of hay are trimmed with gourds and mums, pumpkins lolling at the base. Then they make their way through a long buffet line, grabbing cornbread muffins, salad, fruit, barbecue, baked beans, and maybe a beer.

The day is crisp, and Pat has layered a yellow button-down over a green Edward Jones shirt over a red shirt. After dinner, she takes the mic and tells stories to the people who keep the firm running. Some stay seated, others sit on hard ground, as Pat might have a few years earlier. When the panel talk is over, the guests rush toward Pat, eager to chat, shake her hand, take her picture. One woman scoops up Gunner so he won't feel left out, and he poses, princely, for his own photo, staring into the camera as two people scratch beneath his chin.

§

Jones continues to include Pat in its life, too. When the company decides to streamline the office signs, losing the initial "D.," the "& Co.," and the logo, one of the partners makes a presentation to Pat, showing mockups of the proposed sign.

Pat studies the mockups, not saying a word. Finally Doug Hill says, "Well, Pat, what do you think?"

"I don't care about the 'Co.,'" she says. "I don't care about the 'D.' Matter of fact, I don't care about the whole name—you could make it 'Doug Hill.' But do you have to take the logo off? Every time I go into a town, I know there's an office because I can spot that logo."

They go ahead with their signs, as she figured they would. The logo just takes up too much space. Still, including her was a matter of respect—a continuation of the culture Edward and Ted Jones instilled.

For the five-year anniversary of the Tempe campus, the firm flies her out to Arizona and reserves a seat for her onstage. Barbara Webb clutches when she notices that Pat's skirt doesn't quite cover her knee-high nylons. Then she relaxes: Pat won't care.

Jim Weddle, now the managing partner, asks if anyone has questions for Pat. A young broker stands. "Mrs. Jones, do you see any similarities between Ted and Mr. Weddle?"

Seated next to Weddle, Pat turns and eyes him head to toe. "No," she says, "Jim is quite dapper, and Ted wasn't." Pat Jones may not play politics, but she is far too shrewd to answer a question like that one outright.

As sentimental giveaways for the firm's highest performers, Jones asks Pat to sign a bunch of the red bandanna handkerchiefs Ted used to hand out when people came to the farm. People send back pictures of their signed bandanna—framed. A regional leader asks if Pat will sign his boxing glove, and once word is out, she winds up signing *boxes* of them. Even with a Sharpie, her handwriting is still as small and neat as it was on her wedding certificate. When Barbara Webb asks if she could maybe write a little bigger, Pat says, "No, I don't think so."

The company sends a video crew to interview her, hoping to capture reminiscences that will give future Jones advisors a sense of who she was.

Before the sessions, Webb goes through the Jones merchandise catalog and finds Pat a fresh pink golf shirt to wear, thinking that with her soft gray hair and flushed cheeks, the color will be perfect.

"You know, Barbara, I don't like pink," Pat says.

"Oh, please!" Webb pleads. "It'll look great on camera."

Pat gives in. Now Webb realizes Pat will need a jacket; the wind is picking up.

"There's one hanging in the breezeway," Pat says—and Webb finds herself fetching a tan farm jacket with a corduroy collar that easily could have been Ted's. Which is not a surprise, because one day she came out and Pat was wearing an old pair of Ted's slacks and one of his belts, pronouncing them "still perfectly good." Webb wriggles out of her denim jacket and hands it to Pat. "What about this instead?"

"Well, okay," Pat says. "At least it will cover this pink shirt."

She loves the jacket so much, she forgets to give it back. Webb doesn't have the heart to ask; it looks great on Pat. And it has saved her the ordeal of shopping.

§

The paradox of Pat Jones is how tough she is—reserved, stoic, strong—and yet how secretly tender. For Doug Hill's fortieth anniversary at Jones, Pat shows up. She has dug out Ted's forty-year pin, and she gives it to Hill, who so admired him. Then she hands Hill a bottle of the wine Ted ordered to celebrate the opening of the Katy Trail.

Sentiment for its own sake is hogwash, but people make a deep impression on her—what matters to them; what interests them. When she comes across a book about the U.S. Navy that mentions Jim Harrod, one of the Jones partners in Texas (he commanded a ship that is mentioned) she has the book sent to him. She picks out other books of Ted's that she knows certain people would love. When Bill Christensen sits down next to her at a party and begins to introduce himself—having only met her once a quarter-century earlier—she stops him with a laugh: "Of course I know who you are!"

§

When Barbara Webb nears retirement, she looks for someone who will enjoy working with Pat—that part is easy—and honor her stubbornness (less easy). Someone who can drive the Gator, will not run shrieking from a black snake, and can exist without air-conditioning.

Judy Beckmann turns out to be perfect. She brings Pat inexpensive red wine as a present. When Pat appears in a sloppy favorite shirt, she says, "Oh, just tuck that in, you'll be fine." She even learns to drive a tractor. "Never thought in my wildest dreams that by getting a job at Jones I would learn to drive a tractor," she says, laughing. "There are a lot of gears!"

Soon the farm is important to Beckmann, too. When big groups come out and she sees people smoking outside, she hands them a little box and says firmly, "You are going to bring your cigarette butts back out with you. That is not good for Pat's soil."

§

Pat stood by Ted when he gave his last years to the Katy Trail, but there's a hint of exasperation when she later tells a friend, "He was at a point in his life when he could have done *anything*. He didn't have to be traveling to the capital and arguing with a bunch of knuckleheads!"

Now, because he was that dedicated, the Katy Trail feels like Pat's responsibility, too. "Every time a bicycle wheel goes around, a quarter drops into the Missouri economy," she is quick to remind people. In 1996, she throws a switch at the Connection Ceremony, linking the first two trail sections where they now meet in Jefferson City. Often, she goes to the Katy, and one day a truck driver comes up to her and thanks her. She is bemused. "I got the contract for spreading the limestone on the trail," he explains, "and that was the best job I ever had. It was pretty, and that's a satisfaction." He walked away, leaving her smiling. "You're glad to know that even people who drive lime trucks enjoy a nice place to go do it," she says later.

In 2000, the first five-mile Katy Trail Ride is held, and Pat comes out for the opening—then returns every year, chatting, answering questions, and lecturing people on being good stewards of the land. She joins a lawsuit to make sure the state retains ownership of an old railroad bridge over the Missouri River at Boonville, so the Katy Trail can cross that bridge. Along Highway 94, the trail cuts across the hilly terrain so it can stay flat and easy, but Pat sees the cyclists squinting, their faces masked with misery as they ride uphill. She calls them the 94ers; she's learned they ride those hills to prepare themselves to cycle in Colorado. She wants to keep them safe, and she does not want the Katy to stop at Jeff City. So to prevent both those cyclists and the trail's hikers from risking their lives on a bridge meant for cars and trucks, she donates the cash for a zigzag, bicycle-accessible path. To her chagrin, it is promptly christened Pat's Path.

"That was a no-brainer," Pat says of the path, dismissing praise and cringing at the nickname. "It should have been done. But the Highway Department has never been terribly helpful on bicycle things."

She does enjoy riding across the bridge in a rickshaw at the dedication ceremony in 2010. The same year, the state adds a stone patio and bench to the Katy Trail memorial to celebrate Pat Jones *and* the trail's twentieth anniversary.

John Sam Williamson, one of Ted's staunchest foes on the Katy, comes to the ceremony.

28

The Katy Trail Today

Dave Rice, an experienced cyclist from New York, urges his wife and two friends toward the Katy, promising a crisply defined and peaceful route without long stretches where they'll have to compete with cars. They wind up loving how sociable the trail is, introducing them to people who offer tips about a great place to get ice cream or suggest meeting up to listen to live music at Cooper's Landing. Having promised himself not to take many photographs this time, Rice soon shot past seven hundred—"but without a lot of repetition," he points out in self-defense. Churches, prairie, farmland, river, bridges, the old silos, the vintage cabooses, wildflowers....

Scott and Chris Bigler, who live in Utah, are riding the trail with their grandkids, eager for them to see the Missouri River. "It's amazing!" Scott tells them. "Our rivers here in the West are streams by comparison." They stay in a meticulously preserved historic B&B in Augusta, soaking in claw-foot tubs; in a B&B that converted old grain silos into rooms; in rustic park cabins. And—as though Ted is at their elbow insisting—they stop at every historic marker.

§

The Katy continues to grow. In 1992, Union Pacific Railroad Co. donated thirty-three miles of right-of-way from the Missouri State Fairgrounds in Sedalia to the city of Clinton, making it possible to open a thirty-seven-mile section for horseback riding as well as hiking and biking. In 2011, the twelve miles between St. Charles and Machens opened. A Rock Island spur stretches the trail all the way to Arrowhead Stadium. Someday, you will be able to cycle all the way from Kansas City to Confluence Point just north of the Gateway Arch in St. Louis.

Floods taunt and damage the Katy. In 1993, the Great Flood washed away huge chunks of the trail. There are legendary photos—in one, men are in a speedboat, throwing a rope so they can tow a bridge, cast adrift, back to its moorings. The Edward Jones company helped pay for the damage, and so did the state: Just three years after the Katy's opening, legislators were eager to hand over the money to rebuild. That's how fast the trail proved its worth.

Ted had taken note of the three historic train depots on the trail. The one in Jefferson City was burned down by Halloween-crazed vandals before the trail even opened, but the other two were carefully restored. The Spanish-style depot in Boonville now holds city offices, while the largest depot, in Sedalia, is a heritage museum.

Scores of cafés and other small businesses have popped up along the trail. By 2012, an economic impact study measured $18 to $20 million flowing into these towns that would not otherwise be there. William Least Heat-Moon, author of *Blue Highways*, writes in *Missouri River Country: 100 Miles of Stories and Scenery from Hermann to the Confluence*:

> *"One afternoon, wearied of planting trees, I followed a whistle down to the Katy tracks passing the ghost village of Providence where all that remained were a couple of fishing shacks, a few rock walls, and the yet-standing stone chimney of the old steamboaters' hotel. The place was once the river landing for Columbia twelve miles north. I headed up the tracks toward Rocheport, another early nineteenth-century village, this one larger than Providence and still clinging to an existence. The nineteenth-century brick homes and worn shop-fronts had been declining ever since the Missouri shifted its course about a century earlier and left the village a mile or so from the river. Some time later, when passenger service ceased and the Katy trains quit stopping at the little depot, Rocheport, like a dozen other former steamboat or railroad villages nearby, had the scarcest of reasons to continue."*

Rocheport, he continued, was remade by the Katy:

> *"An old church, a bank, a drugstore got turned into antique shops,*
> *wooden-floor cafés, and exposed-brick-wall bistros serving Brie cheese*
> *drizzled with raspberry vinaigrette, panko-crusted sea bass, gooey butter*
> *cake, and clarets from the winery up on the hill....Former train stations*
> *became visitor centers; closed-up groceries and garages and schools*
> *transformed into bicycle-rental shops, bed-and-breakfast inns; a micro-*
> *publisher even opened a locally oriented press."*

The Katy Trail's aspirations—to educate, to celebrate Missouri's heritage, and to bring tourists to its small towns—"have been validated," says John Ashcroft, "and it has brought life and opportunity in a modest but valuable way to those towns."

Even John Sam Williamson now says, "Ted thought it would be a great thing for people to do, and he was exactly right there. People come from other states and ride this trail, the whole length of it, and they stop at little towns along the way."

Many want to see the McBaine bur oak, the largest in Missouri, which shades the part of the Katy that runs through Williamson's land. It's been growing since 1640, he was told; today it stands 90 feet tall and is tied for national champion with a bur oak in Kentucky. People learn about it through the trail, and they come and paint its picture, or photograph it, or fly a drone to get aerial shots. The appreciation is so gratifying, Williamson intends to put in a parking lot for the tree visitors.

Nothing as dramatic as the Katy Trail has been done by Missouri since. Jay Nixon went on to serve as attorney general during the court challenges, then as governor, and now teaches a Rails to Trails class at Washington University School of Law.

"The first time I personally met Ted, I was kind of looking at what his motivation was," Nixon recalls. "People are generally not coming up saying, 'What can I give you?' I was impressed by his directness, by his professionalism. 'Courteous' is too soft a word, because he wasn't fawning. But he was cordial, and there was an intellectual piercing to it—you really felt like, if this guy is behind the project, it could actually happen. He was saying, 'This isn't my business; this isn't even my charity. This is something we can do for *Missouri*.' The usual stereotype of the businessman wanting credit? He shed that so fast. He just wanted it *done*."

§

In December 2021, Missouri officials gather for a ceremony announcing the formal transfer of the Rock Island Corridor from Ameren Missouri to the state Department of Natural Resources and Missouri State Parks. At least $100 million will be invested to develop the 144-mile section into a bike and recreation trail.

There have been murmurs of dissent, the same sort Ted heard 35 years earlier. Landowners along the route lived with the Rock Island Railroad for decades, growing up alongside it, farming the land around it. A recreational trail is an unknown quantity.

Except—it isn't. The Katy led the way.

The Missouri Department of Natural Resources feels entirely comfortable developing the 144-mile section, the governor is willing to commit millions of dollars in state resources to help, and the state's economic analysts can already project strengthened economies for the twenty communities along the new trail. The Corridor, which includes the Rock Island Spur, will become the southern complement of the Katy Trail.

"I would be remiss if I did not mention Ted and Pat Jones today," Missouri State Parks director David Kelly says at the ceremony, "because we would not be here without their vision." They made the Katy Trail a reality, hoping that someday it could form the backbone for a network of trails across the state. "This is an expansion of that vision," Kelly says, barely finishing before there's a burst of loud clapping and a cheer goes up.

Ted and Pat Jones are not present at the ceremony—but they are very much present at that ceremony.

A Rebel With *Lots* of Causes

Pat's godsend is Jamie Coe, a forester who has worked off and on for Ted since 1980. She asks if he'll continue, and because he cares as much about the trees and the soil and the whole ecosystem as she does, they find an easy rhythm working together. The "one day a week" he agrees to give her soon increases to two, then five.

When Jamie shows up in the morning, Pat doesn't fire off instructions the way Ted would have. She simply asks, with interest but no agenda, what Jamie plans to do that day. Ted always knew exactly what he wanted done. Pat's more organic; she shares her ideas as she goes, but she gives a lot of freedom and lets things evolve.

Honored by her trust, Jamie throws his heart into the place, ridding it of invasive species, thinning the timber to keep the wooded areas healthy, sowing more native grasses, doing controlled burns. There is a gentleness in his approach to these projects, and he works hard but steadily, taking care.

This frees Pat to attend to the causes that have galvanized her all her life.

Back in 1962, Rachel Carson's controversial and ominously prophetic book about environmental destruction, *Silent Spring,* was published. Pat and her mother read it avidly, finding resounding confirmation for everything they already believed. They tired out the rest of the family by talking incessantly about the book. Their only other topic was the nauseating racism of the John Birch Society, which was trashing the *human* environment.

Over the years, the causes piled up, some overlapping, some distinct. The environment always tops the list, and social justice weaves through all the rest.

§

If you know Pat, you know that when she dies, she intends to haunt Ameren UE. It is a goal, oft announced.

Melissa Curry grins when her aunt Pat points to the Callaway County nuclear plant and says, intoning it like a late-night horror host, "There's the bomb." Ted thought nuclear energy was exactly what the future needed; Pat thinks it will destroy us. Her clean and gentle solution is wind and water, and she has thought it through: "Generate electricity with wind over salt water. Then use that electricity to separate the water and the salt, oxygen and hydrogen. Now the salt, you can put back into the ocean," or even distribute it to places that *need* a little extra salt. "The place that needs oxygen is the entire delta of the Mississippi River, so you can oxygenate that. Then take the hydrogen where you want electricity, and generate electricity and water. Both of them are salable."

She takes the Missouri Department of Transportation to task regularly. Her one-woman feud with Ameren started when the utility put a power line—a huge transmission line—near The Shack, her childhood refuge. "They use the right of eminent destruction to do whatever they want," she snaps. "I think that should be eliminated. I think they should be sensitive about where they're going."

She speaks freely of her plan to haunt them, even to the Jones brokers whose clients' portfolios include Ameren stock.

Anyone who pooh-poohs climate change instantly loses her respect (as does anyone who shows a hint of racism). She likes the idea of a carbon tax, if only to remind people that carbon causes real damage—and will burn us up. Asked if she thinks resistance to the reality of global warming is political, she says, "A lot of it is economic. I think people don't like to believe things, and if you're in the coal business, you don't want to be told you're in a rotten business. I wouldn't want anybody to tell *me* that." You can demonstrate profitable ways to reform, converting to clean energy, she says, but "it's so easy to jiggle numbers around and make it look like you ought to do it this way or some other way. That's what a lot of economics is, how you jiggle the numbers."

In 2014, her opposition to the Callaway nuclear generating station is vindicated: Tests by the Nuclear Regulatory Commission reveal contaminated groundwater near the site.

As for billboards, they must be eradicated from the land. They are cluttering the view, obscuring the trees and the sky. She has known this her whole life. When Pat was a kid, her family took the train back east almost every summer. Once, as the train chugged through Pennsylvania, her mother saw a giant billboard for Heinz 57 catsup—and never bought or knowingly ate that brand again.

Pat backs legislation to limit the number of billboards along Missouri's interstates. "The Highway Department should think more of the human use of the highway," she insists. "Get the billboards down. We need Lady Bird Johnson up here to tell you how to decorate your highways!" She quotes a parody of Joyce Kilmer's poem "Trees": "I think that I shall never see a billboard lovely as a tree. Perhaps unless the billboards fall, I'll never see a tree at all."

Against all odds, Pat prevails. The tacky, lurid signs are lifted from long stretches of landscape.

The reprieve does not last long. When the companies find out that billboards are about to be outlawed, they throw up even more of them— blank.

Pat is not discouraged. When she learns that the University of Missouri intends to sell pristine land near Weldon Spring to a developer, replacing gorgeous woods and farmland with tract homes and a golf course, not to mention destroying a stunning view of the Missouri River, she sends a sharp letter to the *St. Louis Post-Dispatch*: "It was my understanding that the university teaches good land stewardship. I feel with the sale of this natural area the university no longer practices what it teaches."

She, on the other hand, practices every day.

§

Sometimes Pat teases that she is "a conservative, because that means you're conserving things." But she lives surrounded by true conservatives—family members, friends, her husband, his colleagues—who are painfully aware of her politics. When Doug Hill takes over as managing partner, he has conversations with Pat that, while thoroughly enjoyable, are as strenuous as climbing Kilimanjaro. She knows every issue in the state of Missouri, he realizes with amused exhaustion—what the Republicans think, what the Democrats think. He begins to warn people before they visit the farm: "The one thing I don't want you to do is ask Pat anything about politics. If you do, we're going to get a forty-five-minute lecture."

One Thanksgiving, she engages a few nieces and nephews who are evangelical Christians in a discussion of abortion (she is pro-choice). The conversation explodes. One of her nephews is a preacher, a creationist, and her answer to him is the sixty-foot core sample of soil from the farm. Four inches thick, it acts as a timeline—and it goes back 800,000 years, all the way to "the Refusal," the point where they hit immovable bedrock. She shows her nephew when the glaciers formed, takes him all the way back, sinks him into a time well before his Bible was written.

These conversations do not change anybody's mind, but they let Pat keep her sanity and hone her ideas. She wins grudging respect even from her fiercest foes, because she knows her own mind and expresses it clearly. With Ted gone, *she* has become the force of nature.

Pat serves on the board of the Missouri Parks Association. She helps start a separate organization, the Missouri Parks Foundation, for fundraising, and is one of the charter members of its board. Organizational meetings are held in her home. Regularly, she writes letters to the editor of the *St. Louis Post-Dispatch,* usually about conservation causes. She pushes to renew the parks and soil sales tax. When the state parks director's salary is sliced in half by the Missouri House of Representatives in order to make a political statement, she does not mince her words of disapproval.

On the flip side, "when she supports something, she doesn't do it lightly, and people know that," remarks Axie Hindman. To those who share her world view, Pat's very presence is persuasive.

One day she calls Jim McKenzie out in Nebraska and asks him to contact the governor of Missouri and tell him that St. Louis needs a landscaped park between the Mississippi River, the Arch, the courthouse, and the other downtown buildings, to conceal the highway and give easier access to the Arch and its museum. She is very specific. Either she has read architect Eero Saarinen's original plan, or she has thought through the details herself. "Jim, call the governor!"

What she is suggesting is exactly what will be done, years later.

§

People don't realize how much the soil matters. Scrape one tiny gram of loam off the top of a fertile prairie and stick it under a microscope: You will find about two million protozoans and fifty-eight million bacteria. "The quality of the soil really makes a big difference in what kind of society you live in," Pat points out whenever she is given an opening. "Whole countries are divided by the ground they're on."

Interviewed by *Town & Style*, Pat no doubt startles the reporter with an urgency few people share in 2013: ""We've got to get carbon emissions out of the air—it's destroying our planet!"

In April 2014, a young man with the State Historical Society of Missouri interviews her for an oral history. They talk at the farm, and it is easy to picture them sitting on that long screened-in porch, gazing out at the wild violets just coming into bloom.

"If you want an opinion, I have one," she teases him. Then she cuts to the chase. "We lack pride in our own state. We kind of denigrate our own place. Maybe it's a good idea. Then people won't come! But we don't self-advertise very often." She has thought about this, and she has decided "it's just in the genetics of the people here…. We're the ones that didn't go on. Got to St. Louis and then didn't go west."

Mind, she does not want to encourage people to flood into Missouri. "We don't want to be just crowded with people. We want space." People here have grown up with the rivers and the bluffs, she

Pat reveled in sending visitors home with a bur oak acorn.

explains. "Have you ever floated on a river?"

Her interviewer, Jeff Corrigan, stammers that he is not from Missouri; he moved here for this job. "So this is all new stuff to me."

"Okay, well, go on a float trip," Pat says. "It doesn't matter which river, but it does matter when. Don't go on when you know it's going to be crowded." The Meramec River she grew up canoeing often has its entire width covered with boats, she adds, wincing. "*That's* not any fun."

Corrigan asks about the Ozark Scenic National Riverway debate: Does Pat think there should be restrictions on four wheelers, loud boats, jet skis, and WaveRunners?

"No motorized vehicles should ever be permitted to play in the water," she says firmly. She begins to make a concession for boating, then changes her mind: "You can wreck a nice canoe trip with a loud speedboat. If you've got a speedboat, go down to the Lake of the Ozarks."

Crowd control should be possible, she tells Corrigan, mentioning that if you want to float the Salmon River, you make a reservation. "There isn't any reason that we can't limit the amount of traffic…. You have to rotate the use on things. The more population we have, the more we have to learn how to properly share."

She shifts the topic to the mess people have made of the river near Pacific, Missouri. "The Meramec River gravel does not have manganese in it, so it's in big demand for mixing cement." She sighs. "I don't care what you want, you shouldn't make a mess. But mining spoils, I think, are always a mess."

She flips back to the ATVs: "These little four-wheeler things can do enormous damage." They used to splash through the creek on her land, smashing the rural peace. When her Congressional rep tried to pass a law to allow ATVs and four-wheelers on the Katy Trail, he gained traction fast—until Pat wrote a scathing letter, and he slammed on the brakes. Give them places, she urges now, hills they can climb without doing any harm. "I don't think that's unreasonable, is it?"

§

Pat's favorite tree is a big bur oak in front of the house. It was a fringed acorn when she and Ted built the house, and she remembers placing

it carefully, a few inches deep. Four decades later, the tree is almost
eighty feet high, its trunk almost two feet in diameter. She loves her state
champion wahoo tree, too—a small bittersweet with dark green leaves that
redden in fall—and the Kentucky coffee trees, and the big twisted Osage
orange tree they think was there when the first settlers arrived. Jammed
into its trunk is a big iron hook that easily could have held a fat hog for
butchering.

Two chestnut trees are brought to the farm by a forestry professor at
the University of Missouri. "Chestnuts died in the blight of the 1930s,"
Pat tells visitors that fall. "They're now bringing over Chinese chestnuts to
cross-breed, because the American chestnuts will still grow—they're even
bigger than oak trees—but then they will die from the disease. The cross-
breeding can save them." Pulling back from the urgency—she has slipped
into preacher mode again—she smiles. "We're going to roast chestnuts as
soon as the weather turns cold."

On a wall of the farmhouse, she hangs a saying: "It's fun to plant a
tree and watch it grow. It will keep you busy for the rest of your life."

Trees even live in her mind, offering ready metaphors. She envisions
a mature tree and holds that picture in her mind every time she plants a
seedling. When an interviewer asks her whether some giant project turned
out as she expected, she will shrug: "What do you envision when you put
an acorn in the ground? You don't have an exact picture of what it's going
to be."

§

Pat is diagnosed with breast cancer and has to have a mastectomy, Susan
Willcoxson comes out to be with her while she recovers. Propped up in
bed, Pat is busy planning what she wants to do with the farm. Her idea of
luxury, Susan realizes, is to say to the accountant, "I'd really like to put in
another pond. Can I afford it?" One can only imagine the accountant's
expression; Pat Jones could afford to put in a hundred ponds. Still, her
generosity to others does have to be kept in check; she will need to keep
enough of the money to live on, and someday she may need another Prius,
her biggest luxury purchase, a gift to the earth.

When they notice Pat's joints stiffening, John Beuerlein and his wife make her a present of a big, comfy recliner. As soon as she leans it back, Gunner—the high-energy (this is an understatement) Jack Russell terrier she rescued from certain death—climbs up and sleeps right above her head. He is normally a handful, this dog, zooming here and there like a cartoon character. But for any chance to cuddle with Pat, he settles right down.

Dozens of friends drop in regularly. They know they can come anytime, no warning needed. Those who know Pat well make sure to time their visit around *Meet the Press*. If you arrive during her favorite program of the week, she might turn the volume down slightly, but she will divide her attention—which is utterly unlike her—between you and the TV screen.

When Susan Willcoxson comes to visit, she knows better than to hug Pat; it might make her uncomfortable. Instead, Susie just leans over and kisses Pat on the cheek, and Pat says, "Well, *hel*-lo!" All the warmth is in that voice, all the welcome. Her eagerness for your company, Susie decides, is the way you know she loves you.

Now that she is alone, Pat celebrates Thanksgiving with the Van Dykes. She brings a bottle of wine. They know better than to ask her to cook.

30
——

Back to the Prairie

In 1997, Pat decides to go ahead and donate the entire farm to—jointly—the Missouri Department of Conservation and the University of Missouri. This is wily of her; she wants to make sure the state and the university collaborate rather than compete. "If those two entities have to work together, then it makes it more interesting," she observes. "And working together gets things done. Nobody's going to solve problems alone."

She watched Ted operate for decades; she knows you have to make sure things happen the way you want them to. That's another reason for her impulsive early gift: She wants to be around when the work begins, so she can make sure it's done right.

The farm is to be used for both research and education. The site will be named Prairie Fork, for the creek that runs through the land. Pat's gift includes, of course, the proviso that she may live there for the rest of her life. But she has already established the Prairie Fork trust with a generous endowment, and it will grow as surely as the bluestem did, providing money to manage Prairie Fork well into the future.

When Jim McKenzie hears about the gift, the implications of its timing floor him: "She trusts people enough that she doesn't need to own the very land she lives on."

Soon after she deeds the land over, a 200-acre farm adjacent to Prairie Fork goes on the market. Pat's longtime friend and neighbor, Jean Smith, hears the news first and instead of going home, rushes to Pat's house. "They're talking about putting in a trailer court!"

Pat gulps. "What does he want for the land?"

Jean relates everything she knows.

A brisk nod from Pat. "I think I'll buy it."

She immediately donates the new land to the Missouri Prairie Foundation, which will deed the land to the state as it is restored to prairie. All told, Pat has handed over more than 900 more acres for conservation, doubling her original gift of the 900 acres her mother amassed.

§

Pat's template for Prairie Fork's restoration is a prairie landscape from 1840. She has chosen that year carefully, because she doesn't want to take the land back to a time when the plantings and practices encouraged erosion. She needs to go back further than that. How was it when the Anglo settlers first got here, she wonders. She is sure there were virtually no cedar trees, because early surveys always emphasize the presence of a cedar tree as though a rare find. The Indians burned the land so often, cedar wouldn't have had a chance; prairie species can survive, but the vascular tissue of a tree like cedar collapses in the blaze. Which was the point, because too many trees would throw shade, inhibiting the understory. So that was *too* far back.

"We're not going back to the Indian culture," Pat announces. "We do burn, but not quite like they did."

Plains Indians called a prairie fire "the red buffalo," wary of its stampede. On a dry and windy day, fire could destroy so much so fast. But their controlled burns, carefully planned, kept the prairie healthy, dissolving the dead, toppled grasses that would otherwise weave a blackout curtain, keeping sunshine from reaching the ground.

The controlled burns Pat favors will have tight boundaries, trenches dug as fire breaks, to leave the woods intact. But she does want to get rid of the thick grass mulch, so sunlight can warm the earth and new grass and wildflowers will have a chance come spring. Some prairie wildflowers are practically fire-eaters, thriving after a burn because it helps their seeds germinate. The ash adds nutrients to the soil. The clearing lets in sunshine.

Back in 1839, the era she wants to revisit, Judge James Hall described "the profusion of light" in an unshaded prairie, and how it can "produce a gaeity which animates the beholder." In *Harrow*, a 2021 novel by Joy Williams, the description of the prairie grasses is elegiac: "They once could have survived the worst, you know, whether fire or ice, their roots went so deep. That's what the worst was thought to be once—freeze and flame. They were eradicated instead by simple human commitment, that and the fact that the determination to survive that other forms of life ofttime exhibit impels many people to extremes of destruction."

There has been enough destruction. It is time to return to nature's original intent. And—secret delight—the restored landscape should also let Pat bring back a population of prairie chickens. Remember the birds her great-grandfather shooed from Fourth Street when he first arrived in St. Louis? Barred brown-and-white grouse, they love to forage in grassland, and they once covered the prairie. To court a female, the males perform-flutter jumps (leaping into the air and flapping their wings while they whoop and cackle) and other acrobatic tricks, and they inflate their chests, making a loud booming noise, and all the while, the females pretend to be bored. They are cool birds, and Pat wants them back again.

§

At least 60 percent of Missouri's land was once covered with prairie. Now, less than 1 percent comes close. It will be hard work, restoring what people tried so hard to get rid of.

The first battle is clearing invasive species. The honeysuckle invited itself, but Ted planted a few exotics—autumn olive for songbird cover, and sericea lespedeza, or Chinese bushclover—as habitat. The conservation department *suggested* those species. Pat doesn't blame them; this was long before anyone realized what harm they could do. Now the exotics have invaded like Napoleon's army, and she pours money and effort into eradicating them from Prairie Fork.

True to form, she treats the project like an experiment, learning as she goes. Sometimes Americorps groups come to help, spot-spraying the exotics. At other times, Roundup has to be sprayed—not Pat's ideal solution—from an airplane, waiting until November when all the native plants are already dormant but the honeysuckle clings to life.

"No amount of sweat or hand pulling will rid the prairie of certain plants," notes Cindy Crosby in *The Tallgrass Prairie*. "We've disturbed Mother Nature. And now, we are responsible for taking care of those areas we've disturbed. Sometimes, drastic measures—such as chemicals—are the only way to repair that damage."

Pat's father was right, it occurs to her, when he warned her mother not to bring in strangers. "We moved out here because we liked it," he used to say. "Don't go changing it!"

§

In 1997, Eric Kurzejeski is a wildlife research supervisor with the conservation department. He is asked to be the state's trustee on the coordinating board for Prairie Fork. Later, he will move into outreach and education, directing a program at the university, and his dean will ask if he'd like to stay on the board, now representing Mizzou.

Pat is relieved. Kurzejeski instantly grasped her vision for the land, understanding how badly she wants to restore natural communities, the ecosystems that existed there before the Europeans razed the vegetation for their own purposes. She wants the prairie grasses and wildflowers, the wetlands and woodland and all the creatures they support, back in place again. It's an idea that still startles many people in 1997 but will seem obviously right a decade or two later.

But where to begin? Do you take a handful of prairie plants and stick them in the ground and call it good? Years earlier, when Ted planted bluestem and called the field a prairie, Pat knew that was a bit too simple. So is Emily Dickinson's version: "*To make a prairie it takes a clover/And one bee,—One clover, and a bee,/And revery.*"

If only. At nearby Tucker Prairie, owned by the university, at least 250 species of grasses and forbs (wildflowers) intermingle in a complex ecosystem. Tucker is a remnant prairie, a bit of land whose vegetation was never chopped down, mowed, or planted over. On Pat's land, the original vegetation was eradicated.

This will take a while.

Botanists from Kurzejeski's division set up a Seed Shed and begin collecting seed. By hand. These are not species you can order from Burpee. You have to know exactly what you're looking for and where it might grow. Sweating in the prairie's peak season, they hunt for shy prairie violets, the only flower the regal fritillary butterfly—saffron orange, black-banded, white spotted—will entrust with its larvae. The caterpillars nibble on the tender bird's foot leaves of these small blue violets—and will eat nothing else. Which is why, like pink katydids and crawfish frogs and prairie chickens and Henslow's sparrows, these butterflies can only be found on remnant prairies.

Wildlife biologist Chris Newbold calls prairie violets "a keystone species for tallgrass prairies. But they bloom early and grow only about two inches tall, and when it comes time to collect the seed, it's hard to collect a large quantity, and it's been hard to germinate in greenhouses."

The quarry also include skullcaps and Indian paintbrush. Downy gentian are also tough to start from seed, but they've been a success, and they're gorgeous, a deep purplish blue, funnel-shaped and blowsy, like a flirty lily. Bumblebees adore downy gentian, but their private dining club is the closed gentian, because bumblebees are the only pollinators big and strong enough to pry their petals open.

Once the botanists have collected in the field, they must strip the seed. As the quantities build, they use a tractor with a flail back to brush the seed off and send it into the hopper. Some of the seed has to be mashed, so they use a hammer mill. By fall, the shed smells earthy, spicy, *alive*.

Each year, the team manages to collect enough seed to cover about forty acres. They always aim for all 250 species, but they often fall short. Pat watches with satisfaction as they process each year's batch. Big muslin bags hang from racks, all neatly labeled: cream indigo, culver's root, asclepias, alum, cluster fescue, gentian, Missouri's evening primrose, quinine, slender false foxglove, white lettuce…. Rattlesnake master is a good find, but its name remains a mystery. The inspiration might be the way its spikes bite your flesh or the soft hiss the leaves make in a breeze, but others say the yucca-like leaves cured snakebite, and still others say rattlesnakes avoid the plant.

Rattlesnake master

The planting will not finish until 2020; she will only miss seeing the final year's assortment. By then, at least 180 species will have emerged, flourished, and begun to self-sow. More continue to pop up; it took bunchflower, a member of the lily family, ten years to agree to bloom. The extra rare or delicate species remain a quest.

§

Whenever anything's happening in the Seed Shed, Pat asks interested questions, but she never intrudes. "What are you doing today?" she will call out from the Gator. "Have fun and get dirty!"

"I really enjoy watching the conservationists work and telling them what to do," she chuckles to a friend, "even though they don't pay a bit of attention to what I say!"

At meetings, her tone is eager, not bossy. "Have you thought of—" she will ask, but she never issues a mandate or an ultimatum, just tosses out good ideas. "I don't think you can tell somebody advice," she tells the new assistant professor who is eager to please the woman who funded her salary. "I think you just have to follow your own leads."

Pat does brim with ideas, though, because just about everything on a prairie has to do with the soil—the micorrhizal fungi that help plants extract the minerals they need to live; the worms that then feed the birds….

Though soil is her specialty, she also honors the larger scope of the biome, its intricate moving parts. Ducks nest in prairie potholes. Up to sixty-four species of bees descend on the purple prairie clover at dawn, often using up its pollen by ten in the morning. Plots of milo and soybeans feed quail, turkey, deer, and rabbits. She makes sure the food is close to protective cover, so the birds don't have to venture far in bad weather. She has Jamie put up snake guards for the bluebird houses. She insists on a weather station for environmental monitoring. Dr. Patrick Market, director of the School of Natural Resources at the university and a meteorologist himself, tells her warmly how much he appreciates her understanding of the role of climate. Briskly, she replies that it would be foolish of her to overlook it.

In 2011, a freelancer hoping to place an article in *People* magazine descends upon Prairie Fork. After spending a day with Pat, the writer christens her the Prairie Godmother. The editor at *People* loves the piece.

For Pat's photo shoot, a stylist sends along several outfits. Pat picks the plainest. Charmed by her, the photographer makes a present of the outfit. Pat promptly gives it away. "Prairie Godmother" sticks; the nickname is copied and used in one bio after another. Pat finds it silly, but barely notices.

She is watching her vision slowly come alive.

§

A big Jones group is out at the farm, and Jack Cahill and Pat are sitting outside in rocking chairs, answering questions. After lunch, Jamie Coe organizes a walking tour, and Pat reaches over and elbows Cahill: "You've taken this tour often enough! I'm going to show you other parts of the farm." Now in her mid-eighties, she climbs into the driver's seat of the Gator, and they take off, Pat doing a running commentary as she speeds over bumps and plows through brush. Scratched by thistle and brush as it scrapes through the open side of the Gator, Cahill glances down and sees that he is bleeding. But that is okay, because now it is raining, water gushing into the Gator, which cleans the scratches.

"You won't melt, will you?" Pat calls. "I've got more to show you."

The rain comes down harder—it sounds like birdshot hitting the roof of the Gator—and when they splash through ditches, water whooshes up against the sides. "There used to be all sorts of big ditches here," Pat yells. "Mr. Jones told farmers if they'd fill in the ditches for him, they could farm the land." They cross bridges and chug past refuge strips, ponds, fields, meadows. Finally the Gator pulls into the garage, and they sit there a while, still talking.

Drenched past inhibition, Cahill says, "When you grow up at Edward D. Jones, you learn about Ted pushing his dad to make it a partnership, and how he wanted anyone who put in a career at Jones to be an owner of the company. People never *do* that. And then Ted said, 'Wait a minute. I think John Bachmann would be a better managing partner than I am,' and gave up his position. People never do that, either. And you gave away your mother's land, and now you're giving away your *farm*?"

Pat's eyes look like gray steel, glinting in the garage's dim light. He sees not a trace of regret. "Jack," she says, "when you love something enough that you want it to last forever, you've got to give it away."

31
—

Tracking Turtles

Loyal as she is to her alma mater, Pat does not hesitate to call the dean of what is now the College of Agriculture, Food, and Natural Resources to make sure the emphasis does not drift. Prairie Fork is to be *educational*, not just an outdoor laboratory for research. She wants kids of all ages to feel the freedom of being outdoors, let their sneakers squish in the mud, stare back at peeper frogs or watch dragonflies or study the structures engineered by beavers, which were almost gone and have now returned to help save the wetlands.

Pat's nephew Truman Young, a restoration ecologist, sits on the Prairie Fork board as the family advisor. He pushes the others to involve people outside the Missouri Department of Natural Resources, so the project doesn't become too incestuous. He pushes the faculty who are involved with research at Prairie Fork to publish, explaining to Pat that "if you don't publish it, you never did it." He also reinforces her demand for more educational programs.

After a few years of Pat and Truman nudging and the university experimenting with different initiatives, the board realizes what Prairie Fork needs is a fulltime coordinator, not a succession of grad students. Once that position is in place, they have continuity and a steady series of educational programs, and momentum builds. Soon as many as five thousand visitors, most of them under eighteen, are descending upon Prairie Fork every year.

Pat meets the buses whenever she can, which is nearly always. She stands there grinning as small humans pour out, shrieking with excitement. "Get dirty!" she urges them. "Have fun!" She still remembers her own favorite field trips, and she knows how those memories can shape you. "I can remember as a child walking someplace and you get in the mud and your whole shoe comes off," she chuckles. "Why shouldn't children have that experience? It's fun to get dirty at any age!"

City kids race around the fields, dart into the Amazing Maze and panic for just a second, then find their way through the corn stalks or sunflowers. Amber Edwards, the fulltime outreach and education coordinator, hands each child a net and directs them to the pond, where they are to venture into the slop at the edge, "catch something alive," and by no means harm it. They start out excited—many have never explored a pond's edges before, stood in damp reeds, felt the underwater tangle beneath serene lily pads. When their faces fall because they have tried and tried, and they still can't find a big croaky frog or scoop up a slippery fish, Edwards seizes her chance to show them all the fascinating tiny creatures they forgot, like the diving beetles and scuttling water scorpions....

When Jamie mentions that it's time to burn a hollowed-out tree trunk, Pat says, "Oh, no, bring it up to the yard, and we'll have kids crawl through it."

It is important to Pat that they have time to investigate on their own, nobody watching over their shoulder. She also likes the idea of pairing good high school biology students with small children. Her idea is for the teenager to "let the little kid talk, because they won't shut up. And do that as long as the high school kid can stand it! That really works."

Always practical, she knows that maybe only one in every hundred of these kids will leave with a new interest and nurture it as it grows. The others, though, will have tasted a new kind of freedom, and they surely they will all learn *something.*

"People need a place where they can be; where they're not fenced in," she says often. "A place where you can take a walk, you can run and jump, you can get dirty, and you can investigate whatever it is you're interested in."

Her father's words come back to her. "I don't care what they're interested in," she adds, "but they have to be interested in *something.*" That's why she wants to catch them young, before peer pressure stifles those impulses.

Childhood is the teachable time, and Pat means to indoctrinate. She explains that there are not many dung beetles on the farm because they don't have any cattle that aren't wormed. Then she shows the kids little antlions and explains that they have to develop a place for them to live. Together, Pat and her visitors watch a wasp build a nest. "Isn't this interesting?" she asks. "Just stay out of its way and we can watch." All spiders are not deadly, she reminds kids who have read too much Harry Potter. A tick will not kill you if you touch it. Soldier beetles, which look like painted fireflies, feed on goldenrods and help pollinate them. The painted lady butterfly loves thistle blooms, and for monarch butterflies, milkweed is a hamburger and a malt and fries all rolled up in one.

When Judy Beckmann pulls the Gator up to the outdoor pavilion where the kids are, Edwards often reaches down, picks something up from the ground, and heads over to show Pat. Beckmann, meanwhile, is easing herself out of the Gator.

"Where are you going?" Pat asks.

"Well, I'm not sure right now, Pat. Let's see what Amber has in her hand."

§

On Earth Day, children flock to Prairie Fork. Tables are set up, and displays are arranged on the tabletops, on the ground, inside booths. The kids can see the different fur coats various animals wear; trace the way water flows underground; look at native prairie plants; and, of course, learn about soil. A hole is dug in the ground to show off the various layers of loam, gravel, sand, and clay. Another lesson, very interactive, involves both soil and water, and, yes, the kids get dirty.

One year, Pat's nephew Mike Young shows up for Earth Day too. As he studies the soil layers, he remembers that back in ag school, soil was her *major*. No wonder she wants kids to get dirty! It's not just about freedom, and it's far more than a good-natured rebellion against propriety. She wants them to feel the stuff, make it part of them, realize they're part of the earth.

Near the Seed Shed, Pat turns a weathered old barn with a rusty metal roof into a Soil Shed. Inside, she puts a display of remnant prairie, never plowed. Buckets labeled LOAM, SAND, SILT, and CLAY. A little stuffed badger tunnels,

Pat, at home on the prairie at Prairie Fork

behind glass, through various layers of soil. For a while, Pat even has a tunnel that visitors can crawl through alongside the earthworms, but too many of the grownups balk.

Outside, a shaded pavilion seems like a good idea for talks and activities. When construction is complete, a sign is hung: "The wood used to build this pavilion came from trees from this farm. The pine timbers used for the main supports were harvested from trees that Pat and Ted Jones planted in the early 1950s and harvested some 60 years later."

The floor of the pavilion is a work of art: Concrete inscribed with the tracks of wolf, bison, elk, bobcat, striped skunk, wild turkey—and here's a scuffle, and then there's no more wild turkey. The floor tells the story of the prairie, its grasses and trees, its showy yellow rosinweed and the pale greenish-white bundleflower with its crazy, twisted seedpods. Pat knows it's working when, told to write a story about something depicted in the floor, a little girl asks if she can write hers from the point of view of a fly.

Pat has plenty of stories herself. She tells young visitors about neglected critters like the American burying beetle (more graphically known as the carrion beetle), which finds a carcass and coats it with secretions to embalm and mummify it. The beetle then feasts, efficiently breaking down and recycling organic material for the rest of us. Pat shows the kids pictures of the beetles' shiny black bodies, the bright orange scallops that add a hint of Halloween, the orange tips on their antennae. Once they crawled around more than half of the United States; by 1989, the only known American burying beetle population was in Rhode Island. On the endangered species list for years, they were then found in six states with prairies, savannas, and Mississippi lowlands. The Saint Louis Zoo bred thousands and, in 2012, reintroduced them in southwestern Missouri.

Everything on the farm is a teaching tool: the meadowlarks with their sweet song, fat lily pads afloat on the ponds, animal tracks, big scraggly nests, mushrooms, lichen, weird tree shapes, butterflies, dragonflies, grasshoppers, water snakes with a disconcerting resemblance to copperheads, bald eagles, glossy red-winged blackbirds, the killdeer doing their dancy little walk, and the small vivid bluebirds, the state bird of Missouri.

"Life is not long, so enjoy every minute of it," Pat encourages the kids. "Have something you want to do, some goal for tomorrow or the next day." On a concrete wall in front of the Soil Shed is her motto: "Learn, Get Dirty and Have Fun!!" Two exclamation points.

§

David Crane brings Boy Scout groups out to Prairie Fork to do work projects, a tradition that started three decades earlier. Ted and Pat always welcomed kids to the farm, and about ten times a year, they came to camp out. Now, the boys are a huge help, building a footbridge, a dock, tree stumps smoothed into stools for nature classes, and cedar benches whose design was the brainchild of naturalist Aldo Leopold. They have a back that swings down to become a desk, and if you put two benches together and swing their backs the other direction, you have an instant picnic table.

The Scouts put their heart into their work, even stamping the tracks of deer, fox, and turkey on one of their bridges. Whenever he brings a work group to the farm, Crane knocks on Pat's door to see if she wants to come out and talk to them. She always does. She's like the best grandma they can imagine, patient, willing to explain anything, thrilled to delve into the nerdy science—but with a dry wit that keeps the kids on their toes. She attaches little plaques to the boys' work projects so they can be proud of what they have made.

When the beavers cut their teeth on the bald cypress trees around Crow Pond, Pat is furious. She calls the Future Farmers of America and sets up a trapping clinic. She does know that beaver have helped create important wetland ecosystems. She just doesn't want them killing her beautiful cypress trees.

Ted's circuses wowed the crowds with all sorts of acrobatic tricks, but nature is the greatest balancing act of all.

§

By the year 2000, all sorts of research projects are running year-round at Prairie Fork. "I'll tell you what to do," Pat jokes with the field scientists, "but you don't have to do it." She turns to Jamie and nods. "They have their own research. They have their own things they're doing. And that's the way it should be."

Researchers dig deep holes, revealing layers called soil horizons. Ted's swamp fills with willows and becomes another laboratory. Camera traps are installed to locate weasels, but because Gunner loves the cat food the researchers use as bait, most of the photos are of Pat's terrier.

One project aims to save the vanishing blacknose shiner, a soft-rayed freshwater fish, like trout, that prefers cool, weedy creeks, small rivers, or sandy-bottomed lakes. Another focuses on the prairie crayfish that live in water below the ground. Once they are located (helpfully, the mud chimneys of their dwellings extend above ground), Phase Two begins: reintroducing the prairie crawfish frog. An endangered species, this frog likes to squat in the crayfish burrows. The researchers want to place frog eggs in a pond, but first all the fish must be killed, or else they will eat the eggs. One day at least fifty vultures darken the air above the pond, their glassy eyes fixed on the dead fish. The look of them, that sense of raw wildness, reminds Pat of her trip to Africa.

The experiment succeeds: Soon the field researchers spot the crawfish frogs, cream with an overall pattern of gold or black circles. Now the scientists will keep an ear to the ground, waiting to hear the loud, guttural old-man snore that indicates the frogs are breeding.

§

"When it gets warm, we're going to do research on where the morels are," Pat announces one day. "And then we're going to eat them."

She is loving all this field work, the fizz of research and speculation and learning. One stipulation she makes again and again: When she's gone, the house should come down. The educational team will not need a house, and the maintenance will only drain money from their projects. The guesthouse is adequate for their purposes, she points out, and there's a sheltered pavilion, "and they still make umbrellas."

All the projects at Prairie Fork thrill her, even the earthworm study and the slow, painstaking tracking of the three-toed box turtles. In summer 2002, Charlie Van Dyke's daughter Nancy, now in college, comes out to help with Operation Turtle. Radio transmitters are glued to the thick, hard, shiny backs of seventy-five turtles, and soon the field workers are scrambling through briars after them, the beeps growing louder as they close in on their particular turtle.

The species was chosen because it would be easy to locate and track— "Eyes on turtle!"—but "turtles can move farther and faster than you'd think!" Nancy tells Pat breathlessly.

The field work runs on a twenty-eight-hour cycle, each worker's shift advancing by four hours every day so the same person isn't always scrambling after the turtles at two in the morning. Only a few turtles go MIA. The young male box turtles are the restless ones, taking off in a straight line, winding up miles away in just a day or two. Older females tend to stay put, hanging out in the same place all summer long, possibly most of their lives. Similarly, translocated turtles (those moved from their original home) travel greater total distances every day, ranging farther from their new home. Resident turtles are more likely to remain homebodies.

Why does this matter? Because when habitats change—degrading or fragmenting because someone has invaded—populations can get isolated, their movements limited. Translocation is one way to help them. Once moved, though, the turtles are in a new environment and don't know where all the resources are, so they have to go exploring. Longtime residents go on shorter, more direct errands, because they know where they'll find what they need. The more scientists know about these patterns, the easier it will be to help the turtles—and therefore, the rest of the ecosystem—thrive.

32
——

Particle Physics After Breakfast

The Young and Jones families are well accustomed to Pat's quirks. As a holiday gift, she invariably sends crates of Florida grapefruit. They are healthy and more luscious than anything available locally, but they could also be an unconscious nod to her seafaring great-grandfather. Effie used to talk about the pomelos, giant teardrop-shaped grapefruit, he brought home from the tropics for his kids to enjoy at Christmastime.

One year, Pat and Ted made the mistake of giving Ted's parents a brilliantly dyed, handwoven Diné rug as a present. "We live in St. Louis, not Arizona!" Ursula snapped. Pat gave the rug to Ann and Pete Key instead, and from then on, she played it safe, giving reusable grocery bags—years before they turned trendy—and baskets stuffed with every delicacy sold at Crane's General Store.

Her own comforts come from her daily trips to Crane's. The place is everything she cares about: historic, founded a century ago, rooted in the land; local and independent; stocked to the gills with "boots, bullets, britches, and bologna." A photograph of the interior would make a perfect jigsaw puzzle: rustic artifacts from floor to ceiling, candy in apothecary jars, old wood beams….

Pat picks up the store's mail when she picks up her own—they've given her a key to their box. At Crane's, she hands over the mail, buys herself a newspaper, and chats a while, catching up on the local conversation

Ted and Pat waiting for a bologna sandwich at Crane's in 1990.

(but not gossip; she has no time for gossip). People gather around the pot-bellied wood stove in the center of the store. In the added-on wings are antiques the Cranes gather from the surrounding area and a museum of local culture, which makes Pat happy. Before she leaves, she might examine a pair of muck boots or sniff a wood-smoke candle, but her usual purchase is hot pepper cheese, fresh off the slicer, to accompany her ritual glass of red wine in the evening.

Always, the wine is pressed from Missouri grapes; their origin matters far more to her than the vintage. If Brie were made locally, she would eat Missouri Brie. The snooty concept of *"terroir"* makes perfect sense to Pat, because the soil in which something is grown *does* make all the difference. For special occasions, she likes to eat at Les Bourgeois, a winery in nearby Rocheport. If someone orders French or Californian wine, she is liable to list a few reasons they might want to drink the local wine instead.

On the few occasions when she buys new clothes, Pat buys those at Crane's, too. She wears a denim Carhartt barn coat so often, it looks like rats have munched on the threads. When Carhartt brought back the same coat fifteen years after she bought the first one, David Crane took the liberty of suggesting it might be time for a new one. It's the biggest personal extravagance he can remember Pat indulging.

Now that lots of workers are busy restoring the farm to prairie, though, she regularly buys a dozen straw hats to make sure everybody protects their noses. Ted's melanoma never leaves her mind.

§

Pat is aging gracefully. Her hair is a little shorter than it was in high school, the bangs now silver, but her dimples are just as deep. Jamie builds her a

ramp so she can still climb easily onto her John Deere mower. The only
ache or pain he has ever heard her complain about is her knee. When
he talks her into a knee replacement, she does the post-surgery exercises
diligently and swats away the pain pills.

At eighty, she takes up yoga, which helps with balance. For walks,
she uses a tall, rustic wooden walking stick, plain as a broom handle. She
cannot wander at will around Prairie Fork anymore, but she hops in the
Gator and, splashing through muddy ditches, meets visitors wherever they
have wound up. She still shows up, in other words, finding sensible ways to
take part in the world she loves.

By five in the morning, she is up watching the farm reports on
television. When Jamie arrives, he calls out "Hey, Pat, Jamie's here," and
gets the wood stove blazing. She starts that fire in October and doesn't let it
go out until April.

First, she has coffee, then oatmeal. Once she bought a fifty-pound bag
of oats for the horses and shared it with them.

After breakfast, she works out. She splurged on a CD set of Great
Courses, probably two hundred of them, and while she walks on her
treadmill for an hour, she listens to a lecture on string theory, astronomy,
Dante, or Shakespeare.

Every day, Jamie drives her up to Crane's. Then they come back and
have lunch together. When he first started working for her, she made his
lunch; now, he makes hers. Usually, she wants a corn tortilla with melted
cheese, so one day, for a change, they try a Mexican restaurant in a nearby
town. When the food arrives, Pat informs the waiter that their food is not
Mexican, because they are serving flour tortillas, not corn tortillas. The
bemused waiter leaves the table as soon as polite, and Jamie threatens,
under his breath, never to bring Pat here again: "You can't tell them that!
It might not be Indian, but half of Mexicans came from Spain!"

After lunch, Pat puts on either her Carhartt jacket or the denim one,
now raggedy, that she nabbed from Barbara Webb. She and Jamie drive
around the farm in the Gator, covering a different chunk of its vast acreage
every day. She likes to go to the spot with the highest elevation and just
take a minute to look. In spring, they make sure to visit the creek, its banks
dotted with delicate white Dutchman's breeches ("britches," to the locals).

If she spots a researcher or conservation scientist, she says, "What's he doing? Let's go find out!"

For a while, Pat has a cell phone, but she can never find it, and when she does, the battery is always dead. Never has she owned an answering machine. "If they want to talk to me and I'm not here, they'll just have to call back," she says when Jamie suggests one.

She reads avidly, mainly natural history (*America's Ancient Forests*, Eliot Porter's *Birds of North America*, an old green book just called *Weeds*) and biographies. Presidents are a favorite category, especially Lincoln and Grant. Her hero is Thomas Jefferson. Television barely interests her. When she cannot receive the local stations for farm and other news, Jamie gets her a satellite tv. One day she can't get it to work, and when she calls for help and some guy in India answers, she jerks the cord out of the socket.

Pat likes local everything. Real experience counts with her, not virtual. She likes the curling, lingering fragrance of wood smoke and the sharper smell of fresh-cut grass. She does make use of her computer, though, keeping all her financial records there, and her curiosity lures her to the internet. When Jamie finds out she's chosen pjones as her password, he groans, already imagining everything that could go wrong when she intersects with all the pjoneses out there. Sure enough, she winds up somewhere she doesn't want to be and jerks the cable out of the router.

At 5:30 pm, she has dinner, most nights by herself. First, a glass of red wine and some hot pepper cheese. In a pinch, red wine and dark chocolate, her only concession to sugar. Peanut butter, catsup, doughnuts, cookies—none of that stuff interests her.

She goes to bed early. Her body tires sooner, now. But her brain is as sharp as an MIT engineer's, and when somebody in conservation hands her the mic, she's not shy. Nor does she take the usual tack of someone her age, dwelling on the past, preferring to think of the years she has already lived, the knowledge already familiar to her. With Pat, it's always the future that's of interest—and of deep concern.

Once in a while, someone persuades her to go out to dinner. When her niece, Melissa Curry, takes her to Les Bourgeois, they walk in and hear a chorus of "Oooohhh, Pat Jones!" Aunt Pat is a bit of a celebrity, Melissa realizes. But she never acts it. Getting dressed up means round-toed flats and a long wool skirt, maybe, if the occasion's really fancy, a pin on her sweater.

When she nears ninety, Jamie worries that she should have somebody around at night. A friend of his moves in upstairs and fixes Pat dinner in the evening. Jamie also orders her an alert necklace in case she falls. She rolls her eyes but puts it on.

At Jones, Doug Hill is worried that the company visits might be too much for Pat, who just took a visiting nurse for a ride in the Gator and drove her right into a tree. "I think these visits are keeping her alive," Beckmann tells him. "She doesn't do much else anymore, and she looks forward to this." The nurse (who was uninjured) agrees. So Beckmann takes over driving the Gator, and Jones slightly reduces the trips' frequency.

Every time Pat meets somebody new on one of those group visits, she has a hundred questions. "How are you? Where is your family from? What do you like to do?" She absorbs new information constantly. What she cares about is everyday stuff, nothing heavy or overly personal, just the details of lived experience.

"Why do people want to take my picture?" she asks Beckmann one day, grumpy about it.

"Pat, you're beautiful," Beckmann says.

"No, I'm *not*," Pat correct her, matter of fact as always.

Instead of automatically insisting, Beckmann says quietly, "I think you are. And people just want to remember that they knew you, and that they are a *part* of this place."

Pat never protests again.

§

In *The Velveteen Rabbit*, a passage explains how a stuffed creature can turn into a real one: "You become. It takes a long time. That's why it doesn't happen often to people who break easily, or have sharp edges, or who have to be carefully kept."

Pat didn't have to wait; she has always been real. Artifice never tempted her. And because she is so fully at ease herself, she has a knack for putting other people at ease, too. Her life out on the farm seems solitary, but if you look more closely, you can begin to trace a giant web of relationships. Pat's solitude is a bit like the hermitage of Thomas Merton, a contemplative Trappist monk who corresponded with friends all over the world.

Her first rule is that her door is always open; no one need call first to make sure it's okay to stop by. Hers is a thoroughgoing hospitality that is almost nonexistent these days: Interruptions are welcome, alerts unnecessary. Friends with all her neighbors, she pays visits and welcomes visitors as an essential part of life.

One day, after she mentions that a friend her age is remarrying, Jamie asks Pat if she ever thinks about getting married again. She bursts out laughing. "No, no way!" She *had* a good marriage, and now she is content on her own. But she enjoys talking with all sorts of people. She'll ask anybody anything: she wants to know what fascinates them, what they care about, who they *are*.

Nancy Freeze—the Van Dykes' daughter, now grown and married—visits Pat every time she comes home. Always surrounded by a pile of books, Pat has little time for small talk or superficial topics, and Nancy likes that Pat assumes she doesn't either. They plunge right into the latest research or environmental topic, Pat sharing what she's learned about mycorrhizal fungi or prairie grouse or controlled burns. They talk about big things, too, like God and freedom. "Well, if He is up there somewhere, He created our brains," Pat says, "and I don't know about you, but I don't recall Him sayin' we weren't allowed to use 'em." When Pat talks about schoolkids wriggling their bare feet in the mud—and sounds as gleeful as they did—Nancy realizes that she truly sees herself as a steward of this land, responsible every day for sharing it.

In his years as the world-renowned director of the Missouri Botanical Garden, Dr. Peter Raven finds every visit with Pat "a delightful experience—what a thoroughly nice and positive person." She is always so *encouraging*, he thinks as he drives away. And she's fun, too: On one visit, she takes him to "that mixed-up taxidermy handicraft place on the other side of the road, a really varied and interesting landmark of rural Missouri, for lunch," and he enjoys every minute. Later he will remark that Pat Jones "left her mark in many ways that she would not even have known herself."

Eric Kurzejeski finds himself stopping by Prairie Fork whenever possible, just because he loves talking to Pat. He can't even explain why it's such a joy. One day she's on the treadmill when he knocks. Eighty-five years old, she is sweating freely and listening to a lecture on particle physics. Kurzejeski doesn't know anything about particle physics, and he's not sure she knows a hell of a lot yet either, but by God, they talk about it.

Always, he leaves the farm feeling both soothed and invigorated; spending time with Pat is like swimming in a cool, clear lake, then letting the sun dry you. She holds fast to her convictions and expresses them firmly, but her outrage is always mixed with compassion, and as a friend, she is staunch. Most days, Kurzejeski is an optimist, but he encounters enough idiocy about the environment that his spirits can flag. Pat revives hope. There *are* things we can achieve, he thinks as he leaves, even if they don't seem possible at the time. It's just a matter of forging forward, building partnerships, finding ways to get things done. Who would have thought you could restore four hundred acres of depleted farmland to prairie in just a few years' time?

Darwin Hindman calls often and brings his wife out for lunch. He thinks of Pat, with her modest lifestyle and totally original thinking, as the model of how everybody should be. They talk about conservation, energy, national politics, local politics….

Jay Nixon, who is reaching the end of his term as Missouri governor, also visits often. Pat has taken a shine to his wife, Georganne Nixon, who loves plants as much as she does and calls trees "slow pets." The two women talk nonstop, Pat sharing expertise freely and unselfconsciously while Jay trails along after them, listening with interest. When their conversation gets a little too far into the weeds for him to follow, he spends the time thinking about the contrast between Pat and her late husband. "She just has this outdoor, natural spirit to her," he summarizes later, "and he had a corporate leader feel. It was a bit yin and yang."

As deputy director of state parks, David Kelly brings every new state park director out to Prairie Fork for a visit. "It's like taking them to the mountain to see a wise person," he explains, dead serious. Yet Pat laughs easily, telling stories, enjoying absurdity. She can still remember jokes she heard as a kid, limericks and little rhymes, and she will recite one whenever it pops into her head and then laugh, tickled. "It takes a lot to get Pat upset," a neighbor remarks. "Some major act of selfishness on somebody's part."

"She's a come-as-you-are sort of person," remarks state parks director Bill Bryan. "She's as comfortable in her skin as anybody I've ever been around." He sees "no sense of inflated importance for the work she has done, no desire for credit. She's just very thoughtful." Again and again she tells him, half scolding, "Missouri needs to be more proud of what we have here. People don't spend enough time recognizing it. They get on a plane and go away."

She is not so interested in raw wilderness, he realizes; she likes the pastoral, agrarian landscape. She sees a place for humans there, and a responsibility to protect it. The state's finest treasure, in her mind, was its vast prairie, and now there are only remnants left to show its glory.

"She could live anywhere she wanted," he reflects, "but she has a little piece of prairie." The land sustains her, connects her to the past, imposes a moral obligation to the future. Restoring it has probably been her idea all along. "She talked about the Katy in terms of Ted, his passion, how much time he invested in it, how important it was to him," Bryan will say later. "But Prairie Fork and the kids and education? That was Pat."

As director of state parks and historic sites for the Missouri Department of Natural Resources, Doug Eiken first meets Pat at a ceremony in Jefferson City, celebrating the connection of two segments of the Katy Trail after damage from the Great Flood of '93 is repaired. They become friends, and he watches over the years as she gives generously not only to the Katy but to all sorts of urban and rural trail efforts. She fights alongside Doug to get the parks and soil sales tax renewed. She backs any effort related to prairie preservation. She's so positive, so confident in young people to fix the future, that he includes her in group presentations whenever he can.

Above all, what he loves is the way she treats people, and how good he feels every time he's with her. The only way he can pin it down is as some sort of spiritual quality, something that flows from deep inside her. There are people in the world, not many, who are so contented, so *joyous*, that he feels uplifted just to be in their presence.

33
———

Spending Ted's Money

For nearly three decades after Ted's death, executives from not-for-profit organizations call on Pat with all sorts of projects they hope she will fund. Sometimes she frowns and says, "I don't think I can spend Ted's money on that." At other times, she gives as much as she thinks responsible. Often she helps out behind the scenes, solving problems that aren't sexy enough to inspire other donors. She has the imagination and the caring to lend a hand when there's no glory in it.

Toward the end, though her mind is still clear, her memory softens into the stereotype of an absentminded professor. People will show up while she and Jamie are having lunch and say, "Gosh, I'm sorry I'm late," and both she and Jamie will smile but wonder to themselves, "Who *is* this person?" Eventually, Jamie pulls out a calendar and takes over the scheduling.

He worries about all these outstretched hands. Pat spends next to nothing on herself, he knows, but she donates, sometimes too readily. "I want to be like Molly Brown," she tells him, "spend all the money and die with a nickel."

She sets up a college fund for all her great-grandnieces and great-grandnephews, making possible a public policy degree from the University of Chicago, a year studying abroad in Scotland, educational experiences tailored to a great-niece with special needs. Then she turns to her causes.

§

"I am certainly having a good time spending Ted's money," Pat tells her niece Melissa, laughing. Ted had given money to the local church and community center. Back in 1979, North Callaway set up its own volunteer fire department, using a building across from Crane's. Ted wanted the community to have a better fire station. He donated money, but he wanted the community to do some work, too. Volunteers donated their time and equipment, and someone else donated the land. And when Ted saw the three-bay station being built, he said, "It might not be big enough. I think we ought to have four bays." And so they expanded the blueprints.

Now, Pat tells the county firefighting board that she wants to buy Williamsburg a fire truck, and she has $100,000 to spend. A few board members ask if she will buy two used trucks instead, $50,000 apiece. "I've got $100,000," Jim Zerr, a charter member of the original group, hears her reply. "You can buy a new truck. If you buy a used one for $50,000, that's all you're going to get." She wants Williamsburg to have a new, well-built fire truck; she doesn't want a worn-out fire truck for her town and a second worn-out fire truck for somebody else's.

Later, the volunteer firefighters find an old regular truck that's been abandoned and try to use it as a brush truck. When Pat finds out, she buys them a new, heavy-duty pickup for a brush truck, too.

Community means a lot to her, and community is local, particular, specific, concrete. Whenever visitors come to talk to her about projects, she brings them to Marlene's for lunch so they can see Crane's museum and get a feel for the place and its history.

§

Most awards commemorate large monetary gifts with standard prose. But in the wording on many of the plaques and speeches honoring Pat, you sense an effort to capture more than generosity. People know the depth of her convictions. This is not somebody who just sits down at strategic times and writes a tax-deductible check.

"It frustrates me that people so focus on the money," remarks Jay Nixon. "I don't mean to underestimate it, but that's not the part that makes the difference. Ted and Pat have been so much *more* than that."

In 1999, two years after deeding her land over to the state and the university, Pat donates money to the Dunn Ranch Preserve, a 3,680-acre holding up in northwest Missouri, almost at the Iowa border. Much of the land has never seen a plow, and soon tallgrass prairie is being restored throughout. A herd of bison stomps through the switchgrass, and at least a hundred species of birds glide overhead.

What makes her happiest, though, is Dunn Ranch's plan to summon back the prairie chickens. "The first chicken they put out at Dunn Ranch thinks, 'This is good country,' and they want to move directly to Iowa," she chuckles. Eventually, she thinks, the prairie chickens will flourish at Dunn Ranch—*if.* "A lot of the survival of birds depends on soil health and bugs. So if you have a restored prairie and you're getting grass to live in this terrible soil, and you don't have any fertilizer on it, there aren't any bugs there. The bugs, of all things, need fertilized ground. So you don't get the birds." She waits a beat. "There isn't any reason to think that this native prairie has to be poor ground. We *made* it poor."

§

In 2006, Pat is named a Master Conservationist, the highest honor bestowed upon a Missourian who has made "substantial and lasting contributions" to wildlife and forest conservation and education.

In 2013, she receives the Outstanding Lifetime Achievement Award from the Conservation Federation of Missouri.

Next, she pledges $1.6 million to her alma mater to endow a youth program and a faculty position in conservation. She goes to the annual dinner expecting only a good meal and finds herself rising to accept the University of Missouri's Frederick B. Mumford Award.

Her response is warm, a little startled, but with no mock humility, none of those protestations that sound self-deprecating but are really designed to draw more attention to oneself. She is interested in the *issues*, not the attention. When she is seated in the rotunda of the state Capitol, waiting to receive an award from the Missouri Conservation Foundation, billionaire Johnny Morris, CEO of Bass Pro, steps to the podium and speaks lyrically of the beauty of fishing in the Lake of the Ozarks. Pat calls out, her voice amplified by the acoustics, "More people need to float than fish! You ever try to float a lake? We need to stop putting up dams."

Everybody laughs, hard enough that most people would be gratified by the attention and settle back in their chair. But Pat does not lose focus. "The world needs a few more streams and a few less dams," she murmurs under her breath.

One day Jamie drives her—using Pat's rusty little Geo—to see the Danforth Plant Science Center. Dr. William Danforth, the founding chairman, and Dr. Roger Beachy, the founding president, are standing outside waiting for Pat Jones. They wave the little Geo on.

Danforth comes to know Pat Jones well enough that he will never make that mistake again. He and Beachy visit Prairie Fork several times. One day, Pat joins them for a special event in front of the Danforth Plant Science Center. All the guests have been given a little paper cup of seeds to plant, and they set off for the designated area. Pat is clutching her cup with a hand wrapped around her walker, and Danforth, one year younger, is managing with two canes. She glances over at him and says dryly, "Want to race?"

§

When the Smithsonian sets out to create a National Soils Display, Pat offers her backing. The idea is to show the various layers of all the soils that cover the surface of America, making life possible here. The exhibit will use monoliths, vertical slices from topsoil down to subsoil, that preserve the colors and textures of each layer. Pat is literally in her element.

She feels the same way when she learns of the Missouri Department of Conservation's Stream Team. She tells the project's manager, biologist Mark Van Patten, how urgently her mother cared about keeping nature as clean as her kitchen, and how she made all the kids pick up litter whenever they went to LaBarque Creek. Pat reaches for her checkbook and pays for all the trash bags, then continues to lend support. She and Van Patten become good friends, talking for hours about science and nature, and when she finds out he teaches fly fishing, she invites the kids out to the farm.

Pat also gives to the Missouri Prairie Foundation's Prairie Garden Grant Fund and Prairie Stewardship Fund. The Missouri Botanical Garden. The Audubon Society, designating the Ark, a floating nature center on the Mississippi River that educates the public about natural resources. The Nature Conservancy, especially for the Grand River Grasslands Conservation Area around Dunn Ranch. The Saint Louis Zoo. MoBikeFed. The Danforth Plant Science Center. Planned Parenthood. Westminster College. The YMCA of Missouri.

Ted racked up his own flurry of awards, including the National Wildlife Federation Award and the Column Award from the College of Agriculture, Food, and Natural Resources at the university he once hoped would be his alma mater. He is already in the Missouri Conservation Hall of Fame, and in 2015, he is posthumously awarded with an even higher honor, a bronze bust of his likeness placed in the state capital in the Hall of Famous Missourians.

Norman Eaker is standing next to Pat when Ted's bust is unveiled. "Well, he looks happy," she remarks. Someone asks where the bust will be placed, and she looks around at Walt Disney, Harry S. Truman, Mark Twain, and the other Hall of Famers. "I don't know," she drawls, "but they better not put it next to Rush Limbaugh's."

The following year, Pat receives the National Lewis & Clark Conservation Award from the Missouri Conservation Heritage Foundation. Called The York Spirit of the Wilderness Award, it is inscribed on pewter and inset in a crosswise slice of a tree. The following year, the award is permanently renamed the Pat Jones/York Spirit of the Wilderness Award, capturing two eras and two kinds of courage.

Whenever yet another invitation arrives, Pat shrugs. "Oh, well, I'll go," she tells Jamie, not exactly exuberant. The *cause* matters; the fuss, she tries to take in stride.

One award, though, touches her to the core. In 2017, her last full year of life, she receives an honorary doctorate in the humanities from her alma mater. After the ceremony, she has the satiny academic hood, the cap, and the heavy medallion placed behind glass in a shadow box, and she *hangs* it—in her home, in a place where she can glance up and see it. Maybe because the award was connected to education, her lifelong love? Or maybe because so much of her life's work these six decades grew right out of that soil science degree.

34

Her Time

Pat is not afraid to die. She talks about it all the time.

"But are you still having fun?" Jamie asks, worried.

"Oh, yes!" she says. "But it's my time."

In late October 2018, she is jouncing along on a tram, taking the Katy Trail from Rocheport to see the McBaine Bur Oak. Famously huge and ancient, the tree stands on the property of Ted's former Katy opponent, John Sam Williamson. Pat holds no grudges; neither does Williamson.

A sharp wind cuts across the tram, carrying a prophecy of winter. Through the damp, bone-chilling hour-long ride, Pat keeps them all cheered up, identifying "just about every tree and shrub we passed," Dan Burkhardt will recall later, "with a running commentary on the conservation value of all of them."

A van is waiting when they reach the bur oak. "Pat, we'll give you a ride back to Rocheport," a state parks staffer calls. The other tram passengers look up, squinting through the drizzle, wondering if there might be extra room in that dry, heated van.

"Oh, I'm fine, I'll ride the tram back," Pat replies. "I want to see what the scenery looks like going the opposite direction."

Abashed, everybody else says they'll take the tram back, too. Can't be shown up by a ninety-three-year-old woman. They reach Rocheport shivering but happy—and far better informed than they were when they arrived.

"I want death to find me planting cabbages," Montaigne wrote, and Pat shares his spirit. Less than a month after that tram ride, her body begins to give up. She has already refused the procedure her doctor suggested for her heart murmur, calmly explaining that she does not *want* the procedure; she has lived "a really good long life," and many of her friends are already gone. She did want to live long enough to see a clean, hydrogen-based economy, but it is taking a ridiculously long time to get people on board.

Jamie knows better than to suggest a nursing home. People have made discreet murmurs about the joys of assisted living in these last years, and it's been the fastest way to upset her. "I will *not* go into a retirement home!" she exclaims. "I will be out here with my dog!"

Out here, on the land where she has lived and worked for sixty-four years. Jamie respects that. So when Pat can no longer get herself up in the morning, he and his wife, Debbie Coe, take turns with Amber Edwards; Judy Beckmann; Terisa Boley, who has been both housekeeper and nurse; and Brian Warren, who lives upstairs. Someone is by Pat's side every hour, day and night. First, she moves back and forth between her bed and the recliner. In her last eight days, she stays in bed, and a hospice nurse comes to help.

There is little to do by way of preparation. Pat has been giving things away steadily to anyone who might want or need them. Rugs, pictures…. she doesn't want anything of value left behind for others to have to deal with. Except she does want to make sure Jamie gives Eric Kurzejeski's little girl, Isabella, the stuffed blind mole rat. Pat would have given it to her sooner, but it was a present from the Zoo, a whimsical token of their gratitude when she funded an exhibition about, yes, naked mole rats. Pat has used the toy as a prop; she loves telling the story of this wrinkly pink sand puppy that burrows deep, as though to hide a face only a mother could love. Naked mole rats huddle together for warmth, snack on their own poop, and care cooperatively for their babies. Next to the glossy black and orange American burying beetle, they have always struck Pat as having a story worth telling.

Hilda Paterson Young Jones dies on December 17, 2018. Gunner is on the bed with her. Over at the guesthouse, Katy Trail folks are meeting; they were hoping to see Pat later in the afternoon. Edwards pulls herself together, goes over to the guesthouse, and for the first time in this job she loves, she lies. If they know Pat is gone, they will end the meeting, and Pat would never want that to happen.

Finally, Edwards finds David Kelly, deputy director of Missouri State Parks. Taking him aside, she whispers that Pat is gone. For the rest of the meeting, he goes through the motions, but everyone can see that he is not quite himself.

Dan and Connie Burkhardt have to leave the meeting early, and as Dan is pulling out, he sees Jamie Coe walking from the house, his shoulders hunched, the news written on his face. Dan rolls down his window, and the two men hold each other's forearms as Jamie says simply, "She's gone." They don't add many words; can't. What's clear is that there will never be another person like her.

§

When Pat's beloved recliner is moved, acorns roll out—either they fell from her pockets in her better days or Gunner brought them when he jumped up to sleep behind her head. "He was pretty spoiled," Jamie laughs, trying to drive away the tears. "She never said no to a dog. Never said no to much of anything."

§

With Pat gone, there is a sort of vertigo; so many people who made it a point to call or visit are now left with only their memories.

"She was intriguing," Jim McKenzie says. "Why did I make a point of seeing her every year? I've always tried to spend time with people who fascinated me, trying to read them like a good book. Pat had a real inner strength. She was smart, real smart. She could think really clearly and express her ideas without caveats. Pat Jones was very comfortable with Pat Jones."

§

Come spring, there is a celebration of Pat's life—at the farm, of course. A tent is set up in case of rain, but the day dawns clear and sunny, and the prairie is coming back to life, the bluebells and wild violets giving way to columbine and prairie larkspur, phlox and wild iris and Indian paintbrush.

Eric Kurzejeski emcees. Hundreds of people come. There is no music, no script. Instead of bereavement's heavy melancholy, the mood is joyous: Everybody is just so happy they had a chance to *know* her.

"She affected me in ways I never expected," someone says, swallowing hard.

"The way she treated people—she made me want to treat everyone that way," someone else says.

"I moved to a career in conservation because of Pat."

"I started teaching because of Pat."

Penny Pennington, the current CEO of Edward Jones, gives an informal eulogy, saying, "Pat Jones never worked at our firm, and yet she was an integral and important part of who we are." Pennington talks about listening to Pat, "full of wisdom and history, as usual," as she shared stories about Ted and showed off the new seed bank. Kurzejeski tells a story about a Jones function where a man broke away from the outdoor dinner and tiptoed up to the house, peering into the windows. A colleague asked what on earth he was doing. He shrugged, embarrassed. "I just wanted to see how Pat lives."

"Look out there," Kurzejeski says now, gesturing toward the rippling prairie grasses. "*That* is how Pat lived."

David Kelly steps to the mic. He talks about driving Pat and Ted in a golf cart to the site of the Katy Trail ribbon-cutting. They had just been presented with matching bicycles and an old-fashioned bicycle horn, and Pat is honking it as they go, clearing a path through hundreds of people. It was the first of many trips he would share with her, people often lining up to thank her, and Pat using the time to talk about the environment. When it came time to celebrate the Katy's twenty-fifth anniversary, Kelly says, the state added a Pat Jones Picnic Shelter. "Pat's only request for that project was that we plant a bur oak tree next to the shelter to provide shade and for visitors to enjoy."

§

Like Ted, Pat has given her body to science and wants no marker, no religious rites, no commemoration. The irony is that people are all the more eager to remember and commemorate them.

In a year or so, the medical school sends Pat's ashes back to the farm. Students have learned from her one last time. Jamie and the other caregivers spread the cremains around her favorite pond, among the bluestem and wildflowers, under clouds of bluebirds that rise from the grass without warning and fly away, bright splotches of blue spattering the sky.

The year after that, COVID-19 shuts the world down, and all Jamie can think is how glad he is that Pat isn't here for the pandemic. It would have destroyed her to see the farm so desolate, emptied of visitors.

Meanwhile, Kurzejeski keeps asking his son-in-law, who works at Ameren UE's Callaway County plant, if he has, er, seen anything unusual. The transparent figure of an older woman, maybe? Her bangs short, her fist upraised, the dimples as deep as a ghost can manifest….

35

The Culture Ted Created

John Bachmann and Doug Hill, current and future managing partners, celebrate an award with Ted in the early 1980s.

Ted always warned advisors not to be flashy; it was obnoxious. Their job was to help other people achieve their goals, not flaunt their own success.

His carefully chosen successor, John Bachmann, drove home the same conservative message. If he saw a pricey little sports car in the parking lot, he warned the owner to rein in their spending. When the company was growing fast but needed to do better recruiting and training, Bachmann did what he thought Ted would have done: set aside the hunger to grow, delayed the 10,000-office goal by four years, and took a year out to recoup before adding any more offices.

The 1999 Harvard case study ties the firm's success to its steady conservatism: "Less than 10 percent of new brokers came from other firms," and Jones did not pay recruitment bonuses to attract transfers. Jones's recommended stock list had a turnover of only 6.3 percent in

1997; the lists of many major brokerages had turnovers of more than 100 percent. Jones clients held onto their mutual funds an average of 20 years. "The average account balance of Jones' 2.85 million customer accounts was roughly $50,000. Over 85 percent of the company's accounts generated less than $500 in annual commissions."

That is the landscape Ted plotted out, the steadiness he cultivated. And hardly a meeting or presentation went by without Bachmann in some way acknowledging the legacy Ted had left them—and pushing to keep it strong.

Ted made five absolutely essential contributions, Dan Burkhardt realized later, that set the company apart and allowed it to grow: "First, the one-broker office. Ted would not compromise on that. He refused to pit salespeople against each other, no matter what you could save in overhead costs."

Norman Eaker was the one tracking those costs, but he approved of the one-broker system wholeheartedly: "Usually, firms have a branch manager, and thirty people are all following the instructions of one person. If you have thirty different financial advisors instead, you're going to tap into their entrepreneurial spirit and unleash their energy. Not everybody can survive in that environment, but those who can, thrive."

Ted's second contribution was picking the right managing partner at the right time. "There is no success without a successor," Drucker says often. In Bachmann, Ted saw someone who shared his principles, could push for the change the firm needed, and had the intellectual ability to adapt to changing times. And Bachmann did adapt, remaining managing partner for a quarter century, from 1980 until 2005. That's when he bumped up against an obstacle even he couldn't overcome, the Jones mandatory retirement age of 65. But he had already more than doubled the ten-year average tenure for a CEO.

Ted's third contribution was not allowing fiefdoms within the firm, separate profit centers that could pile up cash while the rest of the firm scraped along. "When you have profit centers, you get away from the concept of a partnership in which everybody wins or loses together," notes Norman Eaker. "You create internal competition, and now it's 'How do I make my small slice of the pie bigger?'—and maybe it's at the expense of someone else at the firm doing well."

The fourth contribution: insisting that older partners had to sell down their interest and "move over on the bench," making room for younger people.

The fifth: insisting that everyone who worked at Jones, whether they were mopping floors or sealing deals, should have a chance to own part of the company's success.

Those five initiatives were why Peter Drucker agreed to work with Jones, Burkhardt is convinced, and why the *Harvard Business Review* wrote about the firm in such glowing terms.

Ted's latest successor, Penny Pennington, focuses on the principles behind those initiatives: Ted's emphasis on service, wanting everything Jones associates do to be about somebody else; Ted's caveat that to be about other people, you have to be generous with the people who are going to serve them; his willingness to share his company with people who would carry it forward; his refusal to imitate and conform. "Strategy by envy is a non-starter," she says. "Ted did not want to be like anybody else. He made his dad mad because he *refused* to be like anybody else. And what he built was fundamentally different."

Now, what Ted did with his company is even being touted as a neat solution to a current economic dilemma. A 2018 *HBR* article notes that "the gap in wealth in the United States between the ultrawealthy and everyone else has reached its widest point in decades. One way to narrow the divide is through the use of worker buyouts, in which ownership of a company transfers from a single person or a small number of people to the workers of the company." The way Jones did years ago.

If employee ownership gathers steam, it could make a big, fast difference: Privately held companies employ one in six of all U.S. workers, and nearly half of these businesses have owners who plan to retire soon. There is strong interest in keeping local communities viable, and there is mounting evidence that employee-owned companies outperform their competitors, especially during downturns. For those reasons, it is becoming easier for the employees to get financing and invest in the company where they work.

§

The hallway outside Penny Pennington's office was a little bleak until she dug up the oil portraits of the previous five managing partners—and Ted's famous "Why I Am the Richest Man in America" letter—and hung them where she would see them every day. A global pandemic broke out the year after she became managing partner, so she did a lot of thinking about her predecessors and all they shouldered. "Every era," she says, "you can point to something that was existential for the company."

If Ted came back for a day? She imagines him saying, in his folksy, wicked-smart way, "So how the hell have the last 18 months been?" and laughing. And then he'd turn pensive, and his voice would soften, and he'd say, "No, really, how has that been? How has everybody held together? What are we doing for people? What have they needed?" And once she'd answered, he'd say, "Now tell me, *how* many counties are we in? And did you say $1.7 *trillion* assets under care? And we were more successful in 2020 than we've ever been?" To which she would respond, "Yes, and it is wholly because of your vision."

Will Edward Jones continue to grow, or has it reached its maximum?

"We've reached critical mass," Pennington says. "We're not going anywhere, and it'd be very hard for somebody to buy us. But we are serving 7 million clients, and we know there are 41 million serious long-term investors in North America. So actually, we're not nearly big *enough* yet."

§

Like everyone else who has joined the firm since 1990, Maria Pisa (now DiMaggio) sighs over her timing. She "just missed Ted," and she's been hearing stories about him since day one.

In 1994, Pisa was introduced to a man who, upon hearing that she worked for a local bank, said, "Do you know who Edward Jones is? That's who *I* work for." What he said about the company—an independence unheard of at other brokerages, a private partnership that treated you well and allowed you to run your own office—sounded too good to be true. She'd just finished reading John Grisham's *The Firm*, and she was suspicious.

She did some research. Meanwhile, she was increasingly dissatisfied with her own job. When an earthquake hit, "it was crystal clear how unorganized the bank was." Deciding it was time to move on, she interviewed "with *everybody*. Banks, brokerages…and Edward Jones." The Jones process took six months, prompting Pisa's future husband to suggest she grab a great offer from Dean Witter Reynolds instead.

But by then, she was sure she wanted to work for Jones.

When they finally offered her a job, she proved herself so easily that she was branded a fast starter and asked to train and mentor other advisors. By 1998, she was a limited partner; in 2003, she became a general partner.

Along the way, every Jones financial advisor she met had a Ted story; it got to the point that if they didn't volunteer one right away, she'd ask. She was building a composite picture of the man in her head: "Funny; intimidating; all business, but jovial; humble, humble, humble." She decided she would have been a nervous wreck if he ever visited her office, but in the end, she would have gotten along really well with him.

Today, she can trace his influence in "our desire to do what's *right*. Not only for the client but in general. And to work in tandem, not in competition. Don't get me wrong—I think Ted was very competitive. But not internally." At other firms, for example, incentive trips are capped, available only to the top twenty-five or hundred people, so you are vying with your colleagues to go. At Jones, "if I earn an incentive trip, that doesn't mean my mentor can't win one, and so can the person I'm mentoring. All three of us can go, if we just apply ourselves."

In 2007, Pisa was diagnosed with a tumor in her leg. The company sent another advisor to take care of her clients for months while she healed. She'd been doing so much business, the guy won a trip and insisted it was rightfully hers, and the company overrode her protests and suggested that with a wheelchair and her husband's help, Cabo might be just the place to finish recuperating.

Pisa stepped down from her general partner role, but she went right back to the core of her job, advising clients. If Ted were still around, he wouldn't say much—he didn't believe in gushing—but she would definitely not be on his "worry list."

§

In the late Nineties, Jim Goodknight has a crisis of conscience that winds up creating a program so innovative, it is highlighted in the 1999 Harvard Business School case-study. The idea is born when Goodknight finds himself working as a partner and a regional leader with far too many clients. Busy from early morning until late at night, he realizes he is not giving the kind of service he promised his investors when they agreed to do business with him. Guilt drains the pleasure from his work, and he spends all his free time trying to do right by his clients, and he misses the hours he used to spend fishing, the quiet of the lake restoring his equanimity.

Desperate for a solution, he remembers a quote he once heard at a seminar: "At most organizations, 10 percent of your clients provide 90 percent of your income." Looking through his books, he realizes that is exactly true for him. So he brings in a younger broker and strikes a deal: "I'll give you 90 percent of my accounts, and for a time, we'll split the commission." The new broker more than doubles the commissions, because he has the time and energy to devote. Goodknight starts getting referrals again, because he, too, has enough time and energy for the clients he kept. By 1998, the firm is selectively placing additional brokers in offices that have reached 1,500 to 2,500 accounts and can afford to share them, increasing customer service and expanding those portfolios.

This is exactly what Ted did with the firm, Goodknight realizes. *He gave away part of his ownership to all of us new partners, and now it is making the company as a whole much stronger.*

36

The Land Ted and
Pat Transformed

Most of us are lucky if we plant
a few rose bushes that survive us.
The Joneses loved land, protected
it, cared for it tenderly, planned
its future—and then gave it away.
Carefully, with stipulations in place.
As a result, the state of Missouri
now has a nature preserve, a prairie,
a famous trail, and a park that
surrounds the meeting of our great
rivers. All of that land will be kept
as nature intended it, open and free
and a little bit wild, for generations
to come. It connects us, and it sets
an example, continuing to inspire
other trails, other gifts, other
preservation projects.

Pat and Ted spent years turning their
farm into a model of conservation. They
created habitat for wildlife, stopped
erosion, planted trees and prairies,
nurtured the land. And then they gave it
away, so the rest of us could get as close
to the land and nature as they were.

Hilda's Pristine Wilderness

The land Hilda Jamieson Young amassed is now the Young Conservation Area, part of the Missouri Department of Conservation and free for anyone to roam, hike, boat, birdwatch (especially the indigo buntings and green herons), photograph wildlife, hunt (the land teems with deer, turkeys, and squirrels), or reel in sunfish, catfish, crappie, bluegill, or black bass. The land is about 93 percent forested in oak, maple, hickory, cedar, and other natives, with an understory of spicebush and dogwood and a mix of glades, woodland, pine stands, and open fields. Its LaBarque Creek watershed is almost three times more diverse than any of the fifteen other tributaries of the Meramec River below LaBarque.

"It's one of the few places in the St. Louis region that still has a full complement of fish and insects," says Mark Van Patten, who worked for years as a fisheries management biologist for the Missouri Department of Conservation. "It hasn't been compromised by development."

Pat and her mother made sure of that.

After the 1986 purchase that Pat made possible, an adjacent tract came up for sale, and she quietly handed the Missouri Conservation Heritage Foundation $1 million to buy it. When an even larger tract came up for sale and they had $3 million donated toward the $4 million price, she handed over the final $1 million.

The Young Conservation Area now stretches across 1,300 acres. Pat would approve the wildlife habitat management practices, which include plenty of native vegetation, edge feathering, thinning of the woodland, and strategic tree planting. She would also approve the permission granted for dogs to be trained there off lead—and the sharing of the area's abundant nuts, berries, fruits, mushrooms, and wild greens with anyone who forages for them.

The 3.5-mile LaBarque Hills Trail goes up and down gentle hills and along streams, passing seasonal waterfalls and cutting through oak-hickory forests. The sandstone in this part of Missouri is as white as sugar, and LaBarque Creek cuts into the bluffs and forms overhangs, so you feel like you're in a cave looking out at the water.

It's peaceful there.

Prairie Fork

The Jones farm is an extraordinary place. Fifteen miles north of the Missouri River, dense woods in between. Pat calls the farm "the battleground," the place where the trees met the prairie. "This is between places," she explains, "because we're off at the end of the glacier. So we've got flat land behind us. You come down where the glacier ends, and then it falls off into these hills and down to the river. You know, our hills are below the level land; it's not like a mountainous country."

At the gate to the main driveway, the ground falls off, and the prairie breaks. Now you have rolling land, with strips of woods up and down the draw, until you reach the river breaks. Historically, these acres included prairie, wetland, slightly forested woodland edged with wildflowers and grasses—three entirely different ecosystems in 710 acres.

In full bloom, the prairie is now breathtaking.

The grasses are now nearly as tall as their ancestors—which grew so high that a man on horseback could vanish from sight. In March, Virginia bluebells carpet the damp woods in periwinkle, followed by wild indigo that quickly reaches a four-foot height, its branches clustered with creamy white blossoms that precede its black seed pods. Intermixed with the indigo are the delicate, mini-daffodil blooms of yellow star-grass and spires of blue-violet lupine. June brings even more blue—lobelia and spiderwort—along with the rosy, fragrant clusters of milkweed. In July, fifty kinds of yellow bring the sunshine right down to the ground. Lemony prairie dock, with its rough heart-shaped leaves and sticky pine-resin stem, acts as a natural compass, always orienting itself north-south so the leaves' broad faces receive maximum sunlight. Compass plant does the same, of course, its yellow blooms several inches in diameter. Goldenrod, daisies, sunflowers, and coreopsis dot the grasses. All that yellow looks even more intense against the hot magenta coneflowers and ironweed and the saturated purple of blazing star, all of which carry through to late summer.

The World-Famous Katy Trail

At 240 miles the Katy Trail is the longest rail trail in America. Every year, about 400,000 hikers and cyclists follow this winding, tree-shaded trail. "People come from around the world to see the part of the country that Pat and Ted called home," says Bill Bryan, the former director of Missouri State Parks, who has cycled the length of the Katy Trail and found respite there many times. "Here in Missouri, it's part of the fabric of our lives." Families leave their cellphones and laptops behind and hit the trail together. Photographers and historians explore the towns, caves, churches, farms, and bridges along the way.

The Katy runs through seventy-five miles of rolling farmland, from Clinton through Sedalia to Boonville, then along the Missouri River, beneath limestone bluffs decorated with red Virginia creeper in autumn. The trail runs through heavy wooded areas from Boonville to Bluffton, the sugar maples blazing with color, and after passing through Rocheport's stone tunnel, reaches the trailhead where a plaque dedicates the Katy to Ted and Pat Jones.

Near McBaine, part of the trail runs parallel to the Eagle Bluffs Wildlife Area, a wetland developed by the Conservation Department. The nation's most iconic bird is easy to spot here. So are turkey vultures and the Canada geese that Lewis and Clark wrote about, fascinated to see them nesting on cliff ledges. Hollows in the rock, too high for human hands to reach, host tiny, unusual ecosystems.

After reaching the state capital in Jefferson City and crossing the bridge, you ride or walk along flat farmland—emerald green or beige depending on the season. In Augusta, you have entered wine country, and from here to French St. Charles, you can tour a succession of small, spirited German towns. Then there is a peaceful stretch from St. Charles to Machens, and then you can ride almost to the confluence of the Missouri and Mississippi rivers (and the Ted and Pat Jones Confluence State Park).

The Reachable Confluence

In 2004, the Edward "Ted" and Pat
Jones Confluence Point State Park was
dedicated. The name was a bit of a
mouthful, Pat thought privately, but the
state insisted. What mattered were the
trails that would eventually connect to the
Katy. The thousand-plus acres that would be preserved. The chance to see
the confluence of the Mississippi River and the Missouri River, the place
where westward expansion began.

"Ted read history," she remarked soon after his death. "You read about
people coming to St. Louis. And why is St. Louis here? Because the rivers
meet." It was inconceivable that no one could reach the spot where they
met. Meriwether Lewis and William Clark started their great journey at
the confluence, but since then, the spot had been unreachable by land.
"Dickens got stuck in the mud before he reached St. Charles!" Pat groans,
referring to the famous writer's expedition to the American Midwest.

They must have been disappointed—especially if they had read the
1721 journal of Father Pierre Francois de Charlevoix: "I believe this is the
finest confluence in the world. The two rivers are much the same breadth,
each about half a league; but the Missouri is by far the most rapid, and
seems to enter the Mississippi like a conqueror, through which it carries
its white waters to the opposite shore without mixing them, afterwards, it
gives its color to the Mississippi which it never loses again but carries quite
down to the sea...."

The Mississippi became the strong brown god that would carry the
barges of industry; the Missouri remained a wild western river. The land
where they meet is now reachable, and a natural flood plain is returning,
with habitat for the white-tailed deer and beavers and respite for bald
eagles and other raptors. At the park's dedication, Pat placed one hand
in the Mississippi and the other in the Missouri: two of the world's most
powerful rivers, meeting beneath her fingertips. An experience anyone can
now share.

37

———

Keeping Up With the Joneses

So many people have found a way to follow Pat's lead. One of her great-nieces, Maya Hermann, used the college fund Pat set up to study public policy, then went on for a graduate degree. She became a legislative assistant to Sen. Martin Heinrich, who was at one point considered as Secretary of the Interior. She handled public lands, forestry, mining, water, wildlife, and other natural resources issues; her grandmother would have been weighing in constantly.

Pat's nephew, Truman Young, is a respected emeritus professor in plant sciences at the University of California-Davis. She must have been thrilled by his career, though he says she never mentioned it: "She didn't think boosting people's ego was a thing to do."

"As long as you are on this earth," Pat used to say, "it's your responsibility to make it better for those to come."

Dave Adams worked for Jones before becoming a nature photographer, and trips to the farm inspired him. He has since spent years working to eradicate all the invasive honeysuckle from the wooded back half of his property, so the native species that were being smothered could flourish again. Before he met Pat, he had never even heard the term "invasive species."

Beckmann continues to bring Jones groups to Prairie Fork. Being out there makes people feel closer to Pat, she says. "They can feel she's there.

They ask me, 'Is it weird to be at Prairie Fork without Pat?' and I say, 'No, because every blade of grass has her spirit in it.'"

The world is richer for those blades; tallgrass prairie is the most decimated ecosystem in North America, and grassland, according to the Nature Conservancy, is the most imperiled ecosystem in the world.

At Prairie Fork, it flourishes.

§

When she was being interviewed for a State Historical Society of Missouri oral history, Pat said, "We need more and more people that are willing to keep our rivers floatable and clean. And to keep our land where it is. And keep our air clean."

The interviewer nodded politely; he was there to hear about her life, not her causes. She answered his questions for as long as she could stand it, then switched back to what she felt mattered: "We just need to indoctrinate people that it's possible to do it, and let's *do* it."

When Missouri was named America's Best Trail State at the International Trail Symposium, Bill Bryan brought the plaque out to Prairie Fork to show Pat. Clearly the Katy Trail was the reason the state had scored the award.

"This is fantastic," Pat said, "but you can't rest on this. There's still work to do. What are you going to do next?"

He grinned. One more lesson. Pat had already taught him, just by the way she lived, that "the trappings of success don't have to trap you." The luxury of success is the ability to live the way you want, be whoever you want to be. Your life should focus on what makes you happy—really happy, not just temporarily thrilled or sated.

Barb Gilman noticed that "Patsy had a wicked sense of humor." Others noticed that, despite her intelligent conversation, what she really did well was listen to you. Judy Beckmann noticed how, "everything Pat got, she gave away. It was so humbling to me, the way she lived. Especially knowing everything she *could* have had. You always think, 'If I had more money, I could do...' this or that. She showed me you don't need it." Beckmann pauses. "When you look at life as a whole, what's important to you—I look at things simply now. We put too much thought into everything. Ted found simplicity and made such an impact. Pat did, too."

§

Like his wife—but with a tinge more ego—Ted was conscious of shaping a legacy. He could never drive past a highway marker; he sailed off the exit ramp and stopped to learn the story, interested to know what other people left behind. He thought carefully about what *he* wanted to leave behind—and despite an early death, he made it happen.

"When you consider what he *created*," exclaims John Ashcroft, former U.S. attorney general, U.S. senator, Missouri governor, and state auditor. "He was not a towering person, he was a stocky sort of guy who had a capacity to persist." His company transformed people's finances and therefore their lives. And the Katy Trail has played the same sort of leadership role: "There have been other trails undertaken subsequent to it, both in Missouri and elsewhere. The sincerest compliment is imitation.

"I appreciated, profoundly, Ted Jones's dedication," Ashcroft finishes, brushing aside any credit for himself. "I probably could have made it *impossible*, but I don't think I could have made it *possible* without him."

A famous photo shows Ted sitting on a wood bench at his farm. After he died, Jim McKenzie started handing out a photo that showed the same bench—but empty.

"That's your job," he told the brokers.

§

Now the fourth largest brokerage in the U.S., Edward Jones has quadrupled its market share in the past two decades. It has also ranked highest in investor satisfaction, not once but ten times, and dominated *Fortune*'s list of the best companies to work for. The last large partnership remaining in the finance industry, it is now owned, if you include limited and general partners, by almost 25,000 people—making it the most widely-held partnership of its kind in the world.

Ted's sister Ann was asked, late in her life, how he might have reacted to the firm's exponential growth. "I don't think he would be that surprised," she said. "I think our *father* would be *dumbfounded*!"

Long after Ted's death, Peter Drucker continued to talk about the man's genius. Ted had a true entrepreneurial insight and the courage to act on it; he also had "a basic decency and goodness" that made him want to succeed for all the right reasons, Drucker says. "To write off a person was awfully hard for Ted…. He enjoyed people. He gloried in their success. He worked very hard to make them succeed"—not because it reflected well on him, but because it reflected well on the human race. "Jones forced me to do a lot of thinking on the function of finance in a modern society."

§

Ted gave nature-lovers the Katy Trail. He gave a beaten-up farm a chance to come back to life. He gave his wife the farm she had always wanted and the freedom to fight for causes she held dear. He gave money and scholarships and circus memorabilia and fire engines and Christmas trees and his time and his energy and his contacts. He gave his company to its associates, and he gave his clients security and the opportunity to live as they dreamed. Own a house that feels like a home. Send a kid to college and then to med school. Retire early and travel the world. Dreams now accessible to seven million clients, because of Ted.

The name Edward Jones is now ubiquitous, its white-on-green typeface legible on more than 15,000 signs throughout North America. (There are 15,000 Starbucks signs and 14,000 golden arches.) Ted would be over the moon; Pat would be glad but unimpressed. Neither would dwell on the success. Ted would take another road trip, bologna sandwiches in the cooler and a stop at every historical marker. Pat would gaze with satisfaction at her restored prairie, thrilled that in late 2021, their house was finally demolished as she had requested, to make room for a little more native bluestem, a few more wildflowers.

She would have rolled her eyes at this biography, saying dryly, "It seems like you could have found a more interesting subject." Ted would be boyishly pleased and then hide it by quipping, as he often did after a flowery introduction, that he'd always been a legend in his own mind.

But how to sum up the real legend?

We began the Joneses' story with the family members who preceded them, paving a way right through the nineteenth century and into the twentieth. But Ted and Pat took all that courage, intelligence, and spirit and made it their own. Knowing them better now, it is hard to imagine confusing either of them with anyone else. And it is impossible not to feel changed by who they were.

So what was *their* essence?

Simplicity. A refusal to get caught up in the trappings, the nonsense, the ego rush or bureaucracy or unimaginative norms that others follow blindly.

Because they lived so simply, they had energy left over to be curious. To see the world as it really was. To imagine how it could be—and then fight to make it so.

Ted and Pat had no kids; we are all their heirs. What did they want us to know? That it is possible to live freely, laugh down obstacles, change the world for thousands, and die with no regrets. They would never have preached that at us, though. They just put it into action.

Because this is their story, they should have the last word. And because they lived so clearly, it is easy to imagine what they would say: Do what you love, not what the world expects. Work hard but stay light. Plant a tree, then smear your muddy hands on your jeans and feel at peace. Hike or bike the Katy. Go to Confluence Point at sunset and stand with one foot in the Missouri River and the other in the Mississippi.

And then do something to make the same experience possible for somebody else.

About the Publisher

When the idea for this book struck John Beuerlein, he called another former Edward Jones partner, Dan Burkhardt, and asked for advice. He knew Burkhardt had already published several books on behalf of Magnificent Missouri, a not-for-profit organization he co-founded.

This was the perfect project for him to tackle next.

Like Beuerlein, Burkhardt had been inspired by the way Ted and Pat Jones lived. He had a lifelong interest in the Missouri countryside, and he wanted to build on the work Ted and Pat did with Missouri State Parks to create the Katy Trail. Now, it was important to conserve and enhance the corridor along the Katy Trail—and to bring others to that cause, so they could continue to love and preserve it.

The more Missourians are drawn to the beauty of this stretch of countryside, Burkhardt reasoned, the stronger their desire will be to conserve and protect its farmland, rivers, trails, and parks. And so, over the past decade, Magnificent Missouri has created books and television documentaries, published magazines, sponsored events, produced music CDs, planted trees and prairies, and collaborated with countless individuals and organizations, often the same sort that helped make the Katy Trail possible in the first place.

A nexus for environmental, historical preservation, and art organizations, Magnificent Missouri engages people just the way the Joneses would have, with front-porch bluegrass music at the Peers Store, bird walks for kids, murals on the old grain elevators, honeysuckle hacks, bald eagle days, storytelling sessions, and lively lessons in local history, river history, farm history. There's even a Magnificent Missouri wine Pat would have approved, its label a reminder of the lush, historic vineyards in the river hills along the Katy Trail.

In the coming years, Magnificent Missouri and Forest ReLeaf, another St. Louis not-for-profit, will plant hundreds of trees along the Katy, shading the trail and calling to mind the heavily forested river bottom that Lewis and Clark saw. Those trees were cleared for steamboat fuel, then for agriculture, then for the railroad. Now the survivors, the old fenceline

trees, giant pecans and bur oaks, are aging, and these newly planted trees
will be the giants of tomorrow.

READ *Missouri River Country: 100 Miles of Stories and Scenery from Hermann
to the Confluence; Growing Up with the River: Nine Generations on the Missouri;
The Man Who Planted Tree*s by Jean Giono (a special Magnificent Missouri
edition)

WATCH *River Towns: 100 Miles | 200 Years | Countless Stories*, a PBS Nine
Network documentary. (Search for Rivertowns on NinePBS.org.)

VISIT The Country Store
Corridor on the Katy Trail.
Magnificent Missouri has
worked with Missouri State
Parks to create a four-acre
native prairie along the trail
at Peers, west of St. Louis.
You overlook this prairie
from the front porch of the
Peers Store, built for the
arrival of the Katy Railroad.
Four miles west of Peers is

Riders approaching the Peers Store and Prairie

another historic railroad town, Treloar, with its own small store built for
the arrival of the Katy in the 1890s. Nearby are the "Trees of Treloar," a
Missouri River valley native tree planting. Both Peers and Treloar welcome
visitors and educate them about the value of native plants and the history
of the trail. They also tell riders and hikers from around the world about
the people who created this special way to experience the beauty and
history of Missouri: Ted and Pat Jones.

Whose story has many chapters.